Playwork: theory and practice

Playwork: theory and practice

Edited by
FRASER BROWN

Open University Press
Buckingham · Philadelphia

Open University Press
Celtic Court
22 Ballmoor
Buckingham
MK18 1XW

email: enquiries@openup.co.uk
world wide web: www.openup.co.uk

and
325 Chestnut Street
Philadelphia, PA 19106, USA

First Published 2003

A catalogue record of this book is available from the British Library

ISBN 0 335 20944 0 (pbk)   0 335 20945 9 (hbk)

Library of Congress Cataloging-in-Publication Data
Playwork : theory and practice / edited by Fraser Brown.
    p. cm.
    Includes bibliographical references (p.) and index.
    ISBN 0-335-20945-9 — ISBN 0-335-20944-0 (pbk.)
    1. Play. 2. Child development. 3. Recreation centers. I. Brown, Fraser, 1951–
LB1137 .P557 2002
790'.01—dc21   2002023855

Typeset by Graphicraft Limited, Hong Kong
Printed in Great Britain by Biddles Limited, Guildford and Kings Lynn

In memory of **Vanessa Kidd (1972–1999)**, playworker

All royalties from this book go to: White Rose Initiative, whose Therapeutic Playwork Project is the subject of Chapter 11

Contents

List of contributors

Fraser Brown is Senior Lecturer on the BA (Hons) playwork course at Leeds Metropolitan University. For ten years he was Director of the playwork training agency *Children First*, and previously held advisory posts with Playboard and the National Playing Fields Association (NPFA). He developed and ran an adventure playground in Runcorn, and managed a range of projects for the North West Play Association. For two years he was District Leisure Officer in Middlesbrough. His publications include *Working Together: a Playwork Training Pack* (Children First 1989), and *School Playgrounds* (NPFA 1990). He has recently completed research into the effects of therapeutic playwork on a group of abandoned children in Romania.

Brian Cheesman is Course Leader of the BA (Hons) Playwork course at Leeds Metropolitan University. He has been both a residential and generic social worker, a community worker and a professional footballer, and has worked in the higher education sector since 1985. He was an executive member of Fair Play for Children, and has served on numerous committees, including the Oxfordshire Play Bus Association and Wakefield Prison Children's Play Facility. His consultancies include work for Sutcliffe Leisure, Eureka! (Halifax), Play Right of Hong Kong, and Jack-in-the-Box productions. He appears regularly on radio and television, and has presented papers at conferences from Bolton to Melbourne.

Tony Chilton is Play Development Officer for Play Wales. He has been involved in the promotion and development of adventure playgrounds since the 1960s. After working as a playworker in Telford, he moved to Blacon Adventure Playground in Chester, and then became Regional Officer for the

NPFA, during which time he helped to found the Joint National Committee for Training in Playwork (JNCTP). Subsequently he was Principal Play Development Officer for Newcastle City Council, and Community Development Worker for the Rhyl Community Agency. He has always been involved in the training and education of playworkers, delivering courses throughout the country, including those at Newcastle Polytechnic, Mabel Fletcher CFE Liverpool, Durham Technical College and Stockport College of Technology. He is an expert in playground safety, and his writing includes *Children's Play in Newcastle upon Tyne* (NPFA 1985).

Mick Conway has been Director of Hackney Play Association (HPA) since 1995, and has held a number of play development posts within HPA since 1985. Previously he was Senior Playworker at Bermondsey Adventure Playground. Since 1998 he has been helping to develop *Quality in Play* (London Play 2001), a play-specific quality assurance manual which attempts to put children's play at the centre of quality assurance. He was a contributor to *Best Play* (NPFA 2000), *Towards a Safer Adventure Playground* (NPFA 1984) and *Risk and Safety in Play* (PLAYLINK 1997). He is currently a board member of London Play, and a deputy chair of the Hackney Early Years Development and Childcare Partnership (EYDCP).

Keith Cranwell is Coordinator of the Childhood, Playwork and Youth Studies Section, Thurrock and Basildon College. He completed his MPhil in 1996, focusing on organizations promoting children's play up to 1980. He has held posts in community work, child care and social education. He is a member of the Children's Play Council, and Resource Coordinator for the International Association for the Child's Right to Play (IPA). He was a founder member of the National Centre for Playwork Training and Education, London. He is Chair of the Thurrock EYDCP, and a member of the Child Development Association, the British Association for Social Anthropology in Policy and Practice, and the Voluntary Action History Society.

Stuart Douglas is Head of Play Services for Stoke City Council, and was previously Children's Play Manager for Glasgow, where he was responsible for publication of the city's Children's Play Development Plan, and overseeing the development of 'Children in Glasgow' – a project that takes a comprehensive approach to play provision by combining indoor and outdoor facilities that reflect environmental issues, children's developmental needs and best practice in working with children. He was also responsible for Glasgow Playday, the largest event of its kind in the UK. He was previously employed as a community recreation officer in Clydesdale, and a playworker in Carlisle. From 1992 until 1996 he was Chair of the Association For Fair Play For Children in Scotland.

Sylwyn Guilbaud completed a BA (Hons) Professional Studies in Playwork in 1997 with the highest marks ever recorded. As a project development worker with Meynell Games, her role involved helping communities grasp the value of play. She then undertook face-to-face playwork in those same communities.

Now she is developing and delivering playwork training, and writing and evaluating policy. She is also a mother, and while continuing to work part-time, she spends a lot of time watching her own small child creating and discovering play. Through this experience she is deepening her understanding of the impact an adult can have on a child's relationship to their play, and so to their relationship with the world.

Bob Hughes is the National Coordinator of PlayEducation. He has worked as a playworker, regional play adviser and training manager. He was originally an analytical chemist. He has undertaken consultancy work for national organizations, local authorities and small voluntary organizations. His many publications, from *Notes for Adventure Playworkers* (Children and Youth Action Group 1975) to *Evolutionary Playwork and Reflective Analytic Practice* (Routledge 2001) have been an inspiration to playworkers for the last 30 years. He has spoken at conferences throughout the world, and is especially interested in the effects of play deprivation, play bias and adulteration. This was the subject of his award-winning MA dissertation on the lives of children in urban Belfast.

Jackie Martin is Course Leader of the BA in Playwork and Social Welfare at the University of Northumbria. A geographer by training, she has been involved in play development work since 1982, when she was Development Officer for Newcastle Play Council. Before taking her post at the university, she was Development Officer for the National Centre for Playwork Education (North East). She was Chair of JNCTP, and is a member of the Central Council for Playwork Education and Training. She has produced consultancy reports and spoken at many conferences on the subject of playwork training, which is her main research interest.

Sue Palmer is Head of Playwork and Youth and Community Work at Leeds Metropolitan University. She has been involved in play development work since the 1970s. Having worked as a playworker and play development worker, she then worked for Playboard as a play forum officer. She was responsible for developing the BA (Hons) Professional Studies at Leed Metropolitan University and was team leader for the development of the BA (Hons) Playwork course. She has been External Examiner to the University of Northumbria's BA (Hons) Childhood Studies course, and is responsible for teaching, learning and assessment in the School of Applied Social Sciences at Leeds.

Stephen Rennie is Senior Lecturer on the BA (Hons) Playwork course at Leeds Metropolitan University. He has been a playleader, play organizer, development worker and regional adviser, working for voluntary organizations, local authorities and national bodies. He was Vice Chair of the Fair Play for Children Campaign for eight years. He has undertaken research consultancies into juvenile crime, social behaviours and playground design. In 1999 he completed his MA in Playwork Studies by researching the uses of imagined play in the development of interpersonal skills. He reads Braille and holds qualifications in playwork, youthwork and counselling. He spoke at a recent (1999) PlayEducation conference on 'The isms of Playwork'.

Gordon Sturrock is Course Leader of the DipHE Playwork and Youth Studies course at UEL Thurrock and Basildon College. He has been a playleader, community centre organizer, playground manager and freelance play consultant. Since 1993 he has been the senior partner of The Play Practice. He was a member of the government's think-tank on the Children Act, and is founder of the British Association of Therapeutic Playwork. His most influential publication to date was the joint paper with Perry Else, focusing on 'The playground as therapeutic playspace' (1998). His research interests include analytical psychology, neurolinguistic programming, sandplay therapy, analytic groupwork experience and the development of a new field: psycholudics. He holds an MA in Psychoanalytic Studies and a Certificate in Drama Therapy.

Sophie Webb is a graduate of the BA (Hons) Playwork course at Leeds Metropolitan University. She is a specialist in the use of therapeutic playwork to address the needs of severely disadvantaged children. Originally she was concerned with the value of play to children in hospital, but after spending time in Romania, working with children who were abandoned at birth and spent most of their lives tied in a cot, she developed a deep interest in the power of play as a therapeutic tool. She now works as a therapeutic playwork specialist at a respite home for special needs children in Canterbury.

Acknowledgements

I am immensely grateful for the cooperation and hard work of all the contributors to this book. Without their good humour and flexibility it would never have been possible to complete the task. Thanks also go to the students of Leeds Metropolitan University's BA (Hons) Playwork degree. Their hard work and commitment to the development of the playwork profession has provided the inspiration for several chapters. In addition I would like to acknowledge the contributions to specific chapters of the following:

Introduction: Wendy Ensor for a very useful discussion about the theme of this text.

Chapter 4: PlayEducation for permission to draw heavily on the text of a presentation given to the second theoretical playwork meeting: 'New Playwork – New Thinking?', 21 March 2000, Ely. Ben Tawil for permission to rework the notes from a presentation he made to the third-year cohort of the BA (Hons) Playwork degree in December 2000, concerning the application of compound flexibility to the playwork profession.

Chapter 8: Maggie Harris for her amazingly speedy contribution, which enabled us to put a positive slant on the section concerning the child-care lobby. Malcolm King for permission to make use of some of the material contained within his presentation on social inclusion for the 'Spirit of Adventure Play' seminar (Play Wales 2001b).

Chapter 10: Keeks McGarry for his assistance in developing the chapter.

Chapter 11: White Rose Initiative, first for their permission to conduct the research project and second for their permission to report on its remarkable achievements. Dr Cornel Puscas former, Director of the Sighisoara Paediatric

Hospital for permission to refer to the hospital records, and for allowing us to report honestly on the children in his hospital. We would like to place on record the fact that without his support the Therapeutic Playwork Project simply would not exist.

Most of all I want to thank my lovely wife Anne for her patience and forbearance during the long days and nights when I should have been with her but was locked in my office typing furiously.

Photographic acknowledgements

All cover photographs © Warwick Adventure Playground in Knottingley, except: 'Bubbles' © Sophie Webb; 'Lollipop' © Brian Cheesman.

Introduction: childhood and play

Fraser Brown and Brian Cheesman

This may seem a rather obvious statement to make, but most of those reading this book will be adults, and we all have something in common. Whatever our gender, race, physical characteristics or economic status, we have all been children, and therefore share the experience of having had a childhood. That sometimes provides us with unique insights into the world of children, but rarely makes us 'experts'. In reality each person's childhood is a unique experience, and it is that which draws us into the complex and often emotional arenas of debate about childhood. These range from the full spectrum of Nietzsche's ([1872] 1999) Apollonian vs. Dionysian dialectic (broadly speaking, the rational vs. the emotional), to the more specific and focused elements of the discussion – not necessarily the child as 'innocent', but the child as problematic innocent; not the child as 'devil incarnate', but as a mischievous devil having fun. In general, western societies have approached the study of children and their experiences (childhood) in terms of the child's individual problems and/or the problems they pose to society. How do we deal with this problematization? What is the significance of play in childhood? What is the role of playwork in the child's world? Can playwork offer solutions, or is this the wrong question to ask of a profession that seeks to enable children to find their own place in the world? These are the questions at the very heart of this book.

It would appear that the idealization of play was alive and well in the ancient world of the Greeks. Heraclitus is reported to have proposed that the act of play was more virtuous than the act of governing. But Plato and Aristotle both argued that play and seriousness should be distinguished, and of the two, seriousness was the more important (Miller 1973). In its early teachings the Christian Church very much reflected the dictum of St Chrysostom (347–407) – i.e. 'it is not God who gives us the chance to play, but the devil'. The Church's rejection of play continued for many centuries. However, the nineteenth century saw several new themes emerge. The German poet and philosopher Schiller urged that seriousness and play could be reconciled, and Spencer (1873) argued for the close relationship between aesthetics and play.

However, the nineteenth century also witnessed the full flowering of the industrial revolution and the rise of the Enlightenment, with its emphasis on rationality. Play and non-seriousness faired badly, except among the rich. Social reformers worked hand in hand with industry to foster diligence and sobriety, and to regulate the so-called 'free time' of workers as rigorously as their work time. This new alliance of economic bosses with the Church and a multitude of other reformers succeeded in imposing rational control far more effectively than ever before, and as a result play gained new meanings. The start of universal basic education and the new social sciences inevitably led to the development of ideas about play as preparation for seriousness (Groos 1901). So play came to be viewed as educational in function, and throughout the last 100 years, various professional groups have used play as a supposed means to further human well-being.

Today there are playgroups, kindergartens, uniformed groups and after-school clubs – a plethora of places where children are socialized to the adult concept of play. The unwritten assumption is that play must always be *good* for children. It is organized and sanitized, both in physical and social terms. It is important here not to lay blame upon, or criticize professionals, who give so much of themselves in the pursuit of fostering children's play. The critique is not about individual human behaviour, but about the broad-scale hegemony of contemporary society to which play professionals fall victim just as much as parents and children. This is the hegemony of economic rationalism, which demands that humans must be productive; that this requires seriousness and diligence; and that the task of any child is to become a productive adult. The child's world is constructed around the idea of play being a preparation for the rigours of adult life. Adulthood is perceived as being serious and productive. Regrettably, many branches of the play move-ment have fallen victim to this industrial hegemony. They see play purely in terms of developmental preparation, and voice rhetoric about the beneficial results of play in the development of children. Children are not encouraged to run because it is joyful and stimulating, but rather so that they will run faster than their peers, and win races against them. Of course, play has substantial developmental benefits, but that is not its one and only purpose.

The industrial revolution and its accompanying urbanization left us with another important legacy. In spite of the rhetoric about the family, economic efficiency has meant that people are classified in terms of their relevance to the industrial state – so everyone has their place. The child's place is the playground, nursery, after-school club, etc. One of the important results of this is that idealized play, in so far as the ideal is allowed to survive, has been located in the world of children. The extent to which the play movement has focused its attention and vision on children is one of its most striking features. By maintaining that play belongs to the realm of children, the movement may have aided the depiction of play as trivial.

Today the word 'play' conveys a multitude of meanings:

- children play; kittens and puppies play;
- people play sport and games, some so successfully that they become millionaires;
- musicians play pianos, trumpets and other instruments;
- people play psychological games;
- there is sex play and foreplay;
- at the theatre, we watch a play;
- anglers will play a fish;
- light plays on water;
- engineers measure the amount of play in the spacing of components;
- in politics, various forces come into play;
- we play with words.

Some people would claim this demonstrates the ubiquity of the play idea. Helanko (1956) suggests the 'illusiveness' of play is one of its great strengths. Whatever the explanation for this diverse range of meanings, they offer a reminder that there is no common agreement about what play really is, and that its meaning is both ambiguous and paradoxical. It should not surprise us, therefore, that our media can't seem to decide whether to depict children as little angels or evil demons. Nor should it be a surprise that playwork has struggled to gain a foothold in a society whose politicians make a virtue out of getting children into formal education from a younger and younger age.

Most discussions about children's play seem to assume it is freely chosen, personally directed and intrinsically motivated behaviour, undertaken for its own sake (e.g. Hughes 1982; Garvey 1991). However, as Smith *et al.* (1998) point out, even within that framework, there are almost as many definitions as authors, a plethora of explanatory understandings, and a shift in thinking from looking at the extent to which play is good, to asking what it is good for and how it might help children develop into adults. One of the problems resulting from this is that much of what adults do, supposedly in the interests of children, is seriously misguided. In practice it only serves to marginalize play and make its finest realization even more difficult to attain. Many well-intentioned play providers, whether they realize it or not, are merely adults taking control of children's lives – i.e. removing the very essence of play from the child's experience. For example, Hughes (2001) suggests stimulus bias is accentuated by most children's playgrounds, by virtue of their inflexibility. In supervised play settings, our desire to protect children and keep them safe from harm often mitigates against the child's freedom to experiment, take risks and experience challenges (Hughes 1996a). The excessive programming of many after-school clubs interferes with the spontaneity and personal direction that we might expect to be a characteristic of any child-centred provision.

To some extent the playwork movement which grew so fast in the 1960s and 1970s, and whose philosophy and values were, and still are, firmly rooted in the intrinsic nature of children's play, has been outflanked by three very powerful lobbies: after-school care, curriculum-based education and the health and safety lobby (Brown 2000a). All three of these are pursuing predominantly adult agendas. All three have produced something they call 'play provision', often staffed by people who describe themselves as 'playworkers' (Smith and Barker 2000), and yet whose work bears little resemblance to the sort of child-centred approaches that will be discussed in this book. Playwork is not a branch of community work. It is not youthwork with children. It should not be used as a mechanism to enable social workers to make contact with troublesome families. It has little to do with homework clubs. Nor should it be viewed as a fortunate by-product of the drive to increase the nation's workforce. At the root of all those approaches is an adult agenda.

One of the main purposes of this book is to set the record straight, and begin the process of reclaiming the centre ground of play provision for those who regard playwork as essentially concerned with the following:

- creating play opportunities that enable children to pursue their own play agendas;
- enriching the child's world by providing opportunities for experimentation and exploration;
- creating environments that address the negative effects of play deprivation and play bias;
- developing appropriate responses for individual children's play cues;
- facilitating opportunities for children to develop a sense of self;
- introducing flexibility and adaptability into play environments in order to enhance the prospects of children achieving their full potential.

The book is divided into three parts. Part 1, 'The roots of play and playwork', begins with Sylwyn Guilbaud's analysis of what the experience of playing is, how we are when we are playing, and how playing differs from not playing. She argues the essence of any play experience is at the same time specific to itself and universal to all play experiences. In Chapter 2, Stephen Rennie examines the similarities and differences between animal and human play behaviour and, in particular, play cues. He concludes with an exploration of the various techniques that playworkers may use when responding to such cues. In Chapter 3, Keith Cranwell provides a historical analysis of the development of the playworker function as it evolved to meet the changes in society up to the start of the modern era of playwork, just after World War II.

Part 2, 'Theories of playwork', contains contributions from three of the leading thinkers in the field. As the originator of the most commonly used version of the acronym, SPICE, in Chapter 4 Fraser Brown takes the opportunity to set the record straight about its antecedents, most of which have previously been ignored. In particular the concept of compound flexibility is explored in some depth and related to the development of both the theory and practice of playwork. In Chapter 5, Bob Hughes explores the phenomena of play deprivation and stimulus bias, and offers solid advice to playworkers on how they might assess and address children's needs in relation to these complex issues. In Chapter 6, Gordon Sturrock argues that healing practice should be an essential function of playwork, and that playworkers need to develop their understanding of play and therapeutic playwork's association with dimensions of ludic potentiality. He goes on to make the case for a new field of study which he describes as 'psycholudics'.

Part 3, 'Putting theory into practice – the reflective practitioner', provides six chapters of a more practice-based nature. Mick Conway discusses some of the principles and techniques which could be used to keep children's play at the centre of playwork. Tony Chilton explores the history and modern-day relevance of adventure playgrounds. Stuart Douglas examines the difficulties of establishing a play service in a local authority. Jackie Martin uses three case studies to demonstrate the effectiveness of networking in the playwork world. Sophie Webb and Fraser Brown provide evidence of the beneficial effects of therapeutic playwork on the development of a group of abandoned children in a Romanian paediatric hospital. Finally, Sue Palmer summarizes techniques and approaches for developing and supporting reflective practice and enquiry in playwork.

For most of recorded human history, play has been trivialized as secondary to the more mainstream concerns of life. Today it continues in an ambiguous vacuity between the idealism of play as the source of simple joyfulness, and the reality of a socially constructed hegemony which tells us that all of life must conform to the economic imperative of productivity. Until now the play movement has largely responded with a rhetoric which idealizes the joy of play while at the same time arguing the educational and developmental value of play. That is an explicit acceptance of the economic model of society, which contradicts the rhetorical model. In other words, the play movement has itself been a microcosm of the ambiguity. If we are to overcome this barrier to the fullest realization of play, the playwork movement must pay greater attention to the theorizing of its concerns. The productive developmental idea of play has its feet firmly stuck in the mud of a liberal humanist model of society which locates responsibility for social action in the individual, and tends to ignore the structural forces which act upon and constrain us all. It ignores the powerful evidence that play offers much more than 'healthy development'. It reinforces the separation and trivialization of play, failing to recognize its philosophical heritage. Until now the playwork movement has seemed almost oblivious to the far-reaching consequences of the economic hegemony, and the extent to which it dominates the day-to-day reality of play provision in the UK.

Part 1

The roots of play and playwork

Chapter 1

The essence of play

Sylwyn Guilbaud

What do we know of the essence of play? There are different ways of approaching the subject of play. Theoretical perspectives frequently stem from appraisals of the function and value of play for development and competence in the child, the area of development of interest providing the focus for appraising play. For example, Piaget (1951a, 1951b, 1962) focuses on the value of play for cognitive development. MacMahon (1992) and Dockar-Drysdale (1968) view the primary function of playing as its essentialness for emotional well-being. For Bandura (1962) play is a tool of socialization.

The aim here is not to dispute any of the effects that playing has on development and competence in the individual after they have stopped playing. The aim is to disengage with this process of appraising play via the focus of its effect on, and value to, an individual's functioning in non-play life.

In the early part of the last century Parten (1932, 1933) described play in childhood by referring to an observed set of actions and behaviours exhibited by playing children. Many others have since used, and continue to use, such methods of explaining play. While this positivist approach provides much information about what children do while they are playing, it tells us little of the experience of play. Denzin (1982) epitomizes the shortcomings of this approach when identifying that 'one person's play is another person's work, or non-play' (p. 23) and Csikszentmihalyi (1979: 25) adds that 'playing a game is no guarantee that these [play] experiences will actually be encountered'.

Huizinga (1955) takes the approach to play which begins with the player's playing, and aims to document play from the player's perspective. His discussion of the essence of play includes an eloquent exploration of words (Huizinga 1955: 1–7, 28–45) which are used in different languages to explain what is, and what isn't, play. He observes that while it is fairly straightforward to describe what is not play, an adequate description of the essence of play is elusive. Huizinga goes about shedding light on the essence of play through, as he puts it 'describing the main characteristics of play' (Huizinga 1955: 7).

The exploration here is not about seeking to find an adequate description of play. Descriptions of what play is or is not are used not so much to explain play, but with the aim of unravelling and illustrating how we recognize and understand the essence of play, which at the same time escapes definitive description.

Goldberg (1982: 46) identifies play as 'less a set of activities than a way of organising and framing activities'. Nachman (1979: 61) provides a description of the nature of this 'play frame': 'People play because they choose to play; they enter freely into another reality, unique and self-defining – reality that is created by and exists for the participants themselves.' The following observation shows a manifestation of this described play frame:

> Frankie (aged five) and Alex (aged three) are climbing on the frame of an outdoor swing, they are performing more and more demanding and complex acrobatic feats. Alex sometimes doesn't succeed at some of the feats because his body is too small, he seems to pretend that what goes 'wrong' in his attempts is in fact part of what he aims to do, and Frankie is asked to 'try this one'.
>
> One of the challenges involves the use of a tricycle to climb on to the swing frame. Alex takes off on the bike and starts racing round the garden. Frankie gets on another bike and a racing competition ensues. Frankie can go faster than Alex and after a while Alex suggests to Frankie 'lets pretend that my car can go faster than yours'. Alex is 'allowed' to win some races, which causes him to exclaim jubilantly about his outstanding ability.
>
> The racing leads the boys from the front to the back garden, where Frankie climbs a tree to get a look out over the race course. Frankie is quite high up in the tree and Alex starts to climb, struggling with the lower branches. He says he wants to climb as high as Frankie. Frankie says 'No'. Alex says 'Yes'. Then Frankie suggests 'Let's pretend you're bigger than me and the low branches are really hard to climb and the high ones are easy and that only you can climb on the low ones'. Alex agrees, 'Yeah let's pretend that', and the play continues.
>
> (Guilbaud 1997: 15)

The voluntary creation of, and involvement in, a special way of being seem to be in themselves the essence of this play. The very fact that the rules and goals are divorced from those of usual reality can be seen to cocoon the climbing and bicycle-riding in the play context. Csikszentmihalyi (1979: 17) gives an explanation of the way in which, in the creating of their playing, Alex and Frankie redefined how supremacy and mastery are striven for and recognized:

> What play shows over and over again is the possibility of changing goals and therefore restructuring reality: to risk the things that matter most in ordinary life . . . When this happens, it is no longer meaningful to explain the behaviour with reference to ordinary, everyday reality. Whether play behaviour is 'adaptive' to ordinary reality is no longer relevant.

These children seem to have been experiencing competition and attainment, via different means than would provide those experiences outside this particular shared context. Thus, we see that play is not removed from the goals and pressures of everyday reality because it is a less real practice or repetition of action (Bandura 1962; MacMahon 1992), but because it is a creation of a specific reality to hold experiences (Csikszentmihalyi 1979) through metaphor-like 'seeing as' (Bamberg 1983) in relation to self-chosen catalysts.

The view of play as a context being spontaneously created by and for experience, through the nature of involvement of the player(s) (Csikszentmihalyi 1979; Schwartzman 1982; Bamberg 1983; Crowe 1983) explains the diversity of action and behaviour which has been felt to be play by those involved (Crowe 1983; Hoffman 1992). Crowe (1983: 45) exemplifies this. She recalls when as a child she was asked what she had done today. 'Playing' described a 'glorious day, whatever the weather, whatever we had done or not done', and 'nothing' described a 'hateful, rotten beastly' day. Examples provided by Crowe (1983), Bamberg (1983), Kelly-Byrne (1983), Goldberg (1982) and Hoffman (1992) illustrate that the process of involvement in play is not age, gender or culturally specific or exclusive; although life experience is a variable, influencing the choosing of catalysts for evoking play's metaphoric experiences.

Stewart and Stewart (1981) identify the prototype for play as being embodied in the first expression of the joy of self-consciousness. They suggest that the first expression of the 'pure joy of being alive' is 'the laugh accompanied by that unique total bodily response of exuberance' which 'occurs first in active appreciation of self-motion' (p. 45) (see also Hooff 1972). The way in which recognition of oneself in action has resulted in the experience of joy provides the stimulus for subsequent spontaneous voluntary repetition of action, which has been previously attributed with a meaning or function. When an infant mimes an action out of its usual context and recognizes this process, they are aware of themselves. Thus, the pattern of self-experience and reaction to that experience embodied in laughing in relation to the first 'active appreciation of self-motion', which brings about consciousness of the 'pure joy of being alive', is suggested as the prototype for playing (Stewart and Stewart 1981: 45). The play, which occurs between infant and carer, has been viewed as a process by which each is trying to incorporate the other into their own realm of self-understanding – knowing about themselves through discovering about themselves in relation to the other (Stewart and Stewart 1981; Davis and Wallbridge 1981; Trevarthen 1996).

The evidence provided by Bamberg (1983) and Stewart and Stewart (1981) suggests that play – namely the process of spontaneously creating a metaphoric frame for experience – is an 'interactional form' (Denzin 1982) by which 'identity communication' (Schwartzman 1982) occurs with oneself and with others, often in simultaneously. If this is so, then play, as also concluded by Winnicott (Davis and Wallbridge 1981), encompasses the possibility for interrelationship. The memories of playing presented by Hoffman (1992) and the evidence provided by Stewart and Stewart (1981) and Kelly-Byrne (1983), as well as the conclusions drawn by Denzin (1982) suggest that understanding of play is stimulated only from one's subjective experience. Although the catalyst may initially be external, the reaction (which is play) is internal; play is the experience of the catalyst within a spontaneously self-formed context.

Weber's (1964) philosophy of *'verstehen'* differentiates two kinds of meaning: *direct observational understanding*, which one has when one sees $2 + 2 = 4$, when something is understood in relation to its own internal logic; and *explanatory understanding*, which occurs when $2 + 2 = 4$ is interpreted in relation to a context of meaning – for example, the balancing of accounts. In explanatory understanding we understand $2 + 2 = 4$ within the context of an action governed by the purpose and intent of the actor. It is understood in relation to our subjective interpretation of the actor's concept of their situation (Magnard 1989). It would seem that our knowledge of another's play is based in explanatory understanding. We are able to identify with what another person is experiencing because we have played and therefore own the context of playing. However, we are not able to determine the whole or exact nature of that person's play in the way they experience it, simply by observation. In deciding that someone's play is imaginative play or physical play or solitary or parallel play we are trying to grasp what is going on through the use of direct observational understanding. We may gain valuable insight as to an individual's development, ability and skill in relation to the 'norm' in this way but not about the essence of their play experience.

Empathy is defined in *The Shorter Oxford English Dictionary* (Onions 1983) as 'the power of projecting one's personality into, and so fully understanding the object of contemplation'. Ogden suggests empathy is a special kind of projection which leads us to feel how 'a mountain rises' as we climb it or 'a steeple soars' (Ogden 1930: 201). In our everyday use empathy is often linked to our understanding of another's experience based on our own life experience – for example, 'I can really empathize with what you're going through, I remember when . . . happened to me.'

In his work *Memories, Dreams, Reflections*, published after his death, Jung ([1967] 1983) discusses his strategy for learning about the religion of the Pueblo tribe of Native Americans who were very secretive about their beliefs. He recounts, 'I made tentative remarks' (theological) 'and observed my interlocutor's expression for those affective moments which are so very *familiar* to me' (Jung [1967] 1983: 279, emphasis added). Eventually, Jung became so in tune with this people's emotional relationship to the world via their religion that he himself had experiences of the natural environment in the way that he empathetically understood the Pueblo tribe to experience it.

Else's (1999) discussion of play cues offers a similar picture of the role of empathy in coming to the point of sharing experience with another – this time the experience of play. Else notes the way in which a playworker's *experience* of children at play offers them the opportunity of being in tune with the fact that a child has entered play, 'although the external, physical evidence is slight' (p. 8). A playworker's play return (reaction) to the playing child is informed by their understanding of the child's play cues (subtle or overt invitations to the environment and the people in it to play). If the playworker's response is appropriate and resonates with the playing child, the child incorporates this into their play and responds anew, and a shared play experience comes about between child and playworker.

These two examples of empathetic understanding and the accompanying depth of connection between the individuals involved have been included side by side not to suggest links between the realm of play and the realm of emotion. This has already been done by those concerned with the thera- peutic qualities of play, and as stated in the opening paragraphs the aim here is not to look at play in terms of its function. These examples are included because they offer a picture (albeit a somewhat simplistic one) of the way in which it seems we understand another's play. In these examples both Jung and the playworker described by Else rely on empathy and their experi- ence with the material of expression: emotional expression (Jung) and play expression (the playworker). Our experience of the dichotomy of inexactness coupled with depth of understanding of another's emotional relationship to an object, a person or an occurrence, offers us a handle with which to begin to grasp the way in which we tune into another person interacting with their environment in play.

Bamberg's (1983) and Guilbaud's (1994) observations of the play interac- tions of children suggest that in creating their own play frames, the individual has the possibility of empathetically understanding the way others actualize *their* play frames. Additionally, it is the process of continuous involvement in creation necessary for maintaining playing (Csikzsentmihalyi 1979; Denzin 1982; Schwartzman 1982; Bamberg 1983; Hoffman 1992) that is shown by Bamberg (1983) to provide the medium for the growth of intimacy and the meshing of play contexts between two children.

Without the continuous involvement in the creation of play, empathetic understanding of what it is to play does not seem to be enough to create a shared play experience. I spend many hours playing with my 2-year-old daughter, and I also spend time watching her play with her father. All three of us also play together. Recently I have become aware of an interesting occurrence in the play dynamic. One day I was watching my daughter's father playing trains with her. As the resting audience I was very much enjoying the game. Then he had to go and do something and my daughter asked me to play 'choo choo choo'. I tried to repeat the order and actions that she and her father had followed during their play, but felt very divorced from the process. My daughter tried to play her part in the game too, but pretty soon she looked at me and asked me to go and make soup in her playhouse. Here we became once more involved in making the play frame and playing the play together. Later, feeling somewhat guilty for not having played a satisfactory 'choo choo choo' game with my daughter, I was reflecting on the process. I realized that while my husband and I can play the same games individually with her, we both struggle when faced with playing one of the other parent's games. We seem to get stuck. We replay the actions we have observed, but unless we can become involved in developing the game further, at that moment we become uninvolved. Trying to fulfil some pre-created sequence does not work. The moment to moment creation of our play together, and the experience of shaping what happens next, is crucial to the experience being 'play' rather than a repetition of actions.

In order for two or more people to share the intimacy of their play, it seems that each must use the other's expression of experience in their playing, to extend their own play context (Davis and Wallbridge 1981; Stewart and Stewart 1981; Goldberg 1982; Schwartzman 1982; Crowe 1983; Kelly-Byrne 1983), this being the 'meshing' process described by Bamberg (1983). It is here that absorption, or spontaneous voluntary involvement, is illuminated as essential to the process of playing. Playing is a process of active maintenance of a frame or context. It is this active involvement in the moment – notably the foundation of creativity (Maslow 1971; Csikszent-mihalyi 1992; de Bono 1992 and 1994) – that offers the player 'a peculiar vulnerability . . . to the world around him', an 'invitation to the possibilities inherent in things and events' (Sylva et al. 1976: 244).

Thus it seems that when playing we are highly open to being affected by a chosen environment. Trying to attract the attention of a playing child shows us the extent to which what is encompassed in the environment of play is chosen. Perhaps we are highly open and perceptive for the very reason that our willingness to experience comes spontaneously from within, and the context into which the experiences are internally registered is self-created by that spontaneous involvement. Two people, whose expressions in their own play frames become included in each other's chosen environment of perceptual sensitivity encircle the possibility of growth in intimacy with each other, in the blending and joining of their play frames (Bamberg 1983; Kelly-Byrne 1983).

The following exemplifies this process. I was at the park with Rowan, aged 6. I said it was time to go, but Rowan wanted another swing on the swings. We were holding hands:

Rowan [*pulling on my hand towards the swings*]: Yes.
Me [*pulling the other way*]: No.
Rowan [*tug*]: Yes.
Me [*short tug*]: No.

Rowan [*short tug*]: Yes [*annoyed tone turning into giggle*].
Me [*pulling her towards me and taking hold of her other hand*]: No [*smiling*].
Rowan [*pulling on both my hands*]: Yes [*smiling*].
Me [*quickly rocking back the other way*]: No [*laughing*].
Rowan [*quickly rocking back*]: Ye . . . es [*laughing*].
Me [*quickly rocking back*]: No . . . o [*laughing*].
Rowan [*keeping up the rhythm*]: Yes.
Me: No.
Rowan [*getting faster*]: Yes.
Me: No.
Rowan: Yes [*sigh, looks at me differently*].
Me: No.
Rowan: No.
Me: Yes.
Rowan [*pulling me onto the grass*]: Ha! Ha!, you said yes, I tricked you.

Through the lack of giving in by both parties, and through the gradual introduction of rhythm into the exchange of short words and pulling, the reason for the exchange becomes incidental and the exchange itself becomes what is being done. There is no negotiation about the play outside of the play. The internal recognition of a different context of competition which made the activity play might be seen by Csikszentmihalyi (1979) as a realization of a choice of contexts of meaning, essential for being conscious of play.

Based on the viewpoints presented here, the process of knowing the essence of play and using this knowledge in interacting in play with others can be summarized thus:

- We are driven to play by the prototype of joyous self-awareness.
- We understand and identify with another's playing based on our own experience of playing – this is a deep but inexact understanding of the other person's experience.
- We can play with others by incorporating their play expressions that resonate with us into our playframe. The resonance is linked to our empathetic understanding of their play. They can do the same with our play expressions.
- We create something that is shared and is experienced by each of us together, but may well be experienced differently by each player.
- We use our expressions in play and the response of the people or the response of other aspects of our chosen environment (i.e. water splashing, an immovable rock, a curious cat) to continue creating the play.

This must then raise questions as to the creation and understanding of definitions of what play is.

With today's technology we are at the point of being able to do things like probe 'the subjective stream of consciousness of interacting individuals' so as to 'locate the . . . essence in the play form of human behaviour' (Denzin 1982: 24). The kind of answers that come from this type of research can doubtless inform us as to what play is as a function or process. This kind of information can perhaps make pinning down and dissecting the nature of and reason for play as a whole in humans and animals more straightforward. Looking at play through the lens of neuroscience allows us greater clarity as to what play is, because it allows us to use Weber's direct observational understanding rather than subjective explanatory understanding.

I may be able to understand play in relation to other human experiences through understanding the brain, but why do I have an understanding of the following?

> From the position of secular man (Homo sapiens), that is to say, we are to enter the play sphere of the festival, acquiescing in a game of belief, where fun, joy, and rapture rule in ascending series. The laws of life in time and space – economics, politics, and even morality – will thereupon dissolve. Where after, re-created by that return to paradise before the Fall, before the knowledge of good and evil, right and wrong, true or false, belief and disbelief, we are to carry the point of view and spirit of man the player (Homo ludens) back into life; as in the play of children, where, undaunted by the banal actualities of life's meagre possibilities, the spontaneous impulse of the spirit to identify itself with something other than itself for the sheer delight of play transubstantiates the world – in which, actually, after all, things are not quite as real, or permanent, terrible, important, or logical as they seem.
>
> (Campbell 1991: 28–9)

> Children's play is freely chosen, personally directed behaviour, motivated from within: through play, the child explores the world and her or his relationship with it, elaborating all the while a flexible range of responses to the challenges s/he encounters; by playing the child learns and develops as an individual.
>
> (SPRITO 1992)

Some of the playwork training that I am involved in guides participants to recall and share their childhood play experiences and then, discarding all theoretical knowledge, work with others to create simple definitions of play. Having run the course over a period of time with different types of group (face-to-face playworkers, managers and funding agencies, university graduates not taking playwork courses), my colleague and I began to see the same definitions coming up again and again, definitions which also concurred with theoretical perspectives and definitions. There is of course no way of ensuring that participants have really drawn only on their play experiences in creating their definitions, and it is highly probable that their definitions as well as their memories of playing are affected by any theoretical explorations of play that they have encountered. However, it is also probable that if we use our own playframe as the starting point for creating a shared playframe with others, then theorists who made statements about play based on observation used their own experience-based understanding of play in order to give meaning to what they saw. Furthermore, when we encounter a description past or present of the experience of playing, what it feels like or what it is, do we not interpret it based on our own experience?

I understand the above two quotes because we are designed with the capacity to play and because I have played. Though we share the capacity for play my understanding of these statements may well be slightly or largely different from yours because of the uniqueness of our play experiences.

The essence of play is perhaps one of the last aspects of magic and mystery which remains to us. Huizinga (1955) suggests that the secrecy and mystery of play are in fact an aspect of play itself. Play is a layer of living that can encompass all the subject areas and processes of living and it is perhaps this very quality that enables people to analyse and attribute value to play in relation to different areas of life and the abilities of animals and humans (i.e. play in relation to physical development; the therapeutic value of play). However, the fact that the layer of living in play relies on the player(s) to create, maintain and control the world and their experience within it makes play-life more problematic to investigate than non-play life, in which the aspects of existence can be separated from the individuality of the subject and studied more universally and objectively.

There is great value in breaking play apart and looking at what people do when they play: how they look, what their body and brain are doing, what the effect of playing is on all areas of their development and so on. In this way, play-life can be analysed and categorized in much the same way as non-play life. But the part that one experiences when one is playing, and which lets us identify when another is playing, is perhaps as hard to define as the meaning of life and is perhaps as individual and universal. We know the essence of play through the subjective experience of playing, but we are less able to know it through objective analysis and it is this dichotomy which is part of the essence of play.

Chapter 2

Making play work: the fundamental role of play in the development of social relationship skills

Stephen Rennie

For something so core to our being, we treat play very lightly – in too many instances dismissively. If it is valued at all in our development of social policy, it is almost always in relation to its use to attain a goal of seriousness. Our social institutions frequently use play as a reward for children's compliance. Good behaviour earns extra play time. Playgrounds and playschemes are offered with the express purpose of taking children off the streets, where they interfere with our adult pursuits. Organized games are offered on playing fields to promote healthy exercise and lessons in socialization. Play activities are provided to encourage children to take part in things that adults feel will be good for them – socially, intellectually and physically.

Given that we evidently understand children's strong desire to play (why else offer play as a reward or attraction), it is odd that we treat it so lightly. No other human desire is treated in this way. We may use eating as a reward in the form of treats, but we don't stop there in making provision. We offer socialization opportunities as rewards but we also structure our whole way of life around social groups. It is very frustrating as a playworker to be constantly pressured to use enabling skills developed for play for quite peripheral purposes.

The core problem appears to be our lack of a general social consensus on the value of play for its own sake. We recognize it as something that people (especially young people) desire to do, but don't always agree as to why. It may be easy to recognize but it is notoriously hard to define. Bob Hughes's definition, derived from Patrick, Neuman, Koestler, Miller and Bruner, probably comes closest, but it will undoubtedly be further refined (see Hughes 2001: 11–16).

Play also suffers from an absence of clearly recognizable outcomes. As a society, we tend to like processes that evidently demonstrate cause and effect. A serious approach to problem solving sets goals, and not only clearly achieves or does not achieve them, but offers clear indications of the processes involved and progress made. A playful approach does not do this. It may solve the problem, it may not. It may solve problems not anticipated in setting the exercise. It may have quite different outcomes, wholly unpredicted. Logically, play should be less effective than seriousness in problem solving, but it is not. It is more successful and perhaps part of the denial of the value of play lies in the frustrations of those committed to seriousness (Kelly 1989).

In considering the value of play, we are also hampered by two other factors. Children are better at play than adults, and play is pleasurable. The first of these denies our superiority as adults. If play is a powerful process enabling problem solving, creativity and personal development, we are forced to acknowledge that the child we are facing is likely to have greater potential than we have and to be better able to function in a changing world. If that makes us feel insecure, our only defence is denial. The second touches again on our commitment to seriousness. Pleasure is suspect. It must be rationed. Pleasure leads to excess and excess is dangerous. We know from our studies of other things that we find pleasurable that taking them to excess causes problems. We therefore assume that this is also true of play. We can all remember times from our childhoods when we took play to excess. The time we were fascinated by the way water disappeared when poured from a teapot onto a wooden floor (until the cries from the kitchen below interrupted our reverie). The time we played with burning sticks from a fire until we got burnt. The many other times we were lost in play and put ourselves or others at risk.

What is suggested here is not that free play is perfection, free of risk of harm, naturally directed to pro-social choices, but that it must be examined as a powerful drive which is capable of being those things and is worthy of support towards those ends. Playwork is a vehicle for that process. This chapter therefore examines the drive to play in relation to our other drives and seeks to make sense of it in relation to our function. It then takes that information and looks at how it might be supported in our interests. The role of playwork is investigated in respect of supporting and enabling play, and the delicate issue of guiding play is approached, though not necessarily defined or the questions around it fully answered.

Much of the following material refers to studies of animal behaviour. It makes links between very different sources to draw lessons for the reflective practice of playwork. The more accessible research programmes are given as sources, but there is a wealth of other material to interest readers wishing to investigate further. Most of this material is to be found labelled as ethology, sociobiology or evolutionary psychology. In relation to play cues, the most rewarding sources would be Fagen (1981), Bateson and Hinde (1976), Eibl-Eiblesfeldt (1967), Clutton-Brock and Harvey (1978), Smith (1984) and Lorenz (1970).

They are only playing

Alone in a field, far from safe refuge, with eight of the young of the most dangerous species on the planet, I feel safe and happy. All eight are at play. They don't need to tell me that. I can see it and hear it. I will know if and when they want to involve me in their play, because they will signal that, quite unmistakably. These young predators are human beings, but I would get similar signals if they were dogs, baboons, lions or other social animals.

The fact that these young animals are at play does not mean I would be at no risk if I responded to their play cues. Engagement in physical play can be exhausting and the testing aspect can be dangerous or at least painful, as anyone who has been nipped by a puppy can testify. It does mean though, that I can rebuff the cue, by ostentatiously ignoring it or by a slight non-directed threat display, with a high probability that the young animals will accept either signal. It is a characteristic of play that new activities are engaged in tentatively at first (Lorenz 1961).

Play cues are powerful signals. Few people can resist throwing a stick for a young dog to chase. It rushes up with the stick in its mouth and drops it just ahead of its paws, usually backing off a foot or so. Front legs flat on the ground, rear end up, tail wagging, mouth open and panting, it is cueing us to play, and we recognize that cue. We know it wants to play with us and we know it will pester us until we do. How on earth do we know that? (Lorenz 1954).

On the surface there is little that is similar between that dog and the child who tugs our sleeve and says 'Play with me!' We have shared our homes with dogs for thousands of generations, but we are very different species. So how do we know? Not only that, why do we want to play when we get that cue? And why do our children respond to play cues more readily than we do?

Some way off across a park, a child is screaming and running as fast as she can, straining every ligament for increased speed. Several other children are in pursuit, shouting aloud. For a moment we are alarmed, but even as the adrenalin rises in us, it is quelled. They are only playing. We know this before the screams turn to laughter as the child is caught. In that first glance, only slightly slower than the onset of our reflex to protect a child in trouble, we saw and heard things that switched off our anxiety. Almost too subtle to describe, we saw signals that this was *play*. The chase was real, the emotions strong, but they were only playing and something deep within us responds to that knowledge with approval. We experience a distant shadow of the delight they take in their play.

There is something about the play of the young that attracts us to watch. This too works across species boundaries. Favourite sequences of films of animals are very often those of their young at play, and we will stop what we are doing to watch a kitten tussle with a toy, a puppy mock fight a cushion or a foal spring around a field. The play of our own children is even more attractive (Sutton-Smith and Kelly-Byrne 1984).

The playworker then, is at some disadvantage. The term itself is apparently an oxymoron and is often hard for someone outside the profession to understand. The work part is fine, but although we may see in print phrases like 'teaching them to play' we all know that we did not have to learn to play – we were born knowing how to play. Certainly, we had to learn play activities, but the process came naturally. For most of us too, our favourite memories of childhood play did not involve any apparent learning or really any structured activities as such. The delight of the play was in discovery for ourselves. In addition, we all know play is fun. It is inseparably linked with good times in our memories. There is something slightly strange about people who build a career on having fun. Sports coaches have goals. Entertainers work to give us a good time, but are not necessarily having a good time themselves. The comic who laughs at his own jokes is suspect. We appear to prefer the archetype of the pathos of the clown. Playworkers on the other hand join in the play. They are ready and willing at the slightest hint to be part of the process and they evidently enjoy the involvement. This needs some explanation when they claim a share of the public purse for their efforts. Fortunately there is an explanation and it lies at the heart of our general desire to improve the lot of our children.

It's only play

Human beings may well have unique attributes that set them apart from animals, or they may not. The question is a vexed one, very resistant to resolution, as those who believe they can answer it tend to do so forcibly. It is a question that causes us some problems, as we often omit from our consideration of methods of observing and communicating with children those which are not uniquely human – omissions which cost us dear in gaining understanding. Certainly, play is not unique to humans and nor are the cueing behaviours so often associated with it. Cueing behaviour is almost universal in living things. Play may have a more limited distribution (Smith 1984).

It could be that caterpillars play. They may think caterpillar thoughts that are exploratory and creative. They may engage in caterpillar play behaviours of great significance to their development as moths or butterflies. If they do though, they have so far offered no evidence of it that is within our comprehension. We have never seen a behaviour in a caterpillar that was not explicable in terms of instinct – hard wired, pre-programmed response capability. Higher animals do play, especially when they are young. Roughly, the higher the animal, the more complex the play, and it would appear that play is pretty well universal in many respects. We can see and identify play behaviours in goat kids, in antelope fawns, in lion cubs and in apes. Play is something we know by its patterns and therefore it is by those patterns that it is easiest to define (Fagen 1981).

The poet Schiller and the psychologist Spencer saw play as something animals did when they were well fed, when threats were absent and they were comfortable. That view held sway for many years and still has its attractions and adherents. Films of animals at play are usually of young animals, close to their homes, content and carefree. If a threat arises, food arrives or the weather turns, they apparently abandon their play. Konrad Lorenz, an inspirational writer on animal behaviours, recorded matters very differently. He made observations of animals playing even in the face of threat, hunger and bad weather. His passage on jackdaws flying out into a storm is both wonderful prose and a great insight. It ties in much better with our observations of children at play. They play anywhere and at any time, when the need takes them (Lorenz 1961).

Need is a defining characteristic of play. It is a need that arises, a drive that is biological. It therefore ranks with eating, sleeping, threat avoidance, comfort seeking and procreation in any hierarchy that we develop. It differs from all of those though, in its capacity to be fleeting and sustained, so powerful it leads us to expose ourselves to risk, so sustained that we can play to the point of physical collapse, yet so weak it can be disrupted by a sudden breeze or the passing into our vision of a sycamore seed helicoptering by. It can override hunger, deflect attention from pain, mute grief and put off sleep to the brink of exhaustion, yet release us from its thrall in an instant for no apparent reason.

Like all biological drives, play carries an intrinsic reward. This too is a defining characteristic. Play is pleasurable. That pleasure may vary from intense and prolonged to feeble and transient, but it is always there. Memories of play carry with them a warm glow. Engagement in play brings with that act a sense of well-being. Biofeedback mechanisms of this kind are never accidental, nor are they ever incidental. Evolved over aeons, they indicate that the behaviours linked to them are core to individual and species survival (Bateson and Hinde 1976; Hinde 1982).

For something that is so much part of us, something without which we would be greatly lessened, play is curiously hard to pin down. It overlaps with curiosity, but is not quite congruent with it. It includes a good deal of seriousness, but is evidently very different from it in many ways. It is intensely creative, but not identical with creativity. Play is often very physical, but can be entirely intellectual. It is frequently social, but seems just as satisfying when solitary. It can bring tears as well as laughter, but in retrospect is always remembered as fun.

However hard it is to define play, we know it when we feel it in ourselves and see it in others. We can recognize play across barriers of language, of culture, even of species. Fox cubs tussling with a pheasant wing are instantly identifiable as young animals at play, lambs leaping around their mother likewise. This is no flight of anthropomorphic fantasy. We are not attributing subtleties of emotion or consciousness when we do this. We are seeing clear and unmistakable signals with which we are familiar from our own life experiences. They are as evident as the signals that denote fear and anxiety, hunger and thirst or the desire to mate. In many cases, they are even more immediately evident to us than these. The reason for this may be because we share so many play behaviours with other animals. Play fighting and exploratory play are among the most obvious, but there are others too. In addition, there is good reason to believe that play is intended to be recognized. It carries among its behaviours signals designed to be seen and responded to. These signals are part of a set called cueing behaviours and are further evidence that play is a biological drive.

All life forms beyond the very primitive exhibit cueing behaviours. Many are species specific and gender specific within the species. Others are more general. Some of the more specific cues effectively define the species. All Bower birds, for example, come from an evolutionarily recent common ancestor. They live in similar habitats and eat similar foods. Females of the various species can be hard to tell apart. They are small- to medium-sized brown birds that live in wooded areas of tropical islands. Males by contrast are very easy to tell apart. They build 'bowers' to attract females to mate. Bower building appears to have no other function. The bower is not used as a nest or as a shelter. The brighter the plumage of the male bird, the smaller and more perfunctory the bower. The duller the male plumage, the bigger and better decorated the bower (Borgia and Presgraves 1998).

Many flowering plants offer cues, and these cues are often designed to be read across species boundaries. To us, the field poppy has a red flower with an irregular black splotch in the middle. To the bee, whose vision extends into the ultraviolet, it is a precisely marked landing zone with nectar and pollen at its centre. Some insects offer cues across species boundaries too. Bright colours and patterns often denote poisonous or ill-tasting flesh. They may also warn of risk of retaliation in the event of attack, as in wasps. Among reptiles, the rattlesnake's buzz is a cue to its anxiety and the risk it poses to whatever made it anxious. All of these cues evidently benefit the species that proffers them (Shepherd 2000).

We don't know why play cues are general rather than species specific. We do know they are. A playful puppy is instantly recognizable as such. It has special facial expressions and body postures that invite us to play. We can see the same expressions and postures in lion cubs, in young bears and otters and in a variety of other animals. Similarities between animal play cues and those of human children get even more apparent with species closer to us evolutionarily. Baby monkeys play markedly similarly to infant humans. Baby chimpanzees have play cues and play behaviours even closer to ours (Loizos 1967; van Lawick-Goodall 1968).

Play cues have many curious attributes. They are a signal to 'play with me', but they are also the much more subtle signal 'I am only playing'. The playful lion cub can bite an adult lion's tail so hard the adult yelps, but the most annoyed response is usually a swipe at the cub designed to miss. Much slighter offence by another adult can precipitate a serious fight. Young chimpanzees have been recorded playing with young baboons. The play cues of each species are evidently recognized, as serious damage does not often occur, even during play fighting. The Opies noticed this aspect of play cues in their research on children's language. A child who had hurt or offended another child could say 'I was only playing' and retribution rarely followed, even if the hurt or offended child was much bigger or of greater social status (Opie and Opie 1959).

Cueing behaviour has been recognized as having this kind of effect since it was first noticed. 'Feed me' cueing behaviours in birds, for example, evoke responses. They are powerful enough to evoke these responses to a significant extent across species boundaries. It is this aspect of cueing that the cuckoo takes advantage of. The bird in whose nest the cuckoo laid its egg preferentially feeds the cuckoo chick over its own offspring. The cues of the cuckoo chick evidently overwhelm it by their greater intensity.

The argument that play is a core process in animal survival therefore seems well founded. We may not understand why, in the way we understand why eating, drinking, threat avoidance, sex and sleeping are core survival processes, but we know enough to see that play has similar characteristics to those drives and must therefore be classed with them.

Play vs. seriousness

Human beings appear to delight in seriousness. It is the mark of almost all human societies that we seek intellectually to understand our drives, to shape and control them, to direct them to meet planned objectives. Deferred gratification is a major component of our social planning. Its absence is often seen as a lack of moral strength. We may be right in doing this. It may be that it is this capacity for deferred gratification which has made us so successful as a species and brought us to our current dominant position. However, there are problems associated with control of biological drives. We do not always get our planning right and, when we get it wrong, we can cause great damage to ourselves and to each other (Kelly 1989).

Take eating, for example. We must eat to survive, so we are equipped through evolution to recognize a wide range of signals associated with food. When we need to feed, we feel hunger, a prompt to seek and take in food. Our eyesight, by far the most important human sense in this respect, is particularly good at recognizing the colours of ripe fruits and the light, bright greens of young leaves. Our sense of taste reports the sugar content of fruits very effectively and we experience pleasure when we eat high-energy foods of this kind. In hunter/gatherer mode, in which most of our human evolution took place these past 2 or 3 million years, those various abilities matched our hunger drive pretty well. Our species produced relatively tall muscular primates roaming woodlands and savannahs in small dispersed groups. Intensely social, these groups were large enough to bring down prey and defend themselves against predators, but small enough not to exhaust resources in their territory.

Fairly recently though (a few tens of thousands of years), we changed all that. We worked out how to eat grass seeds by artificially pre-digesting them (cooking). Food therefore became abundant and our numbers exploded. Further applied seriousness showed us how to concentrate food resources by planting the seeds of plants we favoured for eating, and how to keep food animals close by and protected from their predators. This allowed us live in larger groups for better mutual protection. Even more of us survived and we lived longer.

Now, at least in some parts of the world, we have a surfeit. We cannot eat all we grow. The seriousness we applied to food production has gone to such excesses that the inhibitions built into our drive to eat have been over-whelmed. Where once we would have eaten a carrot and moved on to other activities, now we eat a mass of them, part pre-digested, salted to enhance their flavour, sugared to appeal to our desire for sweetness, dyed to appeal to our colour preferences and stuffed with preservatives so that we can have them well out of season. A whole industry has grown up to tackle the resulting problems of obesity and bowel disorders.

We must question whether we have done something similar in respect of our drive to play.

Dysfunctional play

Gordon Sturrock coined the term 'dysplay' as a handy abbreviation for a range of behaviours that appear to emerge fairly consistently when a child's play cues are repeatedly ignored or responded to inappropriately. Some of these behaviours feature high on any list of those that distress us when we see them in children and cause us problems in creating a safe and comfort-able society. It is a useful term to distinguish between behaviours resulting from the failure of play cues to elicit appropriate responses and those which are appropriately learned, but from inappropriate environments (Else and Sturrock 1998).

A play cue is a signal that anticipates a response within a fairly small range. At the very least, it anticipates a response. It is a demand for engage-ment and comes in various forms and strength levels. Tentatively offered to a stranger, it is gently exploratory. Taken up, it invites further exploration, but no commitment. Confidently offered in a family or close friendship group, it is a strong signal calling for social engagement. A rebuff calls the understanding of the relationship into question. The rebuff cannot be ignored and the cue is likely to be repeated, either amplified or changed, until a response is obtained.

The process can be seen in many families where there are problems in the relationship between parent and child. The BBC programmes *The Family Game* (QED, 5 May 1993), and *Driving Mum Crazy* showed some very vivid examples of it. The television drama *Jake's Progress* was a fine fictional tale of it, showing that the author is a good observer of children's behaviours. There is a clear underlying pattern. The child offers an unmistakable play cue. The cue is ignored or rejected.

Where the cue is rejected, there are a variety of outcomes. It may be reissued, or directed to another person, if one is available. The child may turn to a solitary play activity, and even become absorbed by that; or the child may react with quite a strong show of emotion, up to and including evident grief. Much depends on the context and the nature of the rejection. Ignoring a play cue tends to produce a narrower range of responses. The cue will usually be repeated, often more strongly, sometimes far more strongly. Displacement may occur, where the cue becomes infused with anger and results in a destructive, but usually still relatively playful, action. This can include a blow aimed at the unresponsive person.

As with everything that is play, lessons are learned very effectively from either of those experiences. The rejection of play cues can fairly swiftly result in a child who seeks strong bonds away from the family or becomes relatively introverted and much given to daydreaming. Without shared play, relationships do not grow as they might. The attitude of the child to the person who rejects their play cues can be strongly influenced by the nature of that rejection.

Ignoring play cues has if anything worse consequences, including some that are downright dangerous. In the worst cases, the child persists in cueing, becoming ever more extreme in the cueing behaviours, until they are smacked. In a strange and unhealthy way, that smack is at least a response. It is better than nothing – at least it is an acknowledgement of the child. Over time, the child may come to accept the punishment as an appropriate response and even appear to seek that response in the relationship. It is the behaviours associated with this kind of situation that most warrant the title of 'dysplay'.

There are implications in this for the playworker. Many children presented as having behavioural problems can be shown to fit this pattern, including in particular some characterized as suffering from attention deficit hyperactivity disorder (ADD or ADHD). These children commonly respond well to a playworker who recognizes their behaviour as a distorted play cue and responds accordingly. Axline's work with 'Dibs' is a good example of this, although her work long predates the widespread use of the ADHD label (Axline 1976).

Antisocial play

The child whose play cues are rejected by close family may well form very strong bonds with those outside the family who do respond to them. Typically, this is likely to be a peer group. If those bonds are formed in conditions where immediate or wider society is seen to be hostile, the emergent culture of that group might well reflect this. The play of these children can then readily teach them how to respond to their perceptions of external threat very effectively (Zahn-Waxler *et al.* 1986).

We should never forget that we are predators. We learned early in our evolution that group attack was a great defence, environmental modification was a good survival strategy and that a clever mind was at least as big an advantage as large size. Our children are not passively waiting to play major social roles. Where possible, they seek them early.

Antisocial play is a misnomer for problematic peer group activities. 'Antisocietal' might better describe them. 'Hanging out' together confers status and claims territory. It is a highly social process. On a barren windswept estate, an empty flat might be the only possibility of having a den. Apparent willingness to be violent is a precise parallel to the adolescent threat displays of our primate cousins. It mirrors that of so many adults at football matches and similar events. Social status is again enhanced and safety is gained from others who might be hostile. Stealing a car comes pretty well top of the list in this context. The car is a major status symbol as much as a mode of transport. As a child pedestrian, the car is a constant threat when away from home, a demonstration of the power of the adult world and utterly unresponsive to the usual interpersonal signals. As a possession, it is a wonderful den, offers great potential for excitement and is the ultimate status enhancer. Small wonder then that the theft of cars and their later destruction is so popular among older children in hostile social environments (Erikson 1951; Box 1983).

Graffiti is simply territorial marking. We all do that. We are mostly content to mark our homes and their immediate surrounding gardens, but we readily extend this to our places of work and to our vehicles. We go further if provoked, and children away from home are constantly provoked. In the absence of security, your own group's graffiti signals familiar space, the likely presence of friends and some sense of belonging. Unfamiliar graffiti puts you on your guard.

As with most – if not all, children's activities – play is very readily incorporated into territorial marking. Individual and group names scrawled or scratched on highly visible surfaces quickly develop into 'tags' – extravagant and often very beautiful designs placed in almost impossibly inaccessible locations. The playful approach not only supports increased creativity in the nature of the markings, but often enables their development to be a social activity and their placing to become a game. The level of cultural creativity involved is demonstrated by the remarkable similarity of these markings across the world.

The term 'antisocial' is also often applied to very intense and solitary play activities. This too is something of a misnomer. 'Asocial' such activities might be, but they are rarely antisocial. Most children are likely to go through periods of self-absorption in their play. We tend to be comfortable with this as long as those periods are neither prolonged nor very frequent. We are also greatly influenced in our attitudes to self-absorption depending on the nature of the activities involved. Activities with which we are familiar, those which are culturally seen as aspirational and those we have been taught are educational, are mostly tolerated or even lauded. A passionate commitment to physical activity in the form of a sport attracts praise. A dedication to chess, music or poetry is usually similarly welcomed. Utter concentration on computer games is denounced vigorously. A strong tendency to reverie (daydreaming) is derided.

All of these things are play based and all can be problematic in themselves, or indications of problems the child is facing. Most children will overcome these problems and their play will broaden to support more balanced development, but not all will manage this without sensitive help. Like all biological drives, play is very powerful and can take the player to extremes. We don't know enough about play to understand in advance how to switch its drive on and off, but we do know some stimuli that can change its orientation. Variation in physical and social environments can be used for this purpose, or changes in the intensity of existing environmental factors. The most common is a new friend or friendship group.

Finally in this section, there is play that leads to bullying, to a disregard for the needs and wishes of others and to a range of other behaviours we adults class as antisocial. This should come as no surprise to anyone who has studied play. As a biological drive, play is amoral. It is not predisposed of itself towards altruism or aggression. It is predisposed to be social, but social roles vary greatly and all can be supported and developed through play (Charon 1995). It is as easy to learn to bully as to learn to be kind through play. A disregard for others is as easily acquired as compassion or tolerance. These lessons are gained by results. The play process makes the lesson more effective, but it does not of itself change the nature of the experience.

Bob Hughes' writings on his experiences in Northern Ireland well illustrate this. Sectarian groups commonly offer children's activities. These are often effectively run and have a good base in play activities. The children learn a great deal about themselves, form lasting friendship groups, gain a thorough if narrow cultural understanding and develop skills in crafts and music. They also often gain a lifelong distrust and even active dislike of a rival group, which later contradictory life experiences may fail to displace (Hughes 2000).

Playwork practice

As an entry level requirement, the playworker is skilled in ensuring children at play do not come to immediate harm. At higher levels of skill, the playworker can enable children to get more out of environments through their play than they otherwise might. Professional playwork practice takes a further step, more qualitative than quantitative, and exercises long-term foresight in respect of interventions.

Building on our innate capability to recognize play cues, entry level playworkers can skilfully respond to children at play when those children welcome or seek intervention. They can spot a child in distress and determine the immediate cause of that distress, even if the child finds it hard to verbalize the problem. They can predict when risk-seeking by children is within their capacity to handle likely outcomes and when it may go well beyond this. Even with only limited training, the entry level playworker can ensure that the play environments offered are sufficiently flexible to meet likely play demands. In many short session situations, this is enough. Play contains its own problem solving mechanisms. A permissive approach by an adult to children at play can enable good constructive solutions to problems to be developed without significant intervention.

The planning of play provision, even of short sessions and especially the reflection on those sessions subsequently, should be supported by a more experienced and qualified playwork practitioner. It is rare for hindsight to suggest that nothing could have been done to avert a problem that proved intractable when it arose in a play session. A playworker with more knowledge and reflection on experience can often spot key factors in advance and help plan practice to minimize their effect or avoid them arising. It is all a matter of balance. Too sterile an environment is likely to give rise to frustration from forced sharing of few resources. Too rich an environment and supervision becomes a nightmare as children exercise their reasonable creativity, or rush round trying everything because they are overstimulated. The right balance, along with sharing, develops naturally as friendships grow. Children can play at the level they want, on their own, in small groups or large. Supervision can become a background matter, releasing the playworker to engage with those children who want such engagement. This is the first example of making play work. Its achievement is the indication of the first key skill of a playworker.

Longer sessions (whole days for example) or long programmes of short sessions, need the presence of an experienced and knowledgeable practitioner most of the time. In times long gone, a Greek general fighting the Persians said that no battle plan ever survived first contact with the enemy. Children are far from being the enemies of playworkers, but the aphorism holds true for session planning, and the longer the session or the longer the period over which sessions are run, the further the plans and reality diverge. In addition, because play is such a powerful developmental tool for children, they very quickly acquire new skills or greater levels of sophistication in the exercise of existing skills. The pace of this can easily catch the inexperienced adult unawares. The experienced playworker will have anticipated these changes and structured the programme accordingly. The play environment will have been structured to cope with change. Where the entry level playworker might well have several programme options – one for dry weather, one for wet, for example – the experienced playworker will have a far more complex range of options available. Some of these will have arisen from discussion with a professional in the field: a highly experienced and qualified playworker, able to advise and support playwork in challenging circumstances (Johnson 1993).

Dealing with challenging behaviours in children, working with children from difficult backgrounds or providing for play in unpromising environments is not easy, despite the claims of too much of the literature aimed at parents. There are no ready formulas for excellent playwork practice that do not presuppose an in-depth understanding of children at play. Friendly mnemonics and activity skills are fine for a great many children and play contexts, but they fall at the first hurdle of non-compliance.

Play is a process that enables change, and the changes wrought through play are rarely simple. The child who overcomes shyness through play may appear to have achieved a simple development, a friendship or friendship group entry. But that change may have far-reaching implications. There is likely to be an accelerated period of learning, as experiences are shared with the new friend. These are likely to include ideas about behaviours and culture, which may or may not prove acceptable to parents, siblings, teachers and others. There may well be an increase in risky behaviours if the new friend has skills the child does not have, or as attempts are made to share.

In most instances, the changes wrought through play are accepted as the inevitable outcomes of growth and development through childhood. Provided they generally fit with preferred patterns of culture in home and community, they are welcomed as indicators of growing up. But there are two areas where they can pose problems.

The first is where the changes do not fit with cultural expectations in home and community. This is less of a problem where the community on which the play provision draws is relatively homogenous, but can give rise to serious problems where there are minorities keen to preserve ways of life intact and unchanging. In practice, social play is such a powerful and culturally creative process, the changes are hard to prevent, even if it is held to be ethical to prevent them. Parents tend to know this and may well describe the changes as problems resulting from children mixing. This does not always mean they will accept them, or fail to blame the playworker for the outcomes.

The second is where a change is asked for, but associated changes are not anticipated. A professional playworker can bring about a great many changes in particular behaviours in a child, but these are always part of a set, and it is likely that the whole set will change. In addition, because play works at depth, there may be evident personality changes apparently quite tangential to the desired change. Dibs is a classic example of this. Virginia Axline, a very competent practitioner of play therapy, worked with a child, Dibs, who was deeply unhappy and uncommunicative. Through her skills, Dibs developed communication skills rapidly, but one of the major things he was able to express through this process was the extent of his hatred for his father. As a therapist, Axline was able to view this as healthy. The ability to express the feeling was a good indication that it was no longer submerged, where it could do far more harm. The feelings of Dibs's father are not recorded (Axline 1976).

Despite intractable problems of this kind, professional playwork is growing in confidence and expertise. As we understand more about play, we are able to develop better playwork practice. As playwork skills grow, its level of recognition grows and more research is done on play. A helpful developmental spiral is created, which can only benefit the child.

Part of that process lies in practitioners questioning the body of knowledge and beliefs underpinning their own practice and the practice of others. We are a very long way from a thorough understanding of the play process. There are bound to be mistakes in what we think we know so far. New insights are not always likely to attract favourable comment. As adults, we value what we have gained and are reluctant to put old lessons aside. As playworkers we cannot afford that luxury. We work with a change process. If we do so with an intent to practise professionally, we must show we can be as flexible as that process and as effective in tackling problems. We have always been good at demonstrating the validity of playwork. We have some way to go to offer reliability.

Chapter 3

Towards playwork: an historical introduction to children's out-of-school play organizations in London (1860–1940)

Keith Cranwell

Study of children's after-school care and leisure provision is a neglected area in the history of education and social policy. A historical appreciation of the nineteenth-century origins of playwork will illustrate the innovative contribution of play organizations to work with children. Historical analysis of bodies that provided activities for children's out-of-school time serves as an introduction to the central themes pertinent to the development of playwork as a profession. In the nineteenth century, evidence suggests organized play facilities were part of the responses to improve children's welfare. This work, it will be shown, adds to our understanding of the way the state defined its support for the family. It will be argued that a historical understanding of children's play agencies suggests they were used to achieve social and economic goals of the state which helped create the case for the extension of statutory powers in education and welfare services. These aims often meant that children's play provision was part of general welfare goals rather than a separate strand of social policy. By exploring the historical development of these services, it is intended to show that children's play provision has always been a contested area of social policy.

This chapter is an attempt to sketch out key developments in playwork up to 1940 and locate playwork within social policy issues that illustrate the debates that have shaped it. The chapter will explore:

- The perceptions of children's play adopted by advocates to support their work.
- The nineteenth-century social context that prompted the development of play organizations.
- The impact of education on identifying the need for play provision and the responses of social reformers to these issues.
- The effect of statutory interventions in relation to the development of Evening Play Centres in London.

The place of children's play provision in society

In their attempts to create provision for children, the pioneers of playwork had to overcome a number of obstacles that arose, initially, from people's understanding of play in society. Throughout history, uncontrolled play was observed as an agent of social change and not just a consequence of greater leisure time for children (Cross 1990: 2). As a result of changing economic and social conditions, ideas about children and their leisure altered. The nineteenth-century promoters of play provision situated themselves in the broader debates concerning social control of children's unregulated time. They were mindful that their views raised issues regarding the state's support of the family that went beyond its contributing to children's education and development.

Between 1880 and 1940, the major function of supervised out-of-school provision was to assist the state in maintaining the responsibility of working-class families to provide and protect their children in the community. Play provision was considered part of education welfare services which facilitated children's transition into work, or safeguarded them from the effects of a poor environment. The effect of city life on working-class children was thought to undermine schooling, lead to criminal activity and cause ill health. In their out-of-school time, children without organized play opportunities were forced onto the streets, which were a breeding ground for behaviour that would undermine the good moral examples that education was trying to instil.

Alerting society to the problems facing children after school brought several groups of social reformers together, who created the different movements for playwork. These social action agencies formed loose alliances that supported a range of provision including: outdoor play in parks; playing fields for sport; organized holidays for children; church-based recreational clubs; and play centres in the community. In the late nineteenth century these groups were part of the moral crusade to improve children's lives through management of their leisure time. Their work reinforced measures of social control that the state was establishing through the extension of statutory education and the regulation of child labour (Cranwell 2001a).

In the late 1890s, educationalists in England began to develop the scientific study of children, influenced by the American academic G. Stanley Hall and his child study methods. The English child study groups investigated children's use of leisure, which provided a vast range of behaviours and contexts for study. The members of child study groups were a mixture of academics interested in developing a psychological understanding of children, social reformers and teachers wishing to improve education. The methods used by members of these groups were dismissed by academics as lacking in rigour. This criticism undermined the potential development of action-based study of children by fieldworkers that might have run parallel to the work of academic psychologists. At the turn of the century, the split between academic and practitioner meant that the theoretical understanding of play was separated from the playground and became located in the classroom or laboratory (Wooldridge 1994). The effect of this tended to make the leaders of the play movement rely on social risk arguments to gain support for their work rather than develop theoretical approaches to play.

Observations of children's play by Victorian social reformers were used to reinforce their views that children were in moral and physical danger if nothing were done to channel their activities. The need for positive outcomes for play was central to reformers' social welfare work with children, which viewed street play as negative (Cranwell 2001a). The vast range of organized pursuits that could be employed to fill children's leisure time indicated that organized play was a flexible answer to meeting social policy goals and did not require major investments of state funding. In the Victorian period, play provision was thought not to interfere with family responsibilities to care for children as it was community based, informal education provided by volunteers. As pressure for statutory education welfare increased, arguments to support play facilities widened to include issues such as child protection, improvements to child health and the amelioration of the effects of poverty.

In the late nineteenth and early twentieth centuries, the breadth of organized children's out-of-school activities make it difficult to source the development of playwork to any one individual or group. An examination of the evidence from the last 150 years of playwork suggests that several key figures and organizations were influential in establishing the different forms of play provision. An understanding of the role of Victorian social reformers in the development of play provision indicates that several of the current debates in playwork had their origins in this period.

The impact of compulsory education on nineteenth-century play provision

In the late nineteenth century, the introduction of compulsory schooling for children under 10 produced circumstances that aided the development of after-school provision. In schools, children's state of health was observed daily and this brought home to Victorian social reformers the need to improve city slums. The effects of legislation to enforce school attendance gradually removed child labour as an economic part of street life and created a need for provision of 'rational recreation' to deter children from antisocial behaviour during their out-of-school time (Cranwell 2001b). Compulsory education divided children's lives between school and home, raising the issue of how the good influence of education could be maintained in the community. These changes made children more dependent on the family for support and, given the cramped conditions of most working-class homes, also meant that children needed an acceptable place to play, other than the street.

In the late nineteenth century the effect of a poor environment on children was a major concern to many social reformers. The clearance of city slums to make way for railways and school buildings impacted on where children could play. As the city expanded, parks and space for recreational activities were inadequate. Children's out-of-school play provision was at the centre of movements for organized sport. Victorian and Edwardian social reformers argued that the effects of the environment were critical causes of the health and behaviour problems of the inner-city child (Bray 1907). The relationship between environmental improvement and the needs of children was a major theme in debates to secure play space by opening playground in schools, and creating playing fields and parks.

Organized play provision in the late Victorian and early Edwardian period

Church work and playrooms

By the 1880s the need to aid education through out-of-school provision was gaining acceptance. Prior to this period, the earliest forms of playwork occurred mainly as church-based voluntary work. In 1847, the Band of Hope introduced play activities to attract children to what were essentially junior temperance meetings. Magic lantern shows, special games and songs were used to promote lessons of sobriety and godliness among children (Shiman 1973). As the popularity of the Band of Hope spread, church Sunday schools began to encourage their congregations to arrange 'treats' such as sports clubs and uniformed groups (e.g. the Boys and Girls Brigade) as a means to maintain church attendance. The role of church community leisure events served both educative and counter-recreational purposes. The types of activity churches arranged tended to replace morally disapproved of leisure activities (such as rowdy street fairs) with morally approved church outings (Laquer 1976: 239).

In addition, churches promoted 'playrooms' which were an early form of play centre in the community. An example of a 'playroom' recorded in *The Quiver*,[1] described a household with cooking, sewing, music and games, taking place in different rooms with parents encouraged to share in the activities (*The Quiver* 1888: 563–6). Work with children was intended to increase the influence of the Church in family life (Cranwell 2001b). The 'playroom' found secular form in Settlements, as family social evenings or Saturday morning sessions of games, singing and dancing.[2] Indeed, Mary Neal's 'play-room', at Marchmont Hall, was the model for the Mary Ward Evening Play Centre (Trevelyan 1920: 1–4).

Play and school

The earliest regular out-of-school provision was an initiative of school managers to use school buildings in the evening for play. In 1889, school governors set up the Children's Happy Evenings Association (CHEA) and for 27 years this body was an important provider of after-school play. The 'happy evenings' programme was a mixture of board games, songs, dancing, middle-class 'parlour' recreations, boxing, running games and skipping competitions. The CHEA programmes introduced two important features to children's play. First, they gave prominence to doll play and toys, which for working-class children would have been a luxury. The dolls were highly prized, as they came from the Royal household and other upper-class families, who gave them to an annual fund-raising exhibition to support the CHEA. Second, in the 1880s, the School Board for London (SBL) did not normally provide a piano as standard school equipment, making the 'happy evening' piano a valuable resource. The CHEA extended school resources and equipment, and gave children access to play materials that were, at that time, additional to educational provision. This aspect of the CHEA reinforced the view of their work as being complementary to education and not a welfare service.

Ada Heather-Bigg, a founder member of the CHEA, saw the work as more than just a support to schools and parents. Her promotion of the CHEA stressed that play created happiness, which was an important factor in the development of children's physical and mental health. Heather-Bigg also believed that the CHEA might bridge the gap between the end of school life and the age when children would be eligible to join the emerging youth organizations such as the Boys' Brigades. The CHEA, she felt, ought to be part of a coordinated movement for children and young people's leisure, not just an adjunct to school (Heather-Bigg 1890). This vision of play organizations providing continuity between school and other recreational provision was a view that could have placed playwork at the centre of the future development of a leisure policy for children. These policy aims slipped from the agenda as the CHEA grew. The time of the executive committee and its local branches was taken up with the more urgent matters of recruiting volunteers to staff the 'happy evenings' and raising enough money to sustain the organization.

In respect of the volunteer worker role during a 'happy evening', Heather-Bigg appeared to appreciate elements of current playwork values. She stressed the importance of allowing children to self-direct their play, where volunteers' skills were to flow as 'a matter of friendship; of good influences unconsciously disengaged, unconsciously received; of individual effort and individual success' (Cornford, undated). She also believed that the child should be in charge of the play activity, as the 'happy evening' was a time that was a release from a life where they were perceived to be 'only instructed in labour'. Any over-instruction in play, she held, inhibited a child's opportunities for wholesome recreation (Heather-Bigg 1890: 131). Heather-Bigg's expectations of the CHEA volunteer reflected the idea that play should be a freely-chosen, child-centred activity. This view was unusual for the time when ideas of 'rational recreation' tended to stress the need for play to be more formally structured. A claim could be advanced that Heather-Bigg saw the potential of play and the importance of the worker's position as being a facilitator and not a teacher.

In 1906, at the height of its operation, the CHEA served the needs of over 32,000 London children in 96 schools, with a volunteer workforce of 1300 drawn from all strata of London society. Membership of the 'happy evening' was strictly regulated and conditional upon good attendance at school. Only children who received eight out of ten attendances were given admission tickets to the 'happy evening'. The CHEA saw its role as arranging amusements that children would find enjoyable, to divert them from play on the street and limiting home circumstances. The CHEA provided children some respite from their impoverished environment, while the volunteers viewed their work as a means to bring the classes together in an increasingly socially divided society. For the SBL education authority, the gains were that schools achieved a sense of continuing influence in the community as well as an improved school attendance. Other cities followed the 'happy evening' model, but the CHEA never aspired to be a national charity, and following closure of its centres at the beginning of World War I they were not active again.

Play outdoors

As early as the 1830s, social reformers were aware of the need to create open space in English cities (Bailey 1978). In 1839, the Privy Council, the forerunner to the Board of Education, saw playgrounds as 'an instrument of education' (Owen 1968: 7). In the period 1850–1900, key figures who supported civic initiatives to promote parks and playgrounds were also at the forefront of children's recreational provision. In the late 1860s, Octavia Hill, the public housing reformer and environmentalist, set an example for what might be achieved in planning for play with her Freshwater Place development. This was the first time a housing project had included a children's playground. In 1867 she employed a playground supervisor to oversee children's play (Darley 1990: 101). Octavia Hill was also prominent in pressing for the 1884 Disused Burial Grounds Act which created parks in disused burial grounds as 'outdoor sitting rooms' (Hoyles 1991: 139).

In the 1880s, the Earl of Meath, as chair of the Metropolitan Public Gardens Association (MPGA), argued that children needed gymnasium-styled, supervised playgrounds in parks to improve their physique. Also, to create greater opportunities for children's play, he campaigned for small parks near to housing. Meath recognized that provision for children's play needed to be near housing and supervised, if it was to be used, rather than in parks or playing fields, at a distance from children's homes. Both Meath and Hill advocated after-school use of playgrounds and actively demanded that local authorities purchase open space as playing fields for games. In the 1890s, the Earl of Meath, through the MPGA, paid school caretakers to oversee school playgrounds during out-of-school time and holidays. Later, he paid for army drill instructors to organize gym sessions on various playgrounds and open spaces managed by the MPGA (MPGA 1887–1900).

In the late nineteenth century, teachers and members of playground and playing fields organizations pressed for games to be part of the school curriculum and not just team sports operating outside the school day. Promotion of outdoor play and team sports added weight to arguments that schools should embrace a wider range of physical activities as part of children's education. However, attempts in 1900 and 1906 to create a physical education curriculum based on organized games received little support (McIntosh *et al.* 1957: 209). By 1911, in London 730 departments of schools (380 boys' departments, 280 girls' and 70 mixed) arranged school games sessions (LCC 1911). Sports bodies and Playing Fields Societies were active in assisting schools to develop outdoor play programmes and were instrumental in urging local authorities to provide organized playgrounds (Roper 1911). Moreover, well into the 1930s, schools without playgrounds relied on subsidies from organizations like the National Playing Fields Association (NPFA) for use of pitches and bus fares to take children to the grounds (NPFA 1928–1935).

Mary Ward, Settlements and out-of-school provision

In the late nineteenth century, Settlements were the backbone of secular work for children's out-of-school leisure in London. Since 1884, London Settlements had organized country holidays for inner-city children. In addition, Settlement workers voluntarily organized clubs for young people, led recreational classes for children and helped arrange 'happy evenings' and Guilds of Play (Cranwell 2001a).

In 1898, the popular author Mary Ward opened the Passmore Edwards Settlement (PES) and began the work to provide comprehensive play provision six days a week and during school holidays, which continued until 1940. In 1902, Ward introduced to England the American vacation school. This was a major innovation in PES work to provide children with 12 different activities in two daily sessions, 10.00–12.30 a.m. and 5.00–7.30 p.m. during summer holidays. The activities were drawn from the recreational club activities and included manual training, housewifery, needlework, nature study, gymnastics and musical drill, kindergarten games, drawing and brushwork, storytelling, singing and dancing, clay modelling and woodwork. The scheme registered 700 children and numbers did not dip below 380 a day. The 'school' was led by a teacher who deployed the volunteers and the 12 paid workers, recruited from teacher training colleges (Trevelyan 1920: 120–46).

The instant success of the vacation school may, in part, be put down to the effects of a cholera outbreak in London that caused country holidays to be cancelled. The vacation school venture provided a cheap alternative to country holidays, which were already working to capacity, and showed how large numbers of children could be occupied in safe, purposeful activities in a small area. The organization of the vacation school also dispensed with the need for a cumbersome administration structure that was a necessary part of the country holiday scheme.

According to the superintendent's report (Trevelyan 1920: Appendix III) the vacation school had a beneficial effect on children's behaviour, as it maintained the influence of education during the long summer holiday. The vacation school attracted a lot of positive publicity in newspaper articles concerning the educational value of play. Public comment focused on the vacation school programme as an example of how the school curriculum needed to incorporate practical activities which were lacking in an education system perceived as overly academic. The summer 'experiment' demonstrated to influential education observers who were encouraged to visit the Settlement, that children were prepared to engage in learning new skills if they were free from the pressure of school organization and were supported by encouraging and enthusiastic workers.

Statutory recognition for play provision

Evening Play Centres

In 1904, following the success of the vacation school, Mary Ward formed the Evening Play Centre Committee (EPCC), which included four Members of Parliament (MPs). This committee proposed that the London County Council allow free use of certain schools on five evenings a week from 5.30–7.30 p.m. and on Saturday mornings 'for the purpose of providing games, physical exercise and handiwork occupations for the children of the district'. The LCC agreed to the free use of school halls but expected the committee to fund the extra cleaning and caretaking required. Through fund-raising letters to *The Times*, Mary Ward raised £800, enough to start this experiment in eight schools (Trevelyan 1920: 12–25). Without Mary Ward's status as a popular novelist, with an ability to paint vivid pen pictures of play centre work, the committee could not have carried out this programme.

From the outset, the committee sought to employ professionally trained staff. The use of trainee teachers on the vacation school prompted Mary Ward to approach the training colleges for staff, as it was noted that play centre work was complementary to their study and the 5.30–7.30 p.m. sessions would not interfere with their studies. In 1905, total weekly attendances were 5846 children, which increased in the following year to 10,030, at a cost of approximately £120 per centre for the year (Trevelyan 1920: 26). The play centres targeted 'in need' children by supplying them with tickets to all sessions. Within a short space of time the EPC was being urged by the

School Care Committee,[3] police and magistrates to open more centres and increase the numbers eligible for all session entry. The endorsement of play centres by education welfare services and the police was evidence of their place as essential agencies for preventative work with children.

In 1906 the Education Minister, Augustine Birrell, was invited to the Somers Town Play Centre. As a result of this and of Mary Ward's persuasion regarding the need for play centres, a clause was inserted into the 1906 Education Act giving powers to local authorities to support the work. The clause (known as the 'Mary Ward Clause' in recognition of her work) was not universally acclaimed. The main objections came from the CHEA committee who felt that this provision was not needed, as their evidence showed that current need for out-of-school play was being met. They also considered that, if provision of play centres became a duty of local authorities there would be an end of voluntary work in schools, and the additional costs of a statutory service would be an intolerable burden on the rates (*The Times* 1906).[4]

The 1906 Education Bill contained more controversial issues than the play clause, and it failed to reach the statute book. The non-controversial parts of the original Bill were reintroduced in the 1907 Education (Administrative Provisions) Act, which was successfully passed. In this Act, a weakened amendment gave local education authorities powers to 'encourage and assist the continuance or establishment of Voluntary Agencies', rather than making provision of play centres a duty. The origin of the voluntary-statutory dichotomy in play can be identified most clearly in this debate between the CHEA and the Evening Play Centres, which highlighted the split in play agencies between support for play as primarily voluntary, and the view of provision as part of a statutory education welfare service.

The 1907 Education Act made it easier for the London County Council (LCC) to loan equipment and premises but did little to ease the financial burden of maintaining play centres. Fund-raising remained an ever-present burden of organizing the Evening Play Centres. Although the Act allowed all local authorities to assist play centres there was little evidence that it had a major impact on local authorities outside London.

Play in parks and open spaces

Between 1904 and 1914 the number of Evening Play Centres in London expanded from 8 to 20. In 1912, in addition to these centres, the committee ran 40 organized playgrounds in schools, with the LCC running a further 40 through the Education Department Central Care Committee.

As envisaged by Mary Ward and the EPCC, the 1907 Education Act implied that play provision was part of the emerging education welfare service. However, the fact that local authorities, like Birmingham, concentrated on organizing outdoor play through their parks departments suggested that children's play could also be seen as part of general leisure requirements. The aims of this work were to increase children's access by arranging regular bus trips to organized play leadership in parks, and to provide supervised games on open spaces near housing (Campbell 1917). The expansion of public housing provision in 'block dwellings'[5] created the need for playgrounds as part of housing estates. The block dwellings increased population density in the cities and the need for play space became a necessity and established the link between play facilities and housing provision.

The increase of organized play run by local authorities had weakened the relationship between out-of-school play and schools. In the 1912 departmental report on playgrounds (Board of Education 1912), evidence presented by local authorities and representatives of schools supported the view that organized play was best supplied in parks and playing fields rather than by using school premises or spending more money from the rates to supply schools with expensive playgrounds. This report gave further fuel to the prospect that after-school play provision need not necessarily be based in schools and thereby not be funded through education budgets.

Diversification of play provision in the early twentieth century

The 1907 Education Act did not make the play centre's position in education more secure since the word 'encourage' in the clause supporting out-of-school work with children could be interpreted to allow assistance to be given to other bodies. In addition, the diversification of play provision through developments in parks, playing fields and outdoor activities meant that headteachers were able to argue that after school, organized playwork was not as critical to school performance as it had been in previous years. The legislation, in favour of play provision, did not make it clear that governmental responsibility for play would rest solely with the Board of Education, but left the issue to local authorities to decide how support was to be interpreted. As different local authority departments became involved in supporting areas of play provision, so the possibility increased that future provision would not be the responsibility of one government ministry. Over subsequent decades, the ambiguous statutory position of out-of-school playwork contributed to an attitude in government that this work was best carried out by the voluntary sector. This in turn weakened playwork's original position as an ancillary part of statutory education.

In London, play centres enjoyed a special relationship with the School Care Committee, where play was considered an important part of education welfare provision. For a voluntary body this was a privileged position within a statutory organization as the Care Committee could mediate between the EPCC and schools. The fact that play centres had support in the community as well as from the Care Committee gave workers strength to argue for the place of play in education, but the voluntary status of the EPCC never quite overcame the feeling that they were marginal to the main business of schools. In other cities, where the liaison with education was not as formal or integrated, play centres remained community-based in Settlements or churches. By 1912 it was clear that progress of children's play provision within education was likely to be difficult. The school was viewed as the major institution with responsibility for the child's welfare outside the family and this effectively undermined the perception of the play centre's significant contribution to preventative work with children.

Training

In 1913 Mary Ward, partly due to a split with the National Union of Women Workers over her anti-suffrage stance, set up a joint advisory committee of MPs and women social workers to look at issues of training and coordination of work with children (Progress 1914: 97). One interpretation of Ward's role in this initiative might have been to maintain her position as a woman of influence in government without the vote (Lewis 1991: 240–50). Though her aims might have had their foundation in her personal difficulties over votes for women, the objective of bringing together different voluntary sector groups to establish a common training agenda was something that it was felt would benefit the children's club and play movement. Increasing the status of playworkers through training was potentially a way for the EPC to advance their claims to be indispensable to the education welfare service. World War I intervened before any work could be undertaken on this initiative and in the intervening years the issue of creating training courses comparable to the standard of teachers or social workers was only sporadically advanced. Between 1920 and 1970, training for playwork remained a low priority and contributed to the notion that play centres were a primarily part-time or holiday provision, supported by trainee teachers.

The effects of World War I and statutory support for play

The necessity for women's employment and conscription of men into the forces during World War I were blamed for increased juvenile delinquency and truancy as they undermined the influence of parental supervision. At the beginning of World War I, play centres had been suspended, but were quickly reinstated by the government who then provided direct funding provision for out-of-school programmes. In 1917 the Board of Education agreed to give local authorities a grant to provide 50 per cent of the costs of play centres and voluntary sector youth provision. All over England new play centres were opened (*TES* 1917). In London, the LCC granted a further quarter of the costs, leaving the EPC to find the remaining 25 per cent. Janet Trevelyan, Mary Ward's younger daughter, felt that this was a strong endorsement of the play centre movement by the state, and would mean that its future was assured (Trevelyan 1920: 64).

Post-war developments in play provision

In the post-war period, consensus about healthy recreation as a deterrent to juvenile delinquency was revised and the view that a poor environment caused juvenile crime was modified to give greater prominence to the psychology of the individual and the effects of home and family (Bailey 1987). In education, psychology was used to detail the problems of children in schools, which undermined the significance previously given to social problems. World War I had put more emphasis on casework solutions rather than community-based provision. The greater acceptance of middle-class women's full-time employment meant there was less call for voluntary workers. As demand for working-class women in the labour market declined, expansion of provision beyond the levels of 1917 became unnecessary. In addition, although the financial support for play was greater, there was more competition between youth organizations and child welfare bodies who were eligible to receive government funding. In the post-war period, the social arguments that had previously given backing to the play service were no longer as strong nor the causes so urgent to give this work greater prominence.

In 1920 Mary Ward's death at the age of 71 meant that the play centre movement had lost its most eloquent and eminent leader. The place of children's play provision in society was changing and play centres would need to adapt to survive.

Play centres and their relation to education

Between the wars the EPC, with Janet Trevelyan as chair/treasurer, struggled to raise the necessary funds each year. As grants were increased by the LCC, the Treasury decreased its funding, thereby necessitating more fund-raising. The support from the Board of Education gave play centres some measure of security but the workforce was untrained and part-time, relying heavily on teachers in the supervisory roles.

In the post-war period, Evening Play Centre work, based on social welfare principles of protecting the child, was no longer unique. The importance of the educational uses of play gained influence through works such as Caldwell Cook's *The Play Way* (1917).[6]

Learning through play was also a feature of teacher training as popularized by such eminent educationalists as Percy Nunn at the University Institute of Education (Nunn 1947). However, Evening Play Centres did not exploit this interest in the relationship between play and education as a means to widen the appeal of their work.[7] After nearly 20 years, play centres had become social institutions that were no longer seen as innovative.

EPC reports to the LCC Education Committee tended to measure effectiveness based on statistics of the numbers of children using the service rather than develop qualitative evidence based on the value of play to children. As a voluntary body outside education, the EPC was dependent on the LCC for support, which left it open to criticism from a number of quarters. For example, in 1925, London school-keepers criticized the unsupervised use of playgrounds by children, forcing the closure of 80 playgrounds. This put pressure on the LCC to develop supervised playleadership schemes in parks. By 1928, despite this apparent weakness, the EPC had maintained a programme of expansion, managing 38 centres and 20 vacation schools.

In the post-war period, the EPC was increasingly drawn into dealing with problems created by the host schools. In 1930, the Headmistresses Consultative Committee complained about play centres being overcrowded; children under 5 being admitted; non-use of cloakrooms; and the difficulties of ensuring proper cleaning of classrooms. The LCC dispatched 12 of its inspectors unannounced to visit 24 play centres. The report from the inspection found that 'not a single inspector has any really adverse criticism either on an individual centre or on the system as a whole' (LCC 1930). This episode underlined the difficult relationship that a voluntary agency had in working with schools.

Clashes between the EPC and schools were an ever-present irritation that hampered the development of play centres. However, because the EPC had strong support within the LCC, objections were often overcome. For example, in 1935, a headteacher objected to the opening of a play centre unless a change of supervisor was made. After intervention by Janet Trevelyan, the head agreed to the play centre being organized in the school. It was also not unusual for an unsympathetic headteacher to complain about not being able to display children's work and the possible destruction of wall decorations because of the play centre (Pearson-Clarke 1984).

Play centres were also drawn into conflicts about the interpretation of schools' policies. In 1935 an incident arose between school inspectors and the EPC, concerning a school's objection to a five-night a week play centre that clashed with the school homework class, which it was felt ought to take precedence over the play centre provision. This criticism was no doubt influenced by the fact that teachers were paid ten shillings (50p) to supervise the class without being required to undertake any tuition. The play centre in Deptford catered for 500–600 children, while the homework class had only 160 children. Payment for the homework classes was funded by the Board of Education and subject to the same regulations as governed the play centre. These facts were revealed during a meeting between Janet Trevelyan and a senior official at the Board of Education. Indeed it was later suggested by the same official that turning the play centre into a homework class might be a possible solution! In 1938, the whole issue was resolved by the withdrawal of funding for homework classes (Pearson-Clarke 1984).

The need for EPC play centres was not doubted by members of the School Care Committees and the police. In 1938, the EPC estimated that to meet the suburban growth in London, 100 play centres were needed. Play centres were seen as offering a valuable form of social help to developing neighbourhoods and they were used in times of conflict to help a local area with a specific social issue. For example, in the aftermath of the violence at the British Union of Fascists anti-Semitic march in London's East End, the EPC were asked to open a new play centre in this area. However, one should not forget that alongside these 'special issues' the EPC addressed the ongoing social welfare needs of children who were being referred by police and education social workers. In many ways, play centres were serving a real social purpose in protecting children in the impoverished neighbourhoods of London and this work was often undervalued as it was never sufficiently highlighted in LCC documentation.

By the late 1930s it was evident that resourcing a pan-London play service was beyond the resources of a voluntary organization. Across the country, 192 play centres were entirely supported by local authorities (Pearson-Clarke 1984). In 1941, as a wartime measure, the LCC took over the running of the play centres and they remained part of London's education service until the 1990 break up of the Inner London Education Service.

New dangers and new needs for play provision

The EPC's difficulties with schools meant that supervising play centres left little energy to encourage fresh ideas or address the new danger to children on the street – the motor car. The task of diverting children from street play was taken up by the parks department of local authorities and voluntary bodies, who initiated play parks, playgrounds, play streets and playing fields. In 1925, the formation of the NPFA created a campaigning organization to lobby for expansion of children's access to play space. Between the wars, advances in playwork methods tended to occur through open access, outdoor play leadership schemes in parks. The NPFA was instrumental in pioneering the philosophy of this work and they provided a network of support to facilitate the introduction of games and play activities adaptable to parks (CCRPT 1937). Play leadership in parks maintained the idea of creating safe places for children where they could participate in active play opportunities under adult supervision. After World War II, NPFA's experience of play leadership was harnessed to assist Lady Allen of Hurtwood's vision of establishing adventure playgrounds. Through this new departure, play organizations created a new community-based form of playwork.

Conclusion

Historical study of provision for children's out-of-school leisure suggests that there is a need to view the origins of playwork as arising from several different sources. This approach would also propose that there is an obligation to conceptualize playwork in terms of distinct traditions or movements in order to appreciate the manner of the development of children's play provision. It is also important to locate the arguments for play provision within: broader social debates concerning delinquency; the dominant perception of childhood prevalent at any one time; and the effects of major social changes on children. By understanding this wider context it becomes possible to see how the conflicts and alliances between bodies have impacted and influenced the importance of play within social policy.

Play organizations have made innovative contributions to the advance of statutory education and provided examples of good practice that have demonstrated the need for change in the school curriculum. As the play centre became the model that society found most easy to accommodate, and as its role was institutionalized, the innovations within education were lost and its work became marginalized. Historical evidence seems to support the view that play remains marginal to mainstream thinking in education, and is undervalued as a method to facilitate social welfare goals. It is only when play centre work aligns itself directly with children who experience the greatest effects of deprivation, that its value to a community is felt.

The failure of playwork advocates to develop a coherent theoretical grounding for practice, equal to social work or education, allowed the discussion of the role of play to be separated from its social context of protecting working-class children. This factor also meant it was easier, for organizations who perceived a need, to be led by their hearts and believe their constituency was the child, rather than to engage in political debate about the child's right to play. Against this background it became easier for representatives of play bodies to attack each other, or see their efforts from the limited perspective of the volunteer or part-time employee, rather than to situate their work within arguments about creating a statutory informal education service. In this vacuum of theory and lack of clarity over the meaning of play, any statutory help for children's out-of-school provision has often meant that non-play organizations have been able to benefit, since they were able to exploit the opportunities offered to greater effect than their playwork counterparts.

Notes

1 *The Quiver* was a nineteenth-century evangelical social action periodical for Church workers. It also mounted a fund-raising campaign to provide playgrounds in London.
2 The first Settlement was established in 1884 in London's East End by Canon Barnett. The aim was to bring graduates from universities to the inner city to study social conditions, set up education programmes for adults and welfare provision for the working-class population. Over the next 20 years, most large towns with a strong university association founded their own Settlement. The movement also took root in the USA where its leading advocate was Jane Addams at Hull House, Chicago.
3 The School Care Committee was an early form of education welfare service. This organization oversaw issues of children's school attendance, health and liaison with educational charities and play centres (see Williams *et al.* 2001).
4 Rates were an old form of local taxation based on the size of a person's house. In the 1980s this form of local finance in the UK was replaced by the Community Charge, which was subsequently replaced by Council Tax.
5 Block dwellings were local authority 5–6 storey flats built as housing estates after slum clearance, as part of providing cheap housing for working-class families.
6 In the 1930s the ideas in *The Play Way* were adapted and incorporated into the Spens Report and carried into new ways of teaching English that had a similar

impact on education as the adoption of the current Literacy Hour measures (Beacock 1943).

7 In *Play Centres* (1937), Dorothy Gardiner wrote about her experience of running play centres as part of teacher training and their value in improving teacher's understanding of children. Until well into the 1950s, teacher training courses regularly incorporated play centre work into their programmes.

Part 2

Theories of playwork

Chapter 4

Compound flexibility: the role of playwork in child development

Fraser Brown

Play is often the only area of a child's life where the future direction of activity or behaviour is not in the hands of an adult. This 'personally directed' (Hughes 1996a) aspect of childhood play leaves most of us with powerful images to take forward into our adult lives. The strongest of these is the idea that play has nothing to do with adults – indeed, that adults (almost by definition) should not expect to be involved with, or understand, children's play. It is generally assumed that children's play is a natural activity which occurs irrespective of adult input. Some adults may even feel a personal guardianship over their own much loved memories of play. This means there is never likely to be a ready acceptance of the concept of playwork. Consequently, playworkers regularly face comments and questions such as:

- 'No one taught *me* how to play when I was a child.'
- 'What do you do for a real job?'
- 'Why should society spend money on that?'

This chapter seeks to address some of that scepticism.

At its most basic level, the thinking which underpins the concept of playwork is fairly straightforward. Children learn and develop through their play. Therefore, children require a range of play opportunities if they are to achieve their full developmental potential. In many modern-day settings children's play opportunities are restricted. This is detrimental to individual children, and an ineffective use of society's resources. It is clearly in society's interest to address the lack of play opportunities, and so reinvigorate the process of child development through play. This is the role of the playworker.

In terms of its structure (not its practice) playwork has similarities with many other professions. For example, nursing encompasses a range of specialisms including paediatrics, mental health and care for the elderly. The social work profession includes child protection work, adoption and 'care in the community'. In a similar way, playwork may be seen as a generalized description of work that includes adventure play, therapeutic work, out-of-school clubs, hospital play, environmental design and much more – all those approaches that use the medium of play as a mechanism for redressing aspects of developmental imbalance caused by a deficit of play opportunities.

Some playwork theorists have suggested this generic view of playwork lacks focus, and the search for a definition would be assisted by isolating the specific play elements within our work. However, in most playwork settings that would be extremely difficult. If we focus purely on the play elements, or the therapeutic elements, or even the care elements, in our search for a definition we risk creating the potential for disagreement where there need be none. The playwork profession has a long history of unresolved disputes between different factions, all claiming the high moral ground, all defending the purity of their view of playwork. This is not good for the future of the profession, nor does it hold much relevance for most playworkers. A generic view of the profession is preferable because the various branches of playwork have so much in common, and so little substantive disagreement.

On balance, I favour an admittedly loose concept – i.e. the playworker's role should be taken to include everything necessary to create the conditions that enable children to play. Once the right conditions are created, it should be possible for a playworker to return to the sort of non-interventionist approach recommended by Hughes (1996a). Ultimately the aim of playwork must be to provide an environment that enables the child to grow towards fulfilment (referred to by Maslow 1971 as 'self-realization'). For this reason playwork takes the agenda of the individual child as its starting point. In an after-school club that might simply mean the children designing and controlling their own weekly play programme. On an adventure playground I have seen children choose everything from den building to country dancing. Each child had a specific agenda, and that was respected by the playworkers. In most settings there are two distinct but overlapping aspects to the work. Playwork involves:

- analysing the child's environment in order to identify and remove any barriers to the process of development through play;
- enriching the child's play environment in order to stimulate the process of development through play.

'Removing barriers to play' might include a wide variety of activities, from a simple task such as removing broken glass from the outdoor site, to more demanding strategies such as tackling racist behaviour. Sometimes simple tasks can lead to complex outcomes. For example, in the Romanian paediatric hospital (see Chapter 11) the playworkers were confronted with malnourished children who found it difficult to engage in physical play. These children had come to regard food with fear and suspicion. The playworkers were able to persuade the children to eat by making mealtimes into a playful activity, which not only improved their physical fitness but also encouraged levels of social play that had previously been non-existent. Obviously it does not take a highly qualified playworker to pick up glass or feed hungry children. These are not essentially play-related activities, but the quality of play opportunities could be seriously damaged if the task was not performed. Any caring individual could perform such a task, but would they – and would they know what to do next? And if no one else is going to do it, then it necessarily becomes part of the role of the playworker. Otherwise it is impossible to achieve anything. With some of those basic issues addressed (i.e. survival, safety, security) it becomes far easier to continue the day-to-day business of therapeutic playwork, adventure playwork, etc.

The playworker should also be concerned with enriching the child's play environment in order to stimulate the process of development through play. There are a number of factors playworkers should take into account when considering how best to create such an environment. For the purposes of the Romanian research study (see Chapter 11) these were grouped under 11 subheadings: freedom; flexibility; socialization and social interaction; physical activity; intellectual stimulation; creativity and problem solving; emotional equilibrium; self-discovery; ethical stance; adult/child relationships; and general appeal (e.g. humour, colour, etc.). By far the most important element in all this is *compound flexibility* – the interrelationship between a flexible/adaptable environment and the gradual development of flexibility/adaptability in the child. The thinking behind this approach, including the reasons for moving away from the SPICE acronym (social interaction, *phys*ical activity, *i*ntellectual stimulation; *c*reative achievement; *e*motional stability), is explored in the remainder of this chapter.

Background

Since the mid-1980s, the acronym SPICE has regularly been used as a description of playwork (see Table 4.1), usually in a form of analysis which is far too simplistic to be helpful. The use of SPICE has become so widespread it is now hard to identify its source. Of course, few things are ever truly 'original', but I can claim to be the originator of one version of the acronym – a version which has subsequently been misquoted, misused and misunderstood. In summary, the argument had two themes, and went as follows:

1 The ideal developmental cycle for a human being (especially a child) involves the gradual growth of an interaction between a flexible environment and an increasingly flexible human being. In other words, given ideal conditions, the growing child makes use of whatever flexibility there is in the environment, and so becomes more flexible, and able to make even better use of elements of flexibility in the environment – and so on.

Table 4.1 SPICE and the three Fs

Developmental focus	Significant opportunities in the play setting might include
Social interaction	Friendship networks; cooperation; sense of community
Physical activity	Development of motor skills; release of oxygen to brain
Intellectual stimulation	Information; knowledge; inspiration
Creative achievement	Imagination; problem solving; make-believe
Emotional stability	Security; consistency; safety
Fun	Risk; challenge; recreation; entertainment
Freedom	Boundary testing; exercise of power and control
Flexibility	Experimentation, investigation; exploration

This process may be characterized as 'compound flexibility' (see Figure 4.1, p. 56).

2 Children's play has great significance in this cycle of child development. Possibly more than any other activity, play engages children in the full range of developmental stimuli (see Table 4.1).

Taken as a whole this argument leads to the conclusion that the adult world should treat children's play very seriously. Therefore, if we identify areas where the day-to-day play environment of our children is unsatisfactory, in particular where it is lacking in flexibility, then we have a social responsibility to take action to improve matters. This is one of the most basic justifications for playwork, and explains the thinking behind the following definition: 'Playwork is the specific act of affecting the "whole environment" with the deliberate intention of improving opportunities for play' (Playboard 1984).

The remainder of this chapter is an attempt to set the record straight by restating the original ideas, while at the same time examining their strengths and weaknesses. The concepts still have relevance at the beginning of the twenty-first century. However, by offering a degree of self-criticism, I hope to move the debate forward.

Source of the ideas

On a purely personal level, where did these ideas come from? The answer is: from playing, or at least, a specific form of playing – i.e. playing with words. In many ways the ideas were a product of the creative process which Bruner (Bruner *et al.* 1976) calls *combinatorial flexibility* – i.e. it involved the combination of a number of otherwise unconnected factors. Combinatorial flexibility is a process that not only enables the acquisition of information about the world, but also encourages the development of flexibility and creativity in problem solving. It is based on the idea that most artefacts in a child's play environment have a flexible potential. For example, a child who is playing with a toy train, a rope and a box has the potential to play many different games and become involved in a wide range of creative activities. Each artefact has its own inherent flexibility, while in combination they have even more flexibility. It probably said 'skipping rope' on the box, but the child may decide to accommodate the train by using the rope as a railway line, and the box as a station. In the case of my word play, the unconnected factors were:

- a draft document, written by a work colleague;
- a conversation about Fogg indexing[1] with a personal friend;
- the purchase of a word processor.

These factors came together at the same time as I had been trying to get my ideas about play and playwork into some sort of order. In particular, the playwork movement needed an effective answer to a question I had often been asked: 'Why should we spend money on playwork?'

In 1985, I was given a piece of work that a colleague had written, using rather convoluted terminology. It was a very general piece about the role of adults in a child's life. Our staff team had agreed it should be rewritten in terms that could be readily understood by anyone, without the use of a dictionary. At first I tried a crude form of Fogg indexing. It was while trying to simplify the structure that I began to notice a number of interesting commonalities. Next, I tried to bring some order through the cut and paste facility on the word processor. Eventually, the piece had been completely rewritten and the finished article bore little resemblance to the original.

This whole process was reminiscent of a very common playwork experience, which is typified by the following example. A group of teenagers once asked me to write a pantomime which they could perform for a toddler's Christmas party. I was reluctant, since the idea of doing the writing myself seemed at odds with the basic philosophy of playwork. However, I was excited by their new-found sense of responsibility, so I agreed and wrote a version of Rumplestiltskin. In the event, the child-centred nature of playwork asserted itself, and after two rehearsals the group began to rewrite the script. By the time it was actually performed, they had a new title: 'Rumpo Meets the Caveman', and most of the script was theirs.

The argument produced by this process had two main themes. The first concerned the significance of compound flexibility in child development, and specifically sought to highlight the role of playwork in the modern world. The second provided a brief summary of the essential characteristics of a positive play environment. It was my intention that these two strands of thought should be interwoven to provide the beginnings of a theory of playwork. This did not happen in the manner intended, but in quite another way – i.e. the acronym SPICE took hold in the minds of many playwork trainers, but only in a rather superficial way. Sadly, the concept of compound flexibility was largely sidelined. It is worth restating.

Compound flexibility

Bateson (1955) suggests that play texts (the play activity) are affected by contexts (the environment within which the play activity occurs). The notion of compound flexibility (Brown 1989) takes this idea one stage further by suggesting that the interactive process encourages the development of flexibility in the child. There is, therefore, massive child development potential in the play setting. This is not a simple interaction but a complex process wherein flexibility in the play environment leads to increased flexibility in the child. That child is then better able to make use of the flexible environment, and so on.

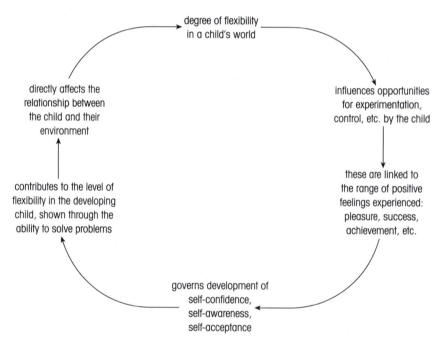

degree of flexibility
in a child's world

directly affects the
relationship between
the child and their
environment

influences opportunities
for experimentation,
control, etc. by the child

contributes to the level of
flexibility in the developing
child, shown through the
ability to solve problems

these are linked to
the range of positive
feelings experienced:
pleasure, success,
achievement, etc.

governs development of
self-confidence,
self-awareness,
self-acceptance

Figure 4.1 Compound flexibility: the theoretical cycle

Figure 4.1 shows an 'ideal type'[2] developmental cycle (which should not be confused with the positive developmental spiral, shown in Figure 4.3). It shows how the developmental process relies on the child's 'whole' environment providing the potential for compound flexibility. The environment in this case includes other human beings, as well as play materials and the rest of the natural and man-made world – anything or anyone that children might use as a plaything. The logic goes like this. The degree of flexibility in the play environment has a direct effect on a child's opportunities for experimentation, because it governs the level of control that the child is able to exercise. The freedom to experiment, where it exists, produces positive feelings, a sense of achievement, pleasure, etc. (Hughes and Williams 1982). This, in turn, encourages the development of self-confidence, self-acceptance, etc. With increased self-confidence, the child becomes more comfortable with taking risks and consequently their reaction to day-to-day problems becomes more varied (Sylva *et al.* 1976). This increasingly flexible approach to problem solving makes the child better able to use the full potential of the play environment. Thus, the child moves closer to their developmental potential than would otherwise have been the case.

I recently observed a child who had been given a teddy bear as a present. She proceeded to create a cradle for an imaginary baby, by using the teddy, the box it was packed in and the string which had been used to tie the box. Clearly play opportunities were not limited by the fact that a teddy is not a baby, a box is not a cradle and string is not cradle straps. At this 'micro' level we have an example of the interaction between a child's imagination and the potential offered by a flexible environment. Such interaction is both stimulating and productive in developmental terms. This is no less true at the 'macro' level – i.e. the child's wider play environment (street, park, school playground etc.). In fact, everywhere children play, flexibility is significant. Those who provide for children's play therefore need to think in terms of the best means of ensuring that children have continuing access to a flexible environment.

But what is meant by a flexible environment? As long ago as 1931 the Danish architect, C.Th. Sorensen wrote: 'Perhaps we should try to set up waste material playgrounds in suitable large areas where children would be able to play with old cars, boxes and timber' (Allen of Hurtwood 1968: 9). This was a line of thought taken up by Bengtsson (1974) when he spoke of play as taking place wherever 'something turns up to move the imagination'. This could be anything, he said, 'but preferably something that can be manipulated and influenced' (p. 49). It also reflects the optimistic view of creativity touched on by Nicholson and Schreiner (1973) when they suggest that children should be empowered to structure their own play environment because human beings are inherently creative, and there is no reason to believe that we loose this talent as we grow older. Hart (1995: 21) has shown a link between children's interest and the availability of 'materials for them to work with'. Why should this be? Nicholson (1971: 30), in developing his 'theory of loose parts', explains it thus: 'In any environment both the degree of inventiveness and creativity, and the possibility of discovery, are directly proportional to the number and kind of variables in it.'

Nicholson is using the word 'environment' in a holistic sense – 'a system of interactive parts that affect us' (Nicholson and Schreiner 1973: 19). Thus, a 'loose part' environment includes everything from the perimeter walls of a building to the flotsam and jetsam that lie within. Nicholson suggests that a beach is a good example of a 'loose part' environment. Here the sand is constantly shifting, the sea is fluid, even the rock pools change with the tides. The debris of past holidaymakers is left on the beach for future children

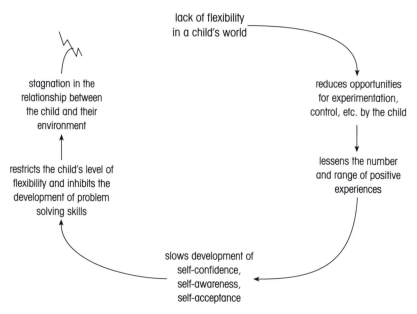

Figure 4.2 Compound flexibility: a negative cycle

to play with. This is presumably the thinking behind e.e. cummings' poem, 'maggie and milly and molly and may', which culminates with the lines

> For whatever we lose (like a you or a me)
> it's always ourselves we find in the sea

(cummings 1977: 53)

Clearly this is where modern society has been most at fault. For example, many children have no access to a garden (let alone the beach); their streets are full of cars; school playgrounds are usually flat, sterile areas of concrete which offer no interest and very little opportunity for interaction (Brown 1990). To make matters worse, we are not very child-friendly in the UK, so children's experience of both the physical and the human environment tends to be negative. The consequences of this are depicted in Figure 4.2, which shows how the compound flexibility process can stagnate if environmental conditions are unsuitable. Children who have little control over their world inevitably have fewer positive experiences, which in turn slows the development of their self-confidence. Children who lack confidence are less likely to take risks or try out different solutions to the problems they encounter.

In such circumstances the relationship with the environment is potentially characterized by three of the 'four dangerous extremes' referred to by Bob Hughes in Chapter 5. It may be either over-negative, erratic or deprived, or any combination of the three (the children discussed in Chapter 11 have experienced a lifetime of all three). Whether such a situation is retrievable is still open to debate. Tobin (1997) has found evidence that certain areas of children's brains become inactive as a result. My own experience in Romania suggests that it may never be too late to help children whose disturbed behaviour is the result of their previous life experience. It is certainly true that children such as these, who have been stimulus deprived, develop 'severe learning difficulties, erratic behaviour, difficulty in forming bonds, depression and withdrawal resembling autistic children' (Hughes 2001: 73). In specific cases we have had great difficulty in identifying whether these behaviour patterns are the result of chronic deprivation or a congenital defect. Most of the children have been assessed by their doctors as 'retarded'. This is not a term we would use, and for good reason. Several of these 'retarded' children have made such staggering progress under the therapeutic playwork regime that it is not unreasonable to describe them as 'normal' (if such a thing exists). By any standard, this is playwork at the extreme limits of its potential. Most playworkers will fortunately never have to witness such abject circumstances. Nevertheless, as a general rule, playworkers will find themselves working with children who have experienced some form of play deprivation, or play bias, and the consequences are potentially damaging to the healthy development of those children.

However, playwork is not simply about redressing the damaging effects of play deprivation. It is more concerned with enabling children to achieve their full potential in developmental terms. Returning to Figure 4.2, herein lies one of the main justifications for playwork: intervention in a child's play world in order to create an environment conducive to stimulating the compound flexibility process. For example, a good adventure playground empowers its users by offering freedom of choice in a stimulating and empathetic setting, with the result that children constantly create and recreate their own play environment. I once worked on an adventure playground where the children did this by designing and building most of the structures, and all of the dens that littered the site. By the end of the first summer they had created something that I thought was beautiful (although a local parent said it reminded him of a 'concentration camp'). On the Saturday before bonfire night, I arrived at the site to find the children tearing everything down to make a giant bonfire. My first reaction was shock at the apparent careless waste of their actions. However, they created the biggest bonfire I have ever seen and raised money for the playground by charging an entry fee when it was lit. The following February, they started building new structures and dens, and thus established an endless creative cycle of construction, deconstruction and reconstruction that continued throughout the life of the playground.

The potential benefits of playwork in the developmental process are shown in Figure 4.3. In such circumstances the word 'cycle' becomes inappropriate. The process would be better described as an ever-growing spiral, self-supporting in nature and generally positive in its outcomes.

Thus, we may be able to justify 'intervening' in the child's play environment, but this begs the question of, what form the intervention should take in order to maximize a child's developmental potential. SPICE (and the three

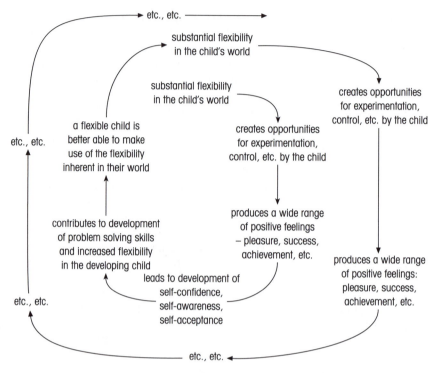

Figure 4.3 Compound flexibility: a positive spiral

Fs) was an attempt to offer some guidance, the idea being to provide a series of generic headings that might serve as reminders for practising playworkers. As can be seen from Figure 4.4, the original idea was quite broad based, bearing little resemblance to the limited interpretation which has come into common use. I did not intend to suggest that all play environments should contain all these characteristics at every moment of the day – rather, that good practice should see playworkers ready and willing to provide such opportunities when called upon to do so *by the children*. This is extremely important, and has too often been ignored. Playwork interventions should only happen at the request of the children. That is why Hughes (1996a) places such importance on the child-to-playworker approach ratio, suggesting it should be far in excess of the playworker-to-child approach ratio. One of the key factors in the compound flexibility process is that sense of the child being in control of their own destiny. For the process to be operating effectively the child must be an autonomous actor. Thus, the first rule of playwork is to work to the child's agenda.

Why then has one part of this concept been so widely used, while the other has been largely ignored? Broadly speaking, there are two possible causes. First, the concepts were misunderstood, and consequently misused. Second, they contained inherent and fundamental flaws.

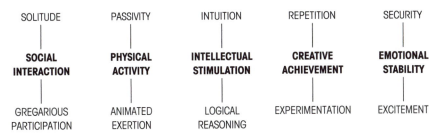

Figure 4.4 Opportunities provided by an effective play environment

Misunderstanding and misuse

The true message of SPICE is uncomfortable for trainers whose priorities differ from those of the early pioneers of playwork. The idea of an interrelationship between the degree of flexibility in a child's world, and the development of flexibility in that child, does not sit easily with a play service that has tended to develop along the path of adult priorities (e.g. specialist coaching, safety, working parents, etc.). I was recently in a public forum where someone mentioned the old adventure playground rule that 'children can do anything so long as it doesn't interfere with the enjoyment of another child'. Another speaker described this as 'sixties hippy claptrap'. The message that play provision should be child centred is one to which many providers offer lip-service, without ever genuinely letting go of their adult power. SPICE was originally designed as a mnemonic, rather than an acronym. Unfortunately, the acronym is striking and many people have assumed that the message is: 'variety is the SPICE of life', when in fact it would be far more accurate to say 'flexibility is the SPICE of life'. Variety implies adults offering children lots of choices. Flexibility, on the other hand, implies children controlling their own play environment. If playworkers and/or their trainers fail to understand this distinction they are short-changing their customers. There are too many projects where the children are offered a wide range of activities, while the control remains firmly in the hands of the workers.

For example, I once witnessed an incident where a 'playworker' had organized a game of football for about 20 children. During the game, a dog chased a second ball onto the pitch. Quite spontaneously the children incorporated that ball into their play, and a very complex, almost three-dimensional game resulted. The adult blew his whistle forcefully, and stopped the game. The children moaned loudly, while he carried the spare ball to the touch-line. The children's body language should have sent a message to the whistle-blower, but he seemed completely unaware of their very obvious 'play cues' (Else and Sturrock 1998). Not surprisingly, during the next ten minutes the players became more aggressive, even to the extent of a fight breaking out. After a while, four of the children simply walked away and the game broke up in disarray. Presumably, having tasted the thrill of creative play, the inflexibility of organized sport was too much to bear. A simple understanding of the compound flexibility process, and the importance of working to the child's agenda, could have saved this playworker a great deal of stress, and made the experience that much more enjoyable for everyone.

Flaws in the original idea

However, it would be foolish to argue that the original idea of SPICE was perfect. When SPICE was originated, its theoretical reference was quite limited. This led to problems of both form and substance, with the result that many leading thinkers in the playwork movement were inclined to dismiss the ideas as being glib or superficial. As originally formulated there was too much loose terminology. First, the phrase 'emotional stability' was far too inexact. It would have been more helpful to focus on 'the pursuit of emotional equilibrium', a far broader concept which would have allowed the incorporation of the thinking of many leading psychologists and psycho-analysts such as Klein (1955) and Axline (1969). Second, the original concept contains no distinction between socialization and socializing. This means, for example, that the reinforcement of cultural norms was overlooked (Tinbergen 1975). One final problem resulting from loose terminology derives from the inaccurate and misleading depiction of compound flexibility as a *cycle*. The word 'compound' does not refer to something that goes round and round. Instead it implies growth, and so it would be far more accurate to say that compound flexibility describes a complex geometric or exponential interrelationship between humans and their environment. This is shown more effectively by Figure 4.3 than Figure 4.1.

Coupled with this there was a lack of clarity in the original approach. It may not have been sufficiently clear that the individual terms which made up SPICE were supposed to be broad in their scope – eclectic headings rather than exclusive terms (see Figure 4.4). To some extent this was inevitable, since 'Fogg indexing' always implies a balancing act between accessibility and intellectual accuracy. This was a deliberate attempt to move away from the approach of an influential group of playwork theorists whose ideas were couched in obscure terminology which could only be understood by a select few. However, my own approach backfired when the acronym was taken up by the after-school lobby, and used as the basis for its training courses. While the playwork movement continued to debate the finer points of the work, the world moved on and we were outflanked by three very powerful lobbies: not just after-school care, but also safety and curriculum-based education.

Finally, it is clear that several concepts were missing from the original approach. Play has value in a number of different ways, most of which are covered by the generic headings of SPICE and the three Fs. Nevertheless, this leaves certain serious omissions, especially where the concept is being related to playwork. There is no room for the ethical stance of playwork, its commit-ment to social inclusion, non-violence and anti-oppressive practice. One of the main functions of play is to enhance the process of self-discovery and self-realization (Maslow 1971), through the development of the spirit, strength of character, sense of morality, etc. Through play the child gradually comes to terms with the external world, while at the same time developing a controllable, secure world of their own – a process Sutton-Smith (1992) calls 'learning to control their own little microcosm of the world'. Garvey (1991) highlights the way in which we develop our concepts of safe practice through the non-literal activity of play. Throughout childhood, the knowledge and understanding gained via play experiences will enable the child to internalize the more abstract complexities of the world. For that reason, Segal and Yahraes (1924) argue that a child's sociocultural environment must not be negative in any way. This has clear implications for playworkers.

Vygotsky (1976) writes about the way in which an adult, or older peer, can help a child to explore their 'zone of proximal development'. This has often been used as an excuse for adult interference in a child's play. However, playworkers have always regarded the idea of adult 'leadership' with suspicion, seeing themselves as fulfilling an enabling or empowering function. This approach to the adult-child relationship is captured beautifully by the artist John Portchmouth (1969: 7):

> I don't remember how it started. There was me, and sand, and somehow there was a wooden spade: and then there were castles! I don't even remember asking how to do it; the need was big enough, and the way was there. Or maybe I'm not remembering exactly; perhaps I only found what someone had provided . . . someone who had anticipated the need . . . and all the time the great world of materials was opening up or waiting to be discovered. It helps if someone, no matter how lightly, puts in our way the means of making use of what we find.

The adult-child relationship is right at the heart of playwork. Who has the power in a play setting? What of the potential therapeutic role of the playworker? These are questions that are fundamental to playwork, and yet they were largely missing from the original SPICE approach.

A way forward

Thus, it might appear logical to argue that my original concept has outlived its usefulness. Certainly the inherent flaws, misunderstandings and misrepresentations are all problematic. Some might argue that it would be more useful to concentrate on 'play types' rather than developmental benefits (Hughes 1996b). However, completely abandoning the idea would serve no useful purpose. The playwork field may be better served by a variation on the theme. The concept of compound flexibility continues to be valid, and highly pertinent to the practice of playwork. As a result of the *Play Value Research project* (Brown 2000b), it is possible to suggest a revised version of SPICE – i.e. a number of generic headings that playworkers might use as reminders to underpin their work. In terms of play value assessment, each heading contains between 20 and 30 specific questions relating to play behaviours and/or characteristics of play that playworkers might ask of themselves and/or their project. A version of this was used to conduct research into the effects of therapeutic playwork on the group of abandoned children mentioned previously (see Chapter 11). The referencing is given as an indication of the theoretical roots of each generic heading.

Play value assessment headings

1 Freedom (Sorensen 1931; Csikszentmihalyi 1979; Bruce 1989).
2 Flexibility (Bateson 1955; Bruner 1972; Brown 1989).
3 Socialization and social interaction (Parten 1932; Harlow and Harlow 1962; Trevarthen 1996).
4 Physical activity (Spencer 1873; Patrick 1916; Garvey 1991).
5 Intellectual stimulation (Froebel 1826; Piaget 1951a, 1951b; Brown and Burger 1984; Roberts 1995).
6 Creativity and problem solving (Nicholson 1971; Sylva *et al.* 1976; Vygotsky 1976; Pepler 1982).
7 Emotional equilibrium (Klein 1955; Axline 1969; Winnicott 1992; Else and Sturrock 1998).
8 Self-discovery (Erikson 1951; Maslow 1971; Hughes 1996a).
9 Ethical stance (Chilton 1985; SPRITO 1992; Petrie 1994).
10 Adult-child relationships (Abernethy 1968; Sturrock 1997; Melville 1999).
11 General appeal (Berlyne 1960; Ellis 1973; Moore 1990).

Recently, Tawil (2000) has shown that the concept of compound flexibility is not only applicable to child development through play, but also to the development of the playwork profession. Figure 4.5 shows the potentially positive effects of the interaction between theory and practice, and the way in which this might aid the development of the profession of playwork and children's services in general.

Tawil is suggesting the degree of flexibility available to a playworker in their workplace has a direct influence on both theory and practice. This results in a wider range of opportunities being available to the children, which in turn provides the playworker with a wider range of experience. In theory this should provide both individual playworkers and the playwork movement with better arguments in support of improved provision. Thus, flexibility at the local level may lead to improvements in the quality and quantity of provision at the national level.

Notes

1 Fogg indexing is a technique, favoured by certain travel companies who recognize that the majority of their customers have limited reading skills. Its methods include:

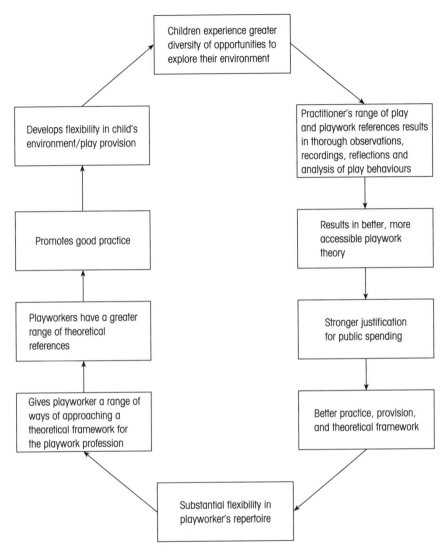

Figure 4.5 The implications of compound flexibility, as applied to the role of a playworker
Source: Tawil (2000).

limiting the length of sentences; restricting the number of syllables in each word; concentrating on 'action' verbs etc. The result is a much more accessible (though often less accurate) piece of writing.

2 An 'ideal type' is a pure model, which specifies the key characteristics of a concept, or organization, against which real-life models can be assessed. It is an abstract conceptual scheme, rather than a concrete description (Selfe 1993).

Chapter 5

Play deprivation, play bias and playwork practice

Bob Hughes

Introduction

Increasingly playworkers ask, 'How important is play to the development and evolution of our children?', when perhaps what we should be asking is, 'What effects does *not* playing, or only experiencing biased play have on them, and what should playwork's response be to those effects?' Consider the following:

- Headlines in the media scream 'Shock 27 per cent rise in muggings say Home Office statistics. Huge street crime rise is blamed on boys as young as 10' (*Evening Standard*, 16 January 2001).
- Current media reports ask 'Should Robert Thompson and Jon Venables, the murderers of James Bulger, retain their anonymity on release from prison?' One analysis of the murder itself suggested that both Thompson and Venables had become trapped between reality and imagination, 'unable to distinguish between everyday reality and the reality of dramatic play' (Jennings 1995: 132).
- The individual responsible for the Hungerford massacre was quoted as being 'unable or unwilling to distinguish between fantasy and reality' (Josephs 1993: 168–9).
- 'Damilola bled to death after being stabbed. Twelve youths have been arrested and released on bail' (*Observer*, 31 December 2000).
- Jeffrey Dahmer, the notorious serial murderer, allegedly played with 'road-kill' – animals that had been run over by traffic. Other serial murderers are reported to have been subjected to 'traumatic events in childhood that

facilitated dissociation, violent fantasies and then homicidal behaviour'
(Hickey 1991: 65–73).

Why do human beings, in particular human children, behave violently
and murderously? Are there predispositional factors like brain damage or a
genetic tendency to violence at work? Do they have access to facilitators of
violent behaviour – alcohol, drugs, pornography and books about the occult
(Hickey 1991)? Are these facilitators the instigators of incidents like the
Columbine High School massacre, or Dunblane, or the killing of James Bulger,
or even Damilola Taylor; or are more subtle forces at work which are having
an increasingly noxious impact upon the children they affect? Could there
be underlying common links that affect many children, irrespective of their
gender or culture, with a form of 'dys-ease' which results in those affected
becoming predisposed to attacking other members of their own species –
sometimes with incredible and indigestible ferocity?

Could it be a play problem, or more accurately a problem of play deprivation? Is it possible that because some children are deprived of play generally,
or of specific play types in particular, they are harmed in some way that
results in violent behaviour? Is it possible that because the environments in
which some children play are biased in terms of the stimuli or experiences
they offer, that those children's view of the world is skewed away from a
biological norm that would facilitate, for example, reasonable social behaviour? Is it likely that because a child does not experience rough and
tumble play, or whose flexibility is not challenged in playing, or whose play
backdrop is constantly dominated by football or fighting, that they might
be developmentally or evolutionarily disadvantaged? Is it conceivable that
because a child's play mainly takes place in a chronically indulgent, erratic or
rejecting space, they could become violent, neurotic or psychotic as a result?

These are important questions both for playworkers and others. They are
at the very root of what playwork is and does. For although many of the
children with whom playworkers work are balanced and agreeable individuals whose behaviour needs little or no intervention on the part of the
playworker, some (others may use the words 'many', or 'a rapidly increasing
number') are not. What should be playwork's response to children who
manifest 'difficult' behaviour?

Behavioural management

In the recent past, playworkers have turned to behavioural management to
cope (what Bonel and Lindon 1996 refer to as 'positive management of
children's behaviour'), but this approach has all too often only resulted in
the exclusion of the 'offending' individuals, rather than a better understanding of what is happening to them.

This chapter proposes that the phenomena of 'play deprivation' and 'play
bias' may act as precursors to many forms of difficult behaviour; that their
effects are manifested when children's play regularly occurs in inappropriate

settings; that the 'behavioural management' approach is a flawed strategy for dealing with their effects; and that future playwork responses to them must be more informed, taking into consideration the form of behaviour and the nature of the environments in which it occurs, prior to the conception of intervention strategies.

Play deprivation

Although play deprivation is defined in Hughes (2000: 21) as the result of 'a chronic lack of sensory interaction with the world; a form of sensory deprivation', it may also be the result of a neurotic, erratic interaction (Hughes 2001). For some years, play deprivation has been predicted as a precursor to non-social and antisocial traits of behaviour in children affected by it (Hughes and Williams 1982; Hughes 1988, 1996b; Frost and Jacobs 1995).

In a study of 26 young murderers, Brown and Lomax (1969) concluded the following: 'What all these studies repeatedly revealed . . . was that . . . normal play behaviour was virtually absent throughout the lives of highly violent, antisocial men regardless of demography. [My] remaining impressions are that . . . play deprivation also takes a devastating toll on women' (quoted in Brown 1998: 249).

Play bias

Described variously as 'environmental imbalance' (Hughes 1988), 'experiential bias' (Hughes 1990), and 'stimulus bias' (Hughes 1996a, 2000), the term 'play bias' (Hughes 2001) refers to 'a loading of play in one area of experience or another', having the effect of excluding the child from some parts of the total play experience. Stimulation theory suggested that this skewed or limited play experience might also be very detrimental to children (Hughes and Williams 1982; Hughes 1996a, 2001).

Stimulation theory

Initially, stimulation theory was devised to demonstrate that:

- play experiences must contain negative as well as positive stimuli if they are to facilitate adaptation/evolution through flexible responses to experience;
- play can be painful and unpleasant as well as pleasurable and fun;
- children need access to both if their developmental *and* their survival skills are to evolve.

However, as the idea developed, it became clear that while playful access to 'optimum' types and levels of negative *and* positive stimulation from the environment might be helpful to children's development of natural skills, certain stimulus extremes might not.

Stimulation theory is predicated on a belief that physical and psychological balance or equilibrium (sometimes referred to as homeostasis) is the preferred human condition; that human beings need balance to feel stable and at ease; and that play is used by them as their balancing mechanism. Thus, when they feel positively biased, they playfully seek out negative input for balance. And when they feel negatively biased, they seek out positive input for balance. However, sometimes balancing stimulation is absent when children play and their experience becomes increasingly biased as a result, eventually moving towards an extreme. Stimulation theory identifies four possible extremes which may act as precursors to increasingly violent behaviour in any children affected.

Four dangerous extremes

The four extremes of environmental stimulation are described as (Hughes 1988, 1996a, 2000, 2001):

- *over-positive*, when the child's play experience is so skewed that they perceive the world as an indulgent place, their toy or plaything;
- *over-negative*, where the child's play experience is so skewed that they perceive the world as a threatening, even hostile place;
- *erratic*, when the child's play experience is so subject to changes outside of their control that their view of the world is one of instability or neurosis;
- *deprived*, where the child's play experience is so impoverished by lack of stimulation that they are forced to search within their own limited experience for the reality they need.

Deprivation, bias and extremes

From the perspective of stimulation theory, the term 'play deprivation' applies to the erratic and deprived extremes, and the term 'play bias' applies to the over-positive/over-negative extremes. Empirical evidence of the effects of play deprivation in children is minimal, and of play bias currently non-existent. Nevertheless many thousands, if not millions of children are experiencing chronic deprivation and bias in their play – because of the impact of commercial developments, fear of traffic, perceived stranger danger, parental fears of children engaging in risky activity, poor housing or diet, violent neighbourhoods or play which does not involve 'live contact' – i.e. contact with other living things. Whether they are suffering, in the words of Lloyd George, 'deep and enduring harm' (NPFA 1926) as a result is open to speculation.

Play deprivation and play bias: possible causes and consequences

Early studies-sensory, social and spatial deprivation

The genesis of stimulation theory was in the heartbreaking but illuminating work conducted by Suomi and Harlow (1976: 492). Experiments published under the title, 'Monkeys without play' explored the effects of sensory, social and spatial deprivation on primates (what we might call play deprivation), and caused them to comment that:

- no play makes for a very socially disturbed monkey;
- when these monkeys reach physiological maturity they are incompetent in virtually every aspect of monkey social activity;
- they are antisocial and will viciously attack a helpless neonate (newborn child) or suicidally attack a dominant male;
- in the absence of social agents they will attack themselves, rending skin and muscle to the bone.

Primates are very similar to human beings and the impact upon them of play deprivation was obviously catastrophic. Similar conclusions were drawn by Jane Goodall. Responding to enquiries relating to the 'murder-cannibalism' by Gombe Stream Reserve female chimpanzees Passion and Pom, she said 'they both were ineffectively mothered, and . . . their early play and later socialisation patterns were constricted' (Brown 1998: 249). Such observations, and the findings of Suomi and Harlow (1976) imply a causal relationship between these kinds of deprivation (deprivation we might expect in children who do not play), and the disintegration of personality, where these beautiful and intelligent beings' social and survival mechanisms were so affected by their deprivation experience that to all intents and purposes the monkey was replaced by something which, if described in human terms, would have been dehumanized. Attacking themselves and everything around them, totally oblivious to the hierarchical and interactive rules that would normally have governed their behaviour, these primates showed powerful symptoms of the distress perhaps caused by the loss of most of the points of reference essential to primate life. Could equivalent circumstances elicit similar reactions in humans?

Play and identity

Thomashow (1995) and Orr (1993) certainly allude to the potential for a similar condition in humans. Thomashow, for example, emphasizes the importance of diverse and intense play experience in the middle childhood period, corresponding approximately to the period of 6 to 9 years of age, stating that it is 'the time of place making, in which children expand their sense of self . . . a time that children establish their connections with the earth, forming an earth matrix . . . which is crucial to their personal identity' (p. 10). Orr (1993: 437) highlights the implications for identity of not establishing those connections, suggesting '. . . we will have succeeded in cutting ourselves off from the sources of sanity itself', implying that without play, human beings may show similar symptoms of distress to those shown by the primates in Suomi and Harlow's experiments, and Goodall's observations.

Like Thomashow and Orr, Cobb (1993), in emphasizing how important play is to the human condition throughout life, demonstrates how powerful is the need to play. She states: 'We refer to a deep desire to renew the ability to perceive as a child, and to participate with the whole bodily self in the forms, colours and motions, the sight and sounds of the external world of nature and artefact' (p. 130).

What is not written, but is implied, is that there is a deep impact on the human psyche if we cannot play, or if the scope of our play is limited. It is interesting to note that access to good quality play itself might be a potential cure for children so affected. Studies by Harlow and Harlow (1962) and Einon et al. (1978) indicate that the effects of play deprivation and perhaps play bias may be reversible. Harlow and Harlow (1962) for example, state: 'yet for all that, twenty minutes of play daily with peers in play cages obliterates the difference between the three groups' (quoted in Bruner 1976: 32). More recent supportive evidence concerning the beneficial effects of therapeutic playwork for a group of abandoned children in Romania is provided in Chapter 11.

As demonstrated above, numerous factors exist in the child's landscape which may inhibit play or bias it in some way. What might be the effects of such factors on a child's identity and sense of self? Grof (1993) alludes to an 'existential crisis' in such circumstances.

Environment and neuronal development

The importance of the environment to neuronal development has been known for decades, and some neuronal recovery as a consequence of playing may in fact be what the Einon et al. (1978) study is identifying. Certainly there is evidence that neurochemical imbalances play a central role in providing the context for violent and antisocial behaviour. Zuckerman (1984), for example, suggesting a model that 'relates to mood, behavioural activity, sociability and clinical states', demonstrated that what he called, 'extremes' of experience caused by neurotransmitters and other brain chemicals could be responsible for violent mood and behaviour. He continued:

at optimal levels of . . . systems activity . . . mood is positive, and activity and sociability are adaptive [implying a happy and flexible organism]. At very low or very high levels [of certain brain chemicals, what might relate to the over-positive and over-negative states described above], mood is dysphoric, activity restricted or stereotyped, and the organism is unsocial or aggressively antisocial.

(Zuckerman 1984: 413)

Perry (1994) has a similar view, stating that 'experience, not genetics leads to the neurobiological factors that predispose people to violence and those that result from exposure to violence are inextricably intertwined'. Thus, as well as the work of Harlow and Suomi (1971), Einon et al. (1978) and Brown (1998) there are other vital scientific strands that underpin the notions of play deprivation and play bias – i.e. those of neurochemistry and neurology.

Environment and plasticity

Over the years, groundbreaking studies, originally pioneered by Bennett *et al.* (1964), Rosenzweig (1971), Rosenzweig *et al.* (1972) and Ferchmin and Eterovic (1979) have increasingly successfully demonstrated the impact of environment both upon levels of neurochemicals in the brain and upon the brain's actual neurological structure. Initially, the Bennett (1964) team suggested that the kinds of change in brain, as demanded by learning theories, could actually be brought about by experience. However, it was Rosenzweig (1971) and Rosenzweig *et al.* (1972) who conclusively showed a link between brain size, activity, environmental type and behavioural interaction with that environment. What they suggested was that, depending on the nature of the experience to which rats were exposed, a neurological capacity known as 'plasticity' occurred. What this meant was that with use the brain expanded, and without use the brain contracted – in terms both of its size and its internal chemical activity.

Rosenzweig's (1971) work had already demonstrated a link between environment and brain growth. Rats kept in what were later described as 'enriched' environments, (Rosenzweig *et al.* 1972), but what he then called a 'lively' environment, showed distinct changes in brain anatomy and brain chemistry when compared with animals kept in an 'impoverished', or what he then called a 'dull', environment.

Thus in the 1960s and 70s, scientists had already formulated links between behaviour, environment, brain growth, and mood and aggression, implying that species reared in enriched spaces (i.e. spaces in which their perceived quality of life was high) had bigger brains, were able to process information more efficiently and more effectively (because of the optimum levels of neurochemicals present), and were less aggressive and moody than their counterparts who had been reared in impoverished conditions.

Theoretical parallels can begin to be drawn between this early work on brain development and environment and the ideas of play deprivation and play bias. For example, that children who are play deprived or whose play experience is biased may experience negative plasticity, where their optimum brain size is subject to contraction, with a consequent reduction in their neurochemical activity, and a consequent increase in both the violent and bizarre types of behaviour shown by the primates in Suomi and Harlow's (1976) experiment. However, caution should be applied lest a purely socioeconomic meaning be attached to the terms 'enriched' and 'impoverished', and playworkers conclude that play deprivation and play bias are primarily the products of poverty, overcrowding and social exclusion. In the studies carried out by Rosenzweig *et al.* (1972), impoverishment did not mean bad hygiene, a poor feeding regime or cruelty. Rather it meant a normal, social/ nutritional regime but a comparatively boring one. Whereas an enriched environment meant that subjects were given access to 'environmental complexity' and a training cage. It was social access to this cage, they concluded, that gave rise to 'brain growth transformation'.

This is important. Playwork has frequently run the risk of having a narrow sociological analysis: that only poor or relatively poor children need access to dedicated provision. What the above data imply is that play deprivation/play bias, brain growth and aggressive and bizarre behaviour are linked less to material factors than they are to more esoteric factors like stress and stimulation, suggesting in a human context that children from any social, economic or cultural background might experience such deficits in their play experience. There may be, for example, a stronger relationship between loneliness and stimulus impoverishment, or indulgence or a violent context and stimulus bias, than between low income and play deprivation *per se*. It is possible, for example, that children whose play does not allow for the development of the capacity of combinatorial flexibility (Sylva 1977) would feel less balanced and perhaps more predisposed to violence than a child whose play did facilitate flexible responses to the environment.

Certainly there is evidence in recent Swiss (Huttenmoser and Degan-Zimmermann 1995), Romanian (BBC 1998), and US (Chugani 1995, 1996a, 1996b, 1998; Chugani *et al.* 1996a, 1996b; Tobin 1997) research that children who grow up and play in stimulus deprived (or what are described as 'battery' as opposed to 'free-range' conditions) experience emotional and other (sometimes severe) neuropsychological disadvantages as a result. This view is further reinforced by Siviy (1998: 236):

if any of the above mentioned effects are specifically due to a lack of play, then play experiences may result in a brain that is better able to deal effectively with specific types of social stressors. In other words those who have had ample opportunity to engage in play as juveniles may be better equipped at a neural level to 'roll with the punches' associated with daily social interactions than those who haven't had this opportunity.

Other recent research also tends to support this view. Originally cited in Sutton-Smith (1997), it was ground-breaking studies by Huttenlocher (1990, 1992) which had the effect of putting play deprivation/bias back into the theoretical playwork frame.

Play, stress and brain development

Sutton-Smith's (1997) book, *The Ambiguity of Play*, provides us with important play-orientated interpretations of Huttenlocher's neurological work which invite the playwork community to ask, 'But what if children do not get proper or appropriate opportunities to play?'

In the context of brain growth itself, Sutton-Smith argues that play's role is in the 'actualisation of brain potential' – in making synaptic connections real, rather than just possible. He describes the function of play as being to save 'more of the variability that is potentially there, than would otherwise be saved if there were no play' (1997: 225). He is suggesting two things. The first is that the human child is born with a neuronal over-capacity – i.e. that at birth it has far more synapses that it needs, which if not used will die. It is play, Sutton-Smith suggests, that enables those synapses to be utilized, thus allowing them to be used in future brain processes. He implies that quirky (apparently), redundant and flexible responses to experience (what we might call play) result in the uptake of this over-capacity. The second, and here Sutton-Smith is drawing from Gould (1996), is that taking up any over-capacity avoids problems which are associated with 'rigidifications after any successful adaptation' (Sutton-Smith 1997: 231). What he is implying here is that play is not only responsible for the uptake and consequent use of any over-capacity of neurones, but when this has taken place, further play enables the brain to remain flexible when there may be a tendency for it to become rigid (i.e. there would be little plasticity or brain growth if the child did not play).

This view is supported by the work of Huttenlocher, from which much of what Sutton-Smith proposes is derived. Huttenlocher (1990, 1992) suggests that in some species there is what he calls a 'sensitive period' for brain growth that roughly corresponds to the first eight years of life in the context of human children. In this period children's brains have an over-capacity of neurones of *twice* that of children over that age, and that over-capacity is taken up by experience. Given that what children do most during their first eight years of life is play, it is reasonable to infer from Huttenlocher's studies that if children engage in regular quality play (i.e. if playing is their dominant experience) they will benefit from plasticity and have bigger brains and more appropriate levels of neurochemical activity than children who do not – particularly if this happens during the first three months of life. Social isolation during the 'sensitive period' has also been cited as being responsible for later persistent social deficits which were independent of social stimulation – i.e. they were not reversible (van den Berg *et al.* 2001).

While Huttenlocher's findings represent a landmark discovery in themselves, it is work by Perry, Balbernie and McEwan that make them relevant to this discussion. Each of these researchers have made significant statements regarding the effects of negative experience on brain development. Research by McEwen (1999) for example, while also emphasizing the important role of environment on brain development, concludes that factors like stress can have a negative impact upon what he terms 'stress induced plasticity', particularly in terms of the early malformation of the hippocampus. He states, 'These effects may be involved in fear related learning' (McEwen 1999: 106), implying that children who experience higher than normal levels of fear (e.g. severe traumatic stress) may suffer stress induced plasticity – a condition which he links to recurrent depressive illness and post-traumatic stress disorder (McEwen 1999: 116).

Other recent studies also highlight the effects of stress, trauma and low levels of stimulation on brain development. Balbernie (1999: 17) states:

A child who has been traumatised will have experienced overwhelming fear and stress. This will be reflected in the organisation of his or her brain, as neurochemical responses to fear and stress have designed it to survive in that sort of environment. By the same token, [a child] who is not being stimulated, by being . . . played with, and who has few opportunities to explore his or her surroundings, may fail to link up fully those neural connections and pathways which will be needed for later learning.

Perry *et al.* (1995: 17) also suggest that trauma in childhood has the effect of influencing the child's brain physiology: 'Children exposed to sudden, unexpected, man-made violence, [are] at great risk [of] profound emotional, behavioural, physiological, cognitive and social problems.'

Gunner (1998) reports that the brains of traumatized children develop 'hair trigger' circuitry for stress reaction, because of high levels of cortisol, which 'increases activity in the part of the brain involved with vigilance and arousal'. However, 'high levels of cortisol also directly effect [sic] the hippocampus', and 'children with disorganised attachment . . . have a permanently higher level of cortisol' (Gunner 1998: 18). Balbernie (1999: 18) also suggests that another adaptive response that can be activated by fearful situations is 'the dissociative continuum – the freeze or surrender response'.

Perry (1994) adds a frightening postscript: 'the very neurobiological adaptations that allow children to survive violence may, as the child grows older, result in an increasing tendency to be violent'. Brain damage, violence and mood changes may be the outcomes when children are play deprived or play biased, but there are other purely playwork analyses too. What follows is but one example:

Hall's theory

Most playworkers will be familiar with Hall's theory of recapitulation, wherein he states: 'the best index and guide to the stated activities of adults in past ages, is found in the instinctive, untaught and non-imitative play of children' (1904: 202). Reaney (1916) expanded Hall's theory, writing that play could be viewed as a 're-enactment of an individual's forebears transmitted activities' – i.e. that the essence of each forebear's past and present (a kind of life summary) was somehow encapsulated into the player's genes, and passed on via procreation to be played out by the next and future generations. This life summary could be 'divided into play periods that correspond to our species' various evolutionary stages' (e.g. the animal, savage, nomad, pastoral and tribal). These stages would roughly translate in a contemporary context into:

- children interacting with the elements;
- cruel interaction with other species;
- ranging for mental mapping;
- mastery play (e.g. gardening);
- membership of gangs and clubs.

There are several interesting and important implications for playworkers within Hall's, and subsequently Reaney's, writings. For example:

- We all (that is, all human beings) need to pass through these various stages during childhood or we will be driven to attempt to pass through them as adults.
- The stages are similar, irrespective of cultural, economic, religious or geographical location.
- This process has been going on since the dawn of human life.
- As we evolve so new stages may be tacked on.
- Manifesting animal, savage, nomadic, pastoral and tribal characteristics is not only biologically legitimate but essential play behaviour.
- Today's play patterns will become tomorrow's recapitulation, and so on.

However, neither these nor similar stages reflect much of what is permitted or allowable in many if not most contemporary play or playwork settings. Fire is frowned on, as is the use of weapons; so is risk and rough and tumble. Movement is restricted, gardening often impossible and the spontaneous development of children's hierarchies disallowed in favour of democratic and equal opportunities policies. In fact, from a Hall and Reaney perspective much of what might constitute an accurate manifestation of recapitulation is not present in the play of today's children – or to put this more accurately, it is not present in many of the play environments currently operated by adults.

Wilber's addendum

Why should this matter? Does it matter? We have to look to another source for an answer. In Ken Wilber's fascinating work *Up from Eden* (1996), he also constructs a stage by stage model for the evolution of human beings, but this time the model relates to the evolution of human consciousness. Whereas in Hall and Reaney's model the suggestion that each and every stage must be manifested to avoid a detrimental impact is only implicit, in Wilber's case it is explicitly stated: 'each stage of human evolution, although it transcends its predecessors must include and integrate them in a higher unity. Failure to do so equals neurosis' (1996: 169).

One interpretation of Wilber's meaning, particularly when juxtaposed with Hall and Reaney's assertions, is that individual and species development and evolution (what Wilber describes as 'a higher unity') can only be successfully accomplished if all previous stages of being are incorporated or amalgamated into each new stage. If this is not accomplished – if, for example, each stage transcends but does not include its predecessor – then the implication of what Wilber writes is that individually and collectively we become 'dys-eased'. The relationship between play, play deprivation, well-being and dys-ease is proposed in Figure 5.1.

The word 'dys-ease' is written so because the thrust of this chapter is that although the causes of the difficult behaviour some see increasingly in

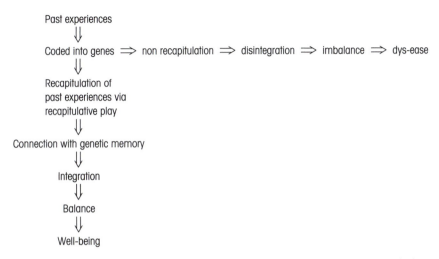

Figure 5.1 Model describing the link between dys-ease, play deprivation and play bias

children are frequently described in sociological terms, this behaviour may actually have its genesis in individuals feeling ill at ease and unbalanced; that something is not right; that an essential biological ingredient for human balance is missing from their experience, in much the same way as they might react adversely if a vitamin or mineral essential to healthy physical development was suddenly missing from their diet.

This is an alternative, although not a mutually exclusive, example of the possible biological impact of the phenomena of play deprivation and play bias upon emotions and behaviour. Human children are born with a genetic expectation that they will experience play and if this does not happen, if children do not enjoy either a comprehensive and to some extent a primitive play experience, or if their play experience is censored for reasons of social protocol, they may become very ill as a result. What 'ill', or 'dys-eased' means in this context is perhaps less to do with physiological change and more to do with affect and mood.

Play deprivation, play bias and playwork practice

As stated earlier, while very little research has been undertaken on play deprivation, and none at all on play bias, there are enough indicators above and in playwork's own theoretical thinking to make the following suggestions.

The first is that it is possible, even likely, that a significant and increasing number of the children attending provision may be suffering damaging stimulus effects from the environments in which they live and play. This means that, from the perspective of stimulation theory, there is potential for increasing levels of the four extremes, which may result in violent, dysfunctional and fantasy-driven behaviour.

The second is that whatever the above studies imply, the indicators they contain make it imperative that playworkers (i.e. those individuals who create and staff play spaces), where they exist:

- begin to apply a behavioural and environmental analysis to the children in their catchment area (see below);
- do not add to the problems children may be experiencing by being either a source of inappropriate stress or of inappropriate types or levels of stimulation;
- leave children to play without interruption or adulteration;
- make it known to children that recapitulative play is allowed;
- adopt playwork, rather than sociological, strategies for intervention;
- avoid censoring or restricting children's chosen play experiences.

The phenomena of play deprivation and play bias provide yet more reasons why good play provision for children should exist where it does not. What is essential is that practitioners ensure that the provision they operate addresses both general and locally assessed need (Hughes 1996a, 2001). This means practitioners should ensure that provision is designed and operated to be physically and emotionally sensitive both to assessed play deficits in a *generic sense* (e.g. that children in general may not have access to open spaces, or that they are not as used to social interaction as they may have been in the past), and to assessed play deficits in a more *local sense* (e.g. that children locally are not allowed fire or water play, that there are no trees to climb, or that there are continually high levels of interruption or stress).

This means that increasingly in the future, playworkers will need to view themselves as technicians assessing the sites and buildings they operate for their suitability and appropriateness for counteracting the potential impacts of deprived or biased play experiences of the children with whom they specifically work (Hughes 1997). They will also need to be kept aware of relevant scientific developments as a part of their professional training and education.

Assessment of individual children

Some assessment approaches are suggested in this final section, and illustrated in Table 5.1.

If the playworker assesses a child as balanced (i.e. well-adjusted, socially competent, happy and confident) any intervention should be minimal, and the child should remain in control of the content and intent of their play. If the playworker assesses a child as imbalanced (if the child is being violently protective or aggressive, if it resists sharing with a show of violence or it takes from others by force) then the playworker may feel that limited balancing intervention (whether in a negative or a positive direction) is appropriate, and the child may by necessity lose some control over the content and intent of their play.

Table 5.1 Assessment/intervention approaches

Play Bias	Playwork Intervention
None (balanced)	Minimal
Over-positive	Balancing exposure to negative $\Rightarrow$ therapeutic intervention
Over-negative	Balancing exposure to positive $\Rightarrow$ therapeutic intervention
Erratic (Z1)	Reliable/forecastable experience $\Rightarrow$ therapeutic intervention
Deprived (Z2)	Contact $\Rightarrow$ inclusion $\Rightarrow$ therapeutic intervention

Note: the terms Z1 and Z2 were used in Hughes (1996a) to describe erratic and deprived biases

If the child is neurotic, untrusting and always trying to second guess the playworker, they may be assessed as erratic (i.e. their play experience has been unreliable and has left them unable to trust their own judgement or predictive mechanisms) then the playworker may need to intervene to provide a more stable, reliable and forecastable/predictable play foundation until that child feels secure enough to leave the stability it now knows to exist for play whose outcome is less stable or predictable. There is a sense in which this child, rather than losing control over their play is actually having control returned after it had been removed by the child's former play context.

If the child is withdrawn, unsocial, irritable, clearly unhappy and unskilled, perhaps even secretive and fantasy driven, then the playworker may assess them as chronically play deprived. That is, the play experience has not just been biased or erratic but much of it has either been missing or accessed at such a low level of stimulation as to be perceived by the child as a very unsatisfactory or unfulfilling experience. The child who is play deprived is invariably lonely, lacking in other human contact and devoid of sensory challenge. Here any playwork intervention must be skilled. In one sense play deprived children are losing contact with reality simply because the sensory mechanisms that provide that contact are not locating stimulation and the child's brain is, to all intents and purposes, shutting off. Tobin (1997) described the brains of children who had been chronically deprived of sensory stimulation as 'utterly devoid of all electrical activity'.

Conclusion

This chapter has argued that play deprivation and play bias, generated within the child's local environment, may damage their identity, their social reference points, their neurological development, their search for homeostasis and even their potential to evolve. Play deprivation and play bias are insidious conditions that undermine children's humanity and may render them dys-eased.

The neurological data is most compelling, demonstrating as it does the relationship between behaviour, environment, plasticity and neurochemical activity. It is a sobering thought and not a little ironic that as the argument for proper play provision begins to be formulated (i.e. provision that authentically facilitates a holistic play experience), provision is being closed and much of what is left is closed access (i.e. restricted in terms of what is on offer and operated for the vocational benefit of parents rather than for the developmental and evolutionary benefit of their children).

Chapter 6

Towards a psycholudic definition of playwork

Gordon Sturrock

Winnicott, like Jung, believed fervently that there is in man a basic and
essential urge to create, to find meaning, and to achieve self-transcendence.
Play, imagination and symbolic process function in the service of this basic urge.

(Squiggle Foundation leaflet)

Introduction

This chapter attempts to set out the basis for a new description of a healing
practice in the playground setting as an essential function of playwork. This
first preliminary exploration looks at the relevance of play within the therapeutic endeavour more broadly, and at the depth psychologies (psychoanalysis and analytical psychology) more particularly. The contention is
simple. By deepening our communication with the analytic and therapeutic
fields, we can only help increase our understanding of play and therapeutic playwork's association with dimensions of ludic, or play, potentiality
(in Latin, *ludo* means 'I play'). It is this perspective – the acute observations
of the playing child and the adult attending to that child within the ludic
ecology, the environment that contains the child's play meaning (the essence
of playwork as I see it) – that goes to form a new field of study I describe as
psycholudics.

By any measurement the depth psychologies and therapies show a deeper
consonance with myth than has been widely explicated or investigated within
playwork's appreciation of these fields. The therapies have much exploited
mythic images and themes to further the impact of their constructs and

interpretations. There has been a consistent and deliberate supplanting of some older established narratives to empower essential new theoretical forms.

It has been argued that we have seen the rise of the therapeutic endeavour with little or no scientific underpinning. What, therefore, might account for its powerful attraction? Is the idea of time, as running backwards, and the reactivation of myth as a container of meaning, of valance, true of every therapeutic practice? At the heart of healing – bear in mind what Freud described as the 'fundamental rule' of psychoanalysis: free association – there is an even more profound metaphor for an essential human truth. For it would seem that in order to build a therapeutic edifice we see the returning of adult desire to the territory of the childhood *world-view*, in an effective adulteration.

What might be seen as the playing child's 'polymorphic freedom' is steadily eroded by an adult need to neuroticize childhood and play by the introduction of rules, or 'games of knowledge'. If so, playwork can readily follow suit with one caveat in mind. While the field of analysis and therapy is steadily moving towards a mind-games ratification, which exploits play and positions the child in particular as the object/ball for strenuous adult interchange, psycholudics, as one of its proposals, attempts to re-privilege the child at play as the central focus of the therapeutic principle. In essence, psycholudics re-inscribes play and the play process as the locus of healing functionality.

This needs to be seen, however, against a background of a playwork field uncertain of its tradition, forced into conformity by increasingly stringent needs for cheapened qualification and child care quick fixes. Playwork values, established over years of practice, are being cast aside in the search for a means of more highly interventionist schema. In effect, we are seeing the usurping of natural and universal phenomena into the strictures of dubious new science. It is in response to the creation of regimes where play is increasingly being regarded as social instruction that what follows should be viewed.

Playwork and healing

I am a specialist, God help me, in events in inner space and time, in experiences called thoughts, images, reveries, memories, dreams, visions, hallucinations . . . We live equally out of our bodies, and out of our minds . . . Here human relations are not the speciality of the therapist. The speciality is interiority and the psychic realities that are beyond the body and the mind in its narrow human sense.

(Hillman 1977: 192)

In order to establish a narrative of psycholudics and to encourage the return of the notion of the playworker's role as having some affinity with that of the therapist more generally, I am taking this opportunity to speculate about the innermost realms of play. But, a first qualitative statement

should be made about the playworker's fitness so to do. The primary justification is that of immersion – that is to say, the amount of time and the
depth of contact that the playworker has with the child at play.

Out of this delicate contact is emerging a whole raft of observations,
in truth most of them based on uncredited, and sometimes uncreditable,
research. Some of this might be dismissed as anecdotal evidence, but these
insights contain some intriguing patterns that are surely worth some further
investigation. They appear to be pointing at a new perspective, a new ecology
of play and the playing child. These novel forms appear to be generated
initially as a range of analogies or metaphors that extend across the accepted
or traditional boundaries imposed by societal, cultural or deductive rationality. They are, to mint a term, *transobjective*, in that the idea, meaning or
intentionality of objects and others is subjected to new laws, values and
verities. New patterns of being are permitted to be essayed, much as the
child does in the intimacy of their playing. It is this nascent construction
that this chapter will concentrate upon. Accordingly, I will briefly examine
four areas:

- the parallels between the role of the playworker and the shaman/therapist;
- the idea of the shared psychic space, the overlapping mutual play projection;
- the deep ludic – physical and psychic grounds for play;
- the 'that darn field' proposition.

Playworker as shaman/therapist

> Where he [Jung] does turn to the creative instinct as such, his descrip-
> tions are given under other conceptions of it: the urge to wholeness, the
> urge toward individuation or personality development, the spiritual drive,
> the symbol-making transcendent function, the natural religious func-
> tion, or, in short, the drive of the self to be realized. He strongly affirms
> that this urge to self-realization works with the compulsiveness of an
> instinct. We are driven to be ourselves.
>
> (Hillman 1992: 34)

The archaic origins of healing predate Greek mythology. It has its roots in
the techniques of shamanism and accordingly in ideas of tribal initiation,
rites, healing and prophesy, and is a theme universally dispersed throughout
cultures and societies. At the centre of many of these ancient and arcane
practices lies:

> the dramatic structure of the shamanic seance. We refer not to the
> sometimes highly elaborate 'staging' that obviously exercises a beneficial
> influence on the patient. But every genuinely shamanic seance ends as a
> spectacle unequalled in the world of daily experience. The fire tricks, the
> 'miracles' of the rope-trick or mango-trick type, the exhibition of magic

feats, reveal another world – the fabulous world of the gods and magicians, the world in which everything seems possible.

(Eliade 1989: 511)

For the greater part, the depth psychologies and therapies have chosen to work within this realm of the fabulous, where everything seems possible, describing it as 'free association' or in a variety of spellings as 'fantasy'. It is little appreciated that 'free association', the 'fundamental rule' of analysis, is common to almost every therapeutic endeavour. It can be seen in psychoanalysis, analytical psychology, drama therapy, art therapy, sandplay – add your own favourites. That the shaman/therapist and the playworker operate in the same way when in contact with this internal zone – the one grouping in an archaeology of affect, the other in a synchronicity of preventative awareness – is not a surprising deduction. I argue that there are strong correspondences between the roles and functions of the shaman/therapist and the playworker.

Though these descriptions seem far removed from the everyday operations of the playground, some cursory examination may well uncover the necessary interweaving of the shared functionalities. Adventure playgrounds, where the ethos has been of child-ordinated activity, often have a curiously tribal cast to their appearance (as do the playworkers for that matter). Many playgrounds sit as reservations of play space in urban blight. The fences are not to keep the children in but to keep adults out. The structures, art and the culture that prevail on the playground could also be viewed as tribal, with the children marking and often defending territory against all manner of incursion. Playworkers act as the mediators between the world of the playground and beyond, between fantasy and reality, play and games, the real and the non-real, the psychic and the material, in an unending whirl of playful enactment.

Playwork in the UK must come to terms with the fact that in a climate where we see a massive rise in learning and behavioural breakdown and a legion of children condemned to the Ritalin cosh, play and play space have a need for a practice more attuned to healing than ever before. That this healing could be ordained through the playing processes of the child seems to be a highly appropriate 'unbending intent' for our task. As Castaneda said (a dictum suitable to the therapeutic playwork application): 'The core of our being is the act of perceiving, and the magic of our being is the act of awareness. Perception and awareness are a single, functional, inextricable unit' (Langs and Badalementi 1996: 166).

The locus of healing – the overlapping mutual play projection

Each time I enter into a fantasy about which diet to begin or group to join, my pathologizing is being given a containing field in which to elaborate and validate itself.

(Hillman 1977: 74)

The playwork and shamanic/therapist connection allows a number of shared elements to be explored between certain ideas common in psychoanalytic/ therapeutic practice that provide theoretical outlines of the operation in this non-physical space, and those of play as I define it. I speak principally of Winnicott's idea of 'potential space' and the concept of the 'analytic third' as it is discussed by Thomas Ogden. Meares gives a useful preamble to this ineffable contact when he says:

> In play, children project the 'basic time-pattern of their lives' (Murphy, p. 119). This seems to have been the case for many thousands of years. Artifacts from the earliest civilisations include miniature representations of people and animals, presumably used as toys. It is difficult not to conclude that the capacity to play is part of our genetic endowment, just as potential for language is biologically given.
>
> (Meares 1993: 151)

Can we therefore suggest that play is driven intent and that the free-flowing imagination of the child and the sharing of this with the playworker has some unexplored consequence? For, if the overlapping of the two free-associated constituents (the analyst also free associates with the analysand to produce curative interpretation) is a therapeutic verity, then is the same not true of the playworker – free associating in the free-associative play of children – as a healer? Is it this new intra-subjective entity, the 'analytic third' as Ogden so poetically describes it, which contains the 'cure' of analysis? Ogden (1994: 62) quoting O'Shaughnessy (1983: 281), explains it thus: 'During the past half century, psychoanalysts have changed their views of their own method. Instead of being about the patient's intrapsychic dynamics, "it is now widely held that interpretation should be made about the interaction of patient and analyst at an interpsychic level".' Consequently, there are some key considerations that need to be taken into account when we examine the import of psychoanalytic and therapeutic thinking (particularly that which is most immediately formed out of clinical practice and encounters), and the theory and practice of playwork as it is presently constituted.

The first point, which must clearly be made, is there is a distinct split between the actual evidence of playwork practice, which is piecemeal and largely anecdotal, and related play-based theory as it is understood. Much of what we read, and this is not a prodigious school of thought, is by and large incidental to the theory, misunderstood, or actually begins to sign departures from play into games, rules and behaviours. Winnicott's 'potential space' is being translated as an actual space, the 'good enough' playworker as a precursor to lowered standards. While some notions of developmental psychology hold a certain sway within the limited jargon of the field, others are used as a confection on project material and politically inspired bids for funding. As a result their influence has been spread through a discourse of misapplied theory.

Yet a conflation of some of the theories most prolifically used in the therapeutic field, allied to the emerging observations and research in play more widely and playwork more specifically, are beginning to offer powerful new potentials. For example: two children active in some shared play are held to be simply taking part in what is described as 'parallel play' (Parten 1932). But what of the possibility that there might be some internally shared potentiality to be explored through an examination of associated free play? That the overlaying of the two intentionalities of the players (or indeed a group of players) has an as yet unexplored effect with which playworkers have been involved for generations? Listen to Langs and Badalementi (1996: 203): 'our research has shown scientifically that, without knowing it, individuals create certain kinds of coordinated rhythmic dances in their dialogues . . . we have fashioned a reasonable hypothesis that there are deep laws of the mind and a communicative or informational field that is activated by human dialogues and interactions'.

Is play one of the ways that these deep laws are explored? Is there a kind of ludic law being played out where we might be able to discern some more profound consonance with the child's playful acts? Piaget, whose ideas have been so contextual to the course of child observation, suggested that play was centred on observable and rudimentary games (Sugarman 1987: 87–9). Hence, you have his three classes: games of mastery; games with rules; and games with make-believe. However, the very form 'game' suggests an external-ized and accepted set of rules. Games of mastery require an encounter with external physical laws (what goes up must come down, manipulation of artefacts, etc.). Games with rules imply there is some agreement, discussion or involvement in arriving at the rules (it might be argued that play is everything that occurs until the rules are established). Games of make-believe also suggest that there is, in the making of a belief, a construction of a reality, an agreed maya or illusion: 'I see not a memory, an imagination, a reconstitution, a piece of Maya' said Barthes (1993: 82). He went on unhesit-atingly to question this form of games with his need to 'outplay the signified, to outplay law, to outplay the father, to outplay the repressed' (Sontag 1993: xxxi). Perhaps we are required in playwork to eschew developmental con-structs that ignore all that prefigures games, and need to outplay them on behalf of play: to resort to the deep ludic as it were; to return our idea of play and playing to the interpsychic level.

The deep ludic – physical and psychic grounds for play

'My view of metaphor starts from Vico, who takes the metaphor to be a mini-myth, "a fable of being"' (Hillman 1977: 156). The deep ludic may be just such a metaphor. Such fables become more crucial as we evolve forms of practice that are redolent of social control rather than entry into the express-ive lifeworld of the children we work with. Playwork, at present, certainly in its UK form, is in danger of a cataclysmic splitting. We can either move away from the internalized acts of playing into a more superficial accord, or we can acknowledge that we stand on the boundary of a deeper engagement with play and its ecological consonance.

Playwork may well need to confront precisely this dimension of the ludic ecology. If we live in denial of the deep ludic then we banish a large part of imaginal play to the peripheries of our practice and the work becomes rather that of societal induction. Play can be seen in this context as a means of achieving communitarian conformity. I contend that playwork is required, out of an environmental obligation, to concentrate on the interplays that lie at the heart of the exchanges between the playing child and the adult attendant to that play.

Playwork is actively seeking perspectives, texts and definitions to describe its methods and techniques. However, it has spent too little time contemplating a more serious immersion in the field of the therapies, depth and transpersonal psychologies and the eastern wisdom traditions for authentification of its values. Yet there are some intriguing parallels between these disciplines and ideas that playwork could usefully explore. (Incidentally, it might also be worth exploring the model of the depth psychologies as a means through which play could emulate developmental success. This though is beyond the scope of this chapter.) There is also considerably more that playwork can offer the therapeutic field in terms of its understanding of work directly with the playing child. As Edith Cobb (1993: 104) suggests, our practice might arrive at a point where it can be an 'entering wedge' in our understanding of the child's transcendent development.

Much of the political machination and social engineering going on at present is determined to move away from the notion of child-centred playwork practice. There is a cosmetic acknowledgement of the worth of play, but on closer examination much that is on offer is a departure from the ludic, away from 'a ludic definition of thought' (Barthes' useful axiom) towards a prescriptive, modifying behavioural change. We have lost the understanding that much of what we attain in contact and continuance with the children we work with is arrived at through our direct involvement in the curative potentiality of the ludic. Just how much is achieved through our skilful intervention in disturbed behaviour as an environmental, cultural adaptation still remains unclear in descriptions of our work.

We have said as a profession little or nothing about the shared impact of entry into the world of the child at play and this contact's directly healing potentiality. We have little information regarding changes we ourselves undergo. Yet there is a wealth of detail about those very factors (the interplay of subjectivities) that the therapies are prepared to deal with in their latest expositions. As Ogden (1994: 64, emphasis added) puts it:

> the task is not to tease apart the elements constituting the relationship in an effort to determine which qualities belong to each individual participating in it; rather, from the point of view of the interdependence of the subject and object, the analytic task involves an attempt to describe as fully as one can *the specific nature of the experience of the interplay of individual subjectivity and inter subjectivity.*

'That darn field' and the ludic ecology

I think we have overrated the brain as the active ingredient in the relationship of a human to the world. It's just a real good computer. But the aspects of the mind that have to do with creativity, imagination, spirituality, and all those things, I don't see them in the brain at all. The mind's not in the brain. It's in that darn field.

(Talbot 1991: 192)

One of the most striking characteristics of working with children in play settings, where the content is freely chosen, is precisely this phenomenon, a phenomenon as yet undescribed in any playwork literature. Over many years of practice it became apparent to me that in the most intimate of play exchanges between the playing child and the playing adult there appeared to be a sharing of an overlapping, externalized cohabited space of 'as-if' potentiality. This phenomenon was also, though more rarely, evidenced in group situations. I, and others, now refer to this effect as the 'ludic ecology'. Within this space, sphere, realm or zone, it was apparent that there was a psychic effect, a unifying communication operating outside the bounds of the known. A sense that incorporated all others into a bonded union, centred around a ludic energy, which appeared to have a number of key factors worth exploring. These were: that a similar effect was described in psychoanalytic literature and indeed was an established part of clinical practice; and that it appeared this area, perhaps like Winnicott's construction of the 'third area' (one which he described as 'that of cultural experience' and 'derivative of play'), has its own curative capacity.

From the perspective of playwork, which insists on this playful context being as untrammelled as possible by anything that could be construed as adulteration, by contrast, most therapies appear to exploit the ludic in a wholly self-serving fashion. In short, their culturally accepted experience of interpretation is indeed derivative of a more original, homeostatic impulse, which the therapeutic endeavour exploits. (This exploitation is most noticeable in the work of Melanie Klein, about whom Winnicott wrote, 'I suggest that in her writings *Klein, in so far as she was concerned with play, was concerned almost entirely with the use of play'* (Winnicott 1992: 39, emphasis added). I cite the example of Klein to suggest the concentration on adult-initiated outcomes in therapy, rather than some child-ordinated healing capacity.

Perhaps the most unqualified acknowledgement of the ludic is in the focus on free association as the starting point of the psychoanalytic application. Laplanche and Pontalis (1988: 169) show that:

The procedure of free association is fundamental to psychoanalytic technique . . . Freud was making use of the technique of free association in his self-analysis – especially in the analysis of his dreams. In this context it is an element of the dreams which serves as the starting-point for the discovery of the chains of association leading to the dream-thoughts.

The ludic, within analytic, free-associated containment, can most easily be discerned by examining the origins of the device and the range of language and definition that surround it (it is perhaps best described by its very alterity). Alfred Binet developed the method of 'provoked introspection'. He inspired the Wurzburg group to consider the subject of imagery. Binet and Janet believed that images arising from this introspection expressed the various unconscious sub-personalities of the patient.

Carl Happich elaborated on Binet's early work by 'encouraging emergent images' through the use of muscular relaxation, respiration control and meditation. He postulated, and this is the important factor, 'that between the conscious and the unconscious lies a zone, the meditative zone', in which 'creations ripened in the unconscious appear to the mind's eye [*geistiges Auge*]' (Roehampton College, undated).

Freud arrived at his solution out of hypnosis, suggestion and the dream. Dream-analysis enabled him, in the first place, to obtain insight into the workings of the 'primary process' in the mind and the way in which it influenced the products of our more accessible thoughts, and he was thus put in possession of a new technical device – that of interpretation. Jung, through his not dissimilar device of 'active imagination', engaged with the same 'chain of associated fantasies' for the same interpretive purposes.

In playwork, the engagement with this same operative area is habitually of a longer duration than the analytic hour and is less interpretive, other than in the sense of working with the ludic content. This consists of the forms and images that the child either spontaneously generates or which are inspired and prompted by artefacts within the play container, the play space, play area or playground, such as toys, clay, earth, other elements, other children (and sometimes adults), found and foraged materials and 'stuff'.

In this space playworkers can see the playing out, the enactment of images and psychic material seeking an encounter in external 'reality'. Here, the various play frames provide a stage on which to register and acknowledge material replete with meaning to the playing child or children. They are, in effect, overlapping projections full of numinous content. These play productions may be beginnings of, particularly, the transference aspect of making and forming relationships. This outline varies little from classic psychoanalytic free association as it is formalized.

The evolution and development of essentially psychoanalytic precepts, more palpably for the playworker, show distinct signs of movement close to a recognition of this ludic principle. I speak mainly of Freud's little-explored idea of *spielraum*, literally a play space. Interestingly, while Klein would be seen as the most play literate of the psychoanalysts from within that field, playworkers could see her as more manipulative of the ludic. The ludic is viewed merely as an instrument: 'the special primitive peculiarities of the mental life of children necessitate a separate technique adapted to them, consisting of the analysis of their play. By means of this technique we can reach the deepest repressed experiences and fixations and this enables us fundamentally to influence children's development' (Mitchell 1986: 68).

Winnicott, perhaps due to his previous paediatric training outside of psychoanalysis, discusses play in a way that has considerable appeal to players and should have some major significance for playwork – an influence not fully realized within the field at present. However, I believe that Winnicott's ideas on the ludic and his notion of 'potential space' will have a growing impact as the issue of adult-conceived 'social fear' begins to neuroticize the idea of the child at play in the environment. His idea was that psychotherapy 'takes place in the overlap of two areas of playing, that of the patient and that of therapist. Psychotherapy has to do with two people playing together. The corollary of this is that where playing is not possible then the work done by the therapist is directed towards bringing the patient from a state of not being able to play into a state of being able to play' (Winnicott 1992: 38).

This is a concept that has much to offer in describing and positioning play and therapeutic playwork. However, that having been said, even within this helpful statement there is a generalized denial of the essential driven nature of playing within therapeutic practice. The idea that we can play and not play is inconsistent with playwork's position, where the expression of play as a ludido, seen as driven internalized material, is the coming-to-be accepted view of the child at play. The Opies succinctly capture the notion 'where the children are is where they play' (Heseltine and Holborn 1987: 23). I might add it is also *when* they play, and that they do so because they must!

The position we seek to take is one of the child's well-being in the environment that pertains. Part of that well-being is the formation of identity and it is to the idea of identity that I now turn.

Play, identity and the teaching of the self

> I have no doubt that most people live, whether physically, intellectually, or morally, in a very restricted circle of their potential being. They make use of a very small portion of their possible consciousness . . . much like a man who, out of his whole body organism, should get into the habit of using and moving only his little finger . . . We all have reservoirs of life to draw upon, of which we do not dream.
>
> (James cited in Walsh 1984: 41)

William Blake takes a friend to a window, and pointing at some children playing outside he remarks 'That is heaven'. The seemingly commonplace nature of this observation in some way denies a deeper truth. It is this deeper truth that this section will examine. The form of expression chosen, with more than a passing nod to the great Hindu yogic traditions, attempts to outline a kind of 'perfected' idea of play. I try here to set play into the frame of meditative and contemplative systems. The extended argument sees play as a kind of awareness. Many of the terms of reference are from religious practice, for which I make no apology. The preliminary point to be made is that the purpose of play, described as a kind of mindfulness, is little explored and I do so briefly now.

I take again the idea of play as having some environmental or more accurately an ecological aspect. I propose that in play the microcosm mirrors the macrocosm. That is to say, what goes on within goes on without, a notion that has particular applications for play. The idea that the play of the child and her dolls is reflective of a universe is something of a truism in our therapeutic understanding of play. Robert Wright (1995: 375) expands this idea through inclusion of the 'wisdom traditions' when he says:

> The Hindu scriptures teach that a single universal soul resides in everyone; the wise man 'sees himself in all and all in him'. As a metaphor for a great philosophical truth – the equal sacredness (read: utilitarian worth) of every human sphere of consciousness – this teaching is profound. And as the basis for a practical rule of living – that the wise man refrains from harming others so that 'he harms not himself' – this teaching is prescient. The ancient sages pointed – however, ambiguously, however selfishly – to a truth that was not just valid, and not just valuable, but destined to grow in value as history advanced.

The discussion that follows sees this as being more a universal law than a 'moral'. We play as a kind of enactment that has, in some traditions of the East, religious overtones. In Sanskrit, *lila* is seen as the cosmic play of the gods, as it is in Hindu mythology, and is in some teachings connected with the worship of the Lord Krishna. John Lash (1990: 345) describes it as 'a paradigm in religious and metaphysical teachings of the East. In Hinduism, the world is produced from the dreaming of Vishnu, a kind of hide-and-seek game in which the supreme Lord who is dreaming us plays at being us so that he can delight in the countless ways of discovering himself.'

David Spangler envisages play as a necessary phase of creative experimentation in the inceptive unfolding of a new spirituality. In Zen, as expounded by Suzuki, it informs and energizes a *sartori* (enlightenment) which 'stands at the point where potentialities are about to actualize themselves . . . It is in fact the moment itself, which means that it is life as it lives itself' (Suzuki 1977: 62).

We may need to understand, as a necessary 'healing fiction', that where we have disruptions in play and in the play habitat, we also create disturbances of the self. Evidence is growing of the emergence of this disturbed self in many of our children. It is the notions of identity and self, the ludic ecology and the balancing of these twin aspects of development, that go to form the core of the psycholudic enterprise.

The self and the ludic ecology

In any investigation of childhood, play should form the most salient aspect of inquiry. That it does not, that our understanding of play and our adult colonization of play goes unheeded, is a matter of some environmental consequence. Yet the signals are there to be seen, children are beginning to evidence behaviours that show they are suffering from deprivation of some kind (I suggest a particular kind). A whole gamut of erratic behaviour, hyperactive syndromes, violent outbursts, suicide and drug use is now steadily being recorded. The question that this generalized dis-ease raises could be expressed thus: is the loss of the ludic habitat, the diminution of playing potential, directly contributing to the now widely registered disaffection of our children?

I argue that the case is clear. There is a direct correlation between the loss of play potential in the wider environment and the signs of increasing angst (the idea of *dysplay* may have some relevance) in our young. This is more than a simple change in comportment or demeanour. Rather, it can be seen as a widespread reaction to repressed play needs. It is the consequence of the loss of the ludic habitat. We have so successfully adulterated the potential play space of our children we are now seeing negative reactions to this pollution in the form of emotional, learning and behaviour breakdowns.

It is the concept of play as a formative ludic domain that is the key idea of this section of the chapter. What is determined in this ludic domain, our notions of identity and selfhood, and their developmental environment, has in playwork never been fully explored. It could be argued that, as a result, we treat the ludic and the worth of play therein with a kind of mature oblivion. The theme I take therefore is of a developmental process that we have, out of forms of profane adulthood, ignored at a certain cost. That cost can be measured in the loss of our civilizing humanity. Winnicott (1992) says that we should not think of creativity as something that can be destroyed utterly. He speaks of pathological communities where people no longer suffer because they have completely given up hope. As such, they have lost the characteristic that makes them human – i.e. they do not regard the world as a creative place. Winnicott suggests that this has a destructive influence at a later date in terms of personal growth.

This deficit of civilization can be seen first in the disintegration of what might be described as the capacity to form identity and self. It promotes an examination of what I hold to be the deeper intentionality of our playing acts. Here I make the argument that play is something far beyond the way it is represented in current playwork literature. I will argue that play provides the medium through which the idea of self is explored against a backdrop of the playing habitat. This is the notion of the self culled from eastern religious perspectives, from transpersonal psychology and from a Jungian, rather than a Freudian, tradition. It suggests that the enactments of our playing are to do with our self, seen (according to Gerhard Adler) as being, 'not only the foundation and ground of the personality but at the same time its fulfillment in an all-embracing and meaningful relation to the world' (Adler 1989: 15).

When we engage in descriptions of the self we are somewhat confined by the language that predominates; in the main, either philosophical or psychological. The description of the self, I venture, is as it is understood in transpersonal psychology. Here, in the work of Ken Wilber (1989), we see the idea of self being stratified into collective levels. In these levels, which are evident across peoples and cultures (hence the term transpersonal) there can be discerned the unfolding of higher and higher forms of self in a transcendent progression.

These levels Wilber summarized as the pleromatic self, the uroboric self, the typhonic self, the centauric self and so on. The idea is simply that to progress to the next level the self is transformed and moves to the new level, which contains the previous iteration. Wilber (1989: 2) says:

> psychological growth or development in humans is simply a microcosmic reflection of universal growth as a whole, and has the same goal: the unfolding of higher and higher unities and integrations. And this is one of the reasons that psyche is, indeed, stratified. Very like the geological formation of the earth, psychological development proceeds, stratum by stratum, level by level, stage by stage, with each successive level superimposed upon its predecessor in such a way that it includes it but transcends it.

Where we see disruption of the self-formation process, through disturbances of either the play process or of the ludic habitat, we see distorted self-formation and identity occurring. It is this idea of malformation that lies at the heart of therapeutic playwork and the approach to dysplay as we see it in playwork practice.

The psycholudic application

> The picture I am drawing for humans is that of an organism that comes to life designed with automatic survival mechanisms, and to which education and acculturisation add a set of socially permissible and desirable decision-making strategies that, in turn, enhance survival, remarkably improve the quality of that survival, and serve as the basis for constructing a person.
>
> (Damasio 1995: 126)

If, as adults, we gaze unflinchingly at the child at play we are bound to recognize that we stand apart from its mystery. The enigma of the encounter centres around our engagement with the child in their 'condition of freedom'. As a result, in the search for definitions and descriptions of play, a grand narrative, we encounter nothing other than its irreducibility. All descriptions become partial, all attempts to pin it down are thwarted, every finality only opens up alternate vistas and perspectives, but circumstances oblige us to try – certainly in the context of play and playwork in the UK, as it presently stands.

For the greater part the question of why we do this work is an unexplored area of investigation. Though the application procedure, the job description guidelines and the techniques of interview that ensure full equality and appropriate appointment are all firmly established, we spend little time in examining the play background of applicants. Though extensive qualification in competence is being pursued under the guise of a benevolent governance, much is being lost in the process. The deepest influences the adult playworker has on a child's play are widely disregarded, while superficial safety and security protocols predominate. The contamination of the play space by intervention is now written into practice as accepted procedure. It goes without saying that we pay no regard to the possibility of the potential playworker having, as they are almost bound to have, unplayed-out material that may be unconsciously compelling them into the field.

Once on the job we then seldom, if ever, spend any time on such esoteric matters as intentionality and motivation while we are busy on our actual play contacts. Yet, it is in the depths of this unplayed-out material, and the daily engagement, the face-to-face component of the work, that one of the most crucial exchanges of playwork takes place. An exchange that could be seen as the stage of dialectical interchange between the playworker and the child or children. It is this interplay that I will maintain is the essence of playwork and is the source point of our strategies for intervention and containment. It is this area of operation seen from a new perspective that the psycholudic application attempts to address.

On examination we can see in the descriptions of playwork (and they are beginning to show some variation) that the concentration has been on the range of tasks that surround the work. Thus we have extensive input on equality of opportunity, safety and security, issues of quality, play value and service delivery. In addition, and more usefully, we have taxonomies of play, assessments and audits of environments etc. However, this could be seen as the more manifest, that is to say the more obvious, apparent and tangible aspects of the task. What we have been less able to explore or explain is that which might be described as the intangible nature of the work, playwork's 'inscapes', to borrow a term from Manley Hopkins; its latent content. It is this latent content that I maintain playwork has inadequately accounted for, and from which a new understanding of our practice could be generated. From this position, the playworker's involvement in the psychodynamic processes of the child's play is accounted for and is indeed extended to incorporate interpretation and analysis. A move that suggests the playworker operates in what might be advanced as a field of insight.

It is for this reason that I telescope the range of playwork function, choosing to focus on the exchanges that lie at the heart of playwork. As there exists no narrative or vocabulary extant in the work of the field itself, I have borrowed some key terms from the depth psychologies, or have created new terms to define our perspective. That having been said, it is important to state that the purpose of psycholudics is not to place playwork in the psychoanalytic or therapeutic traditions. Rather I am suggesting that much of analysis, the remit of the depth psychologies and 'healing' practices of a whole range of therapies, is based on an essential play-based or ludic underpinning. It is this ludic background (we might better appreciate it as a ludic ecology) that forms the basis of almost all therapeutic practice. It is in play that the potential to heal psychic ill lies, and it is to play of this kind that the playworker attends. As such I argue that the playworker is inevitably involved in a form of healing practice.

I see the purpose of the continuum of containments of play in the playwork context as an essential part of a ludic repertoire. One that seeks meaningful enclosure (*temenos*, as a collective, psychic verb) within which to play out love and hate, conflict and resolution, creativity and destruction as a prelude to growth. The drive to play, the ludido, in the psycholudic construct, has this higher purpose. These contained rehearsals have an accord with Wilber's ideas of developing consciousness where the psychic ecology is described in layered strata of growth. As Wilber (1989: 51) says, 'I have frequently commented that the primary process and the infantile bodyself must eventually be surrendered and transformed.'

Playwork practice could ensure that these transitions be negotiated with the minimum of pain and disruption. Thoughtful containment within the play environment provides the means that enable this transformation. In arcane societies this was held in the rites, rituals and observances of the tribe or community. Eliade (1974: 27) explains this in a definition that has overtones of the psychotherapeutic project, as 'the legitimisation of human acts through an extrahuman model'. My contention is that this modelling also takes place within a wider psychic ecology as part of a ludic consciousness and is the function of playwork.

Play is a gift of Creation, not an artefact of culture. It is the still-point and the energy from which all else is evoked. In mathematics it is often suggested that it is the absence of number that makes numerical play possible. Likewise it is play's underlying emptiness or absence of cultural categories and boundaries that enables it to encompass the fullness of life. Anything less could not include the fullness of life. Play's patterns, forms and movements are our mother tongue, what Laurens Van Der Post has called the 'forgotten language of God' (Donaldson 1993: 14).

Conclusion

The modern vision of ourselves and our world has stultified our imaginations. It has fixed our view of personality (psychology), of insanity (psychopathology), of matter and objects (science), of the cosmos (metaphysics), and of the nature of the divine (theology). Moreover, it has fixed the methods in all fields so that they present a unified front against the soul.

(Hillman 1977: 3)

By understanding that we are driven to play as part of a more playfully attuned ludic environment, we can create a psycholudic application that enjoys some overlap with therapeutic practice. There are parallels between the movement from an individual encounter, the analytical dyad and the analytic frame, the play process, the idea of neurosis as unplayed-out material, the setting, and above all the ludic dimension and activity of the play space. We could encourage playworkers, as an element of their own personal development, to be self-regulating in terms of their psychic health and observant of the appearance of their own unplayed-out material in the child's play frames.

A preventative therapy could become activated that recognized ludic enactment and entry into the imaginal, internalized play zone, and its working in the play space that pertains. One which conferred the ability, homeostatically, to reorder and balance the equilibrium of the psyche at the behest of the child. Playwork may have to face up to Hillman's (1992: 6) wider proposal for psychology: 'Consequently, psychological work must be rethought. If soul-making is not treatment, not therapy, not even a process of self-realization but is essentially an imaginative activity of the imaginal realm as it plays through all of life everywhere and which does not need analyst or an analysis, then the professional is confronted with reflecting upon himself and his work.'

If we are to work in the fashion that Hillman outlines, the 'ground' where this reflection should take place is the shared play space, the space for potential within which we are required to strip off the accoutrements of adulthood, standing first as humans. Not an artificial de-maturing, but more authentically a return to innocence. We are asked to recognize, as Rilke (1964: 21) suggests: 'Always at the commencement of work that first innocence must be re-achieved, you must return to that spot where the angel discovered you when he brought the first binding message . . . If the angel deigns to come, it will be because you have convinced him, not with tears, but with your humble resolve to be always beginning: to be a beginner!'

This may chime with ideas of playwork as the elaboration of internalized content in a mediated contact with external 'reality'. The point being that through this contact (by playing out the internalized fantasy, within the no bounds, the out-of-timeness of the play space) we can then re-enter the external world, which operates in time; and this can heal. We may be able to realize that children need not relive repressed fantasy, if neurosis is all unplayed-out internal fantasy! If we playfully interact with the external environment we avoid the build-up, the constellation, as Jung would have it, of neurotic complexes in the first place.

We are in a position to argue that the entire field of therapeutic encounter is exactly equivalent to an internalized construct of the play experience enacted in the outside, external world, and made painfully serious by adults who are themselves deprived of play needs; to suggest that therapists project through free association their internalized play drives onto the subject client/analysand and in the process use the patient, in effect, to cure themselves. Or, more accurately, the curing itself then cures.

Within our psycholudic view of play we see much of the work that has anteceded our views in playwork as being concerned with only that area that is the manifest obvious. We need not deny the work at the manifest, arte-factual level, simply set it into our novel context. We can provide explanations for a whole variety of factors/phenomena for which there have been only secondary levels of thinking and clarification. So, we can examine issues like 'Satanic abuse', False Memory Syndrome, the concern about retained hypnotic influence, the ADD/ADHD epidemic etc. from an entirely unique viewpoint. In short, the psycholudic perspective might, as we develop a discourse about our reflective constructions, and in the long-term our practice base, enable us to analyse and prevent these and similar situations arising, to great effect.

The descriptions of that weight, our interpretations, our analysis, could stem from exactly the same basis as the therapies, depth and transpersonal psychologies. Out of the same essential, shared structure we can draw certain conclusions because we have been in free association with the children. The crucial difference might be that whereas psychotherapy is the archaeology of neurosis, psycholudics is its therapeutic avoidance. Our interpretive methodo-logy can thus be precisely, and in the most dynamic sense, preventative!

A psycholudic involvement with the child can permit an amplification of necessary play expressions to be essayed. The child in the play setting could be approached, through entry into the shared intra-subjective psychic space of the player, not as an expert, or a doctor, or therapist of whatever ilk, but merely as a fellow player rapt in the same ludic consciousness – a meditation which is at the core of imaginal play. Here problems and delights can be rehearsed, rules exchanged and developed and the 'as-if' proposition extended within a realm that offers a form of prophylactic and homeostatic security. Psycholudics and playwork could devise a meaningful myth as just such a means of exploring interpsychic potentiality.

Part 3

Putting theory into practice:
the reflective practitioner

Chapter 7

Professional playwork practice

Mick Conway

I did a simple and slightly depressing bit of research for this chapter by looking through the more commonly available English language dictionaries, thesauruses and computer spell-checkers for the word 'playwork'. I couldn't find a single entry, not even in the *Concise Oxford Dictionary* (Pearsall 1999). While the word 'play' is extensively featured, and many dictionaries mention 'playground', 'playscheme' and 'playgroup', there is no hint of a job or profession related to children's play. The nearest I could find was an occasional reference to children being supervised in playgroups or playschemes. Possibly it is because playwork is a relatively new and even rare profession, but I was nevertheless able to find entries for the much more recent and arguably esoteric 'arbitrageur' and 'spin doctor'.

I think the reason may lie in our past. In his fascinating book, *Childhood: A Multicultural View*, Melvin Konner (1991) points out that in hunting and gathering societies around the world, play is consistently the main waking hours activity for children. These societies are thought to be the nearest equivalent to how our ancestor's children lived before the neo-lithic domestication of plants and animals, and the invention of agriculture around 10,000 years ago. In contemporary examples such as the Kung people of the Kalahari, children from about the age of 2 all the way through to adolescence play together for most of the day, but this is not a task assigned to older children by adults. These societies seem to accept that the role of children is to learn and develop through play, and that it is natural and normal for them to get on with it by themselves, though the studies show they typically play within sight or hearing of adults most of the time.

In contrast, for children in agricultural and herding societies such as the Masai people, in which life probably corresponds most closely to the experience of childhood during the period between the invention of farming and the Industrial Revolution, the time for play averages around 45 per cent of waking hours, compared to around 90 per cent for the children in hunting and gathering societies. The reason is that children from about the age of 6 are routinely required to help adults with work or to look after younger children. Again, there is no adult role comparable to our notion of playworker. In most mature industrialized societies, the play time percentage for most children is broadly the same as in the agricultural and herding societies, which at first seems odd. The reason is that in these societies formal education has tended to replace work time, and in some societies, like our own, has started to eat into play time. In both agricultural and mature industrialized societies, the studies also show that play tends to be much more segregated into distinct age bands and peer groups, quite different to the wide age range in the hunter gatherer societies (Konner 1991).

Thus it would appear that the history of human technological advance is also the history of a significant amount of children's play time being usurped, first, by work and subsequently by formal schooling. In the earliest societies children of all ages just played together, while in the later agricultural societies it seems that the older children were child-minders overseeing the play of younger children, and in their remaining non-work time they played together in their peer groups. It is only very recently, and then only in some societies, that anything resembling what we call playwork has emerged, and I believe that this is because of a very high level of intervention in children's play in our highly urbanized and mechanized society. This intervention is not obviously apparent at first sight because it takes three quite distinct forms.

The first is the significant loss of space for children to play in as urban development, the growth of traffic and agribusiness have encroached on their ability to range across the environment. Intimately bound up with this is the gradual disappearance of extended families living in tightly-knit communities, which provided a kind of safety net for children playing on streets or in fields. Most people would agree these developments are regrettable consequences of technological advance and potentially damaging for children, but I suspect far fewer see them as the direct adult interventions in children's play that they really are.

Because much of our environment is perceived as being no longer suitable or safe for children to play in on their own, we have a second form of intervention where we attempt to compensate for the loss of play space by providing designated play spaces, some of them with playworkers to facilitate children's play in a safe and supervised setting. The concept of play as a child's right, and the emerging evidence of an innate human imperative to play are often used by policymakers and playworkers to argue for and justify this kind of compensatory intervention. Parental and community perceptions of new and different dangers facing children reinforce the argument, and frequently lead to successful demands for compensatory provision.

The third form of intervention is about directing and channelling play provision, and indeed children's play itself, to help produce educational, social and ultimately economic outcomes in the wider interests of a complex and fast-moving society. The financial and political investment in expanding child care provision is in my view a clear example of this type of intervention, and non-play outcomes are now being made more explicit in both government and other funding programmes.

There are obvious and perhaps not so obvious implications for professional playwork practice within these three forms of intervention. Taking the first, there is the problem of squaring the principle that playwork is predicated on the assumption that children's play is freely chosen, personally directed and intrinsically motivated (Hughes 1982), with the reality that the playwork offer (as opposed to a play offer) is generally only available to children in designated play spaces at designated times. Very little playwork happens where children spend most of their time.

Research carried out by Wheway and Millward (1997) has shown that children's play on housing estates and other high density residential areas happens everywhere and anywhere that interests them, and that designated play spaces come fairly low down the list. For me the most interesting finding was that the journeys to and from the places they choose to play appeared to be at least as important to them as the play experience at any particular location. This endless journeying, which often didn't have an obvious purpose, was clearly purposeful for the children given the amount of time they spent doing it.

It certainly reminded me of the endless and thoroughly enjoyable journeying I did as a child in rural Northern Ireland in the 1950s. I recently met up again with my closest play friend from my childhood, and we reminisced about how we had treated the whole environment as a playground, and how much we played in and around rivers, streams and ponds, and particularly under bridges with their magical interplay of water, light and sound. He told me that his own children had never been able to share our experiences because bridges had often been used as locations for planting bombs to attack security forces, and more recently, drainage schemes had made most streams and rivers too deep, fast-running and polluted for him to allow his children to play in the same way as we did. Here was a uniquely Northern Irish, and another more universal example of the erosion of children's play space through adult intervention.

Turning to the compensatory play spaces we've created, let's examine what is actually going on in and just how much compensation has really been made for what children have lost. While there are a number of honourable exceptions, many play environments look and feel uncannily similar. In the early 1980s I was told about (but unfortunately never saw) a slide show which was a sequence of images of cars, housing, streets, hairstyles, clothing fashions and so on over the previous 30 or so years, interspersed with contemporaneous images of both unsupervised fixed equipment and staffed adventure playgrounds. Everything changed with bewildering speed as hats disappeared, hair grew longer and then shorter, cars went from boxy to more rounded shapes and back again, and tower blocks and huge estates sprouted as terraced streets were pulled down.

The one and only constant was that the playgrounds stayed very much the same, and I strongly suspect that if the exercise was repeated now it would show something similar, because in playwork we tend to copy mistakes from each other rather than learning from them. The playwork profession has generally not been good at recording its experience of what does and doesn't work, and in this respect is a bit like one of those lost civilizations which built lots of monuments but never got round to inventing a written language to record their achievements and failures for the benefit of future generations.

We have unintentionally developed a culture in which there are recognizable templates for play spaces, with an implicit assumption that children must come to them to get 'real play' delivered through playwork. By templates I mean sets of characteristics based on received ideas of what play spaces should contain, and which bear very little, or at best a very stylized, resemblance to the natural environments in which children have played for thousands of years. Few play spaces genuinely and fully compensate for what's been eroded, not because their creators can't be bothered, but because it is an almost impossible task to do this on designated sites and during designated times. If we were brutally honest, we would describe many play spaces as ghettos rather than oases of play; we would acknowledge the comings and goings of children as a major component of their play time; and we would accept that our playwork is an irrelevance for most children most of the time. I have my own confessions to make in this respect.

Sixteen years after I left Bermondsey adventure playground in London, one of the most regular users (now a mother of four children and working as a care assistant in a special needs school) cheerfully explained that while she and the other children loved their time at Bermondsey during opening hours, some of the best times they had there were when it was officially shut and they could play freely without the benefit of what then passed for playwork. I suddenly remembered one classic example of how we playworkers got it wrong in the official hours and the children got it right when they weren't supposed to be there. We were very proud of an innovative sandpit we had built, complete with platforms, working cranes and sand chutes, and especially the fully-working rope-operated wooden mechanical digger. We were equally proud of the nearby timber and tarpaulin splash pool fed by a hose trickling down a water slide. We came to work after a weekend closure in the summer holidays to find that the children had made some changes. They had integrated the sandpit and pool by realigning the heavy timbers of both, and engineering the tarpaulin and several cubic metres of sand to make a leak-proof beach, complete with a surprising number of real seashells. For the rest of that long hot summer, every day was beach day, with deck-chairs, transistor radios, sunglasses and sun cream, cooler boxes and sandcastle building. The sandcastles were frequently washed away in realistic seaside manner by the waves created as children cannoned down the slide and splashed into the pool. It had never occurred to us alleged play experts to do anything like this, and we were suitably humbled by the amount of invention, coordination, engineering and the sheer physical effort involved. In true playwork style it took years before I first got round to writing it down so that other people could learn from our mistakes and share the magic of the children's invention.

The third form of intervention with its non-play agendas has been troubling many playworkers for decades, during which time playwork has been seen as a back door route for delivering community development and crime prevention agendas. This approach is now being extended right into the heart of play itself, where play must have a purpose with measurable outcomes. The danger is not only that the concept of children's play having no external goal or reward is corrupted, or even destroyed by the demand for outcomes, it is also that these outcomes are being determined and calibrated according to measurements of educational achievement, citizenship, community safety, employability and so on. The pressure to join up with child care, education and economic agendas is very powerful, and the amount of money on offer under these agendas coupled with the uncertainty about funding for traditional 'pure' playwork seems to have the potential to corrupt the ethos and integrity of the play profession.

But consider Jerome Bruner's insight into what is actually going on in play. He said 'the main characteristic of play – child or adult – is not its content, but its mode. Play is an approach to action, not a form of activity' (NPFA 2000: 6). This is a difficult idea for playworkers, who tend to think of play as being *the* key activity of children, but I think his point is that play is not in a separate box from activities like eating, walking, creating, learning, thinking, climbing, or concepts such as socialization and developing self-esteem. It is a way of approaching them.

Think about a child digging a hole. What they're actually doing is just digging a hole, but the way they go about it is very likely to be playful. They could be digging for treasure, looking for skeletons or worms, going through the centre of the earth and out the other side, or perhaps just exuberantly flinging soil everywhere for the sheer fun of it. They might suddenly and completely change the 'purpose' of the digging, or stubbornly continue it over a period of hours or even days. They might or might not give out play cues to start a short-term or longer-lived epidemic of hole-digging by other children, or invite an adult to help them to extend their play. The invitation to an adult is much more likely to be about extending the basic activity (digging a bigger hole or preventing the existing one from collapsing) than extending their playful approach to it, though of course this will also happen.

Professional playwork practice is thus faced with squaring the circle of maintaining the child's sense of autonomy and control over their own play experiences within adult interventions in their play space and time. This is a central and underpinning theme of *Best Play* (NPFA 2000: 6): 'The impulse to play comes from within the child, and is intentional only in the sense of

being about what interests children themselves . . . The intrinsic motivation
of play, the fact that for children play does not involve the pursuit of any
external goal or reward, raises challenges when defining objectives for play
provision.'

One challenge is acknowledging that while there are clearly play environment deficits in the wider environment, perhaps there aren't quite as many
as the playwork profession has liked to think. Where there is high quality
play provision, easily accessible to children in a particular catchment area,
given the choice, most of the children will spend most of their time playing
or journeying around other places that interest them. Many of the busiest
and best open access adventure playgrounds typically have less than 30 per
cent of the child population in their catchment areas on their register, and
even on those days when there might be a hundred or more children on site,
hundreds more of their users are doing something else, somewhere else at
any given time.

Another challenge is to tear up what I've called the templates for play
provision in our designated play spaces and replace them with questions.
Long before deciding to buy or build a swing or create an environmental
pond, we should ask: why a swing or pond? An example from the commercial
sector illustrates this point. I have never been a great admirer of manufactured fixed play equipment because the design parameters of low maintenance and resistance to vandalism in most cases seem to come a long way
above the primary purpose of facilitating children's play. The result is a cycle
of diminishing returns – the more boring the equipment, the more it has to
be vandal-proofed, becoming even more boring in a downward spiral. The
Richter Speilgerate company has a very different attitude, and gets this free
plug more for their design approach than for the undoubted excellence of
their products.

About a year after the children had remodelled the sandpit and pool, I
came across Richter's play equipment catalogue, which impressed me for
several reasons. First, they seemed to put play value at the centre of the
design process. Second, their policy was to observe and record how children
actually used the equipment over a considerable period of time before putting
it on the market. Each item had an explanation of its play value alongside
the usual technical information in the catalogue. In some cases they actually
abandoned what at first appeared to be good designs because an unaccept-
ably low level of play value emerged during observation. But what really
amazed me at the time was the incredible similarity of the rationale for their
sand and water structures to what the children had done at Bermondsey.
Several years later, having seen one of their six-sided swings in use and built
a version on an adventure playground, I met Julian Richter at a play conference and (after a pathetic attempt to soften him up with the story of the
parallel development of the sandpit) I nervously admitted that I'd copied
one of his company's ideas. Instead of setting the lawyers onto me, he
animatedly questioned me in great detail about what play values I thought
were present in the design and how the children used the swing. He was

particularly interested in a six-sided football swinging game the children had spontaneously invented. Playwork has a lot to learn from this approach, where the first step is to question the play value of any design and relate it to what is known about children's play, then observe and record the children's interaction, then make modifications (or abandon the idea) before going into full production, and then continue to be interested in new uses by the children.

This could be a model of what should become a much more symbiotic relationship between children's play and playwork. I use the idea of symbiosis to underline that children's play is one thing and playwork is very definitely something else – children play, and playworkers playwork. To those who say that playworkers can and should play too, the riposte is that we need to be very clear about what constitutes 'playworker's play'. I would argue that it is not intrinsically motivated in precisely the same way as children's play, nor in the same way as adult play – alone or with other adults. Further, the freely chosen and personally directed elements should primarily come from the children through play cues or more direct invitations rather than from the playworker. The play of playworkers is a much more knowing and self-conscious activity than the direct unmediated play impulse of children, and much of the time the children themselves are aware of a subtle difference between the two. Just reflect on how often children say 'play with me' to an adult, but how rarely they phrase the request this way when wanting to engage other children in their play.

Playworkers are beginning to observe children's play more systematically, to reflect on and record their observations and playwork interventions, partly because it is now seen as good practice, and partly because it is required for National Vocational Qualifications and other qualification awards. However, we need to be clear about the two different things we are recording – children's play behaviours on the one hand, and playwork interventions on the other. An even more important distinction needs to be made, which at its crudest is the question of which comes first. In a true symbiotic relationship, cause and effect are not necessarily clearly separated between the partner organisms, and in something as organic and complex as the relationship between play and playwork this ought to be especially the case. At the risk of a self-inflicted destruction of the symbiosis analogy, it seems to me that children's play should cause the playwork intervention, and from here on I'm going to use the term 'playwork response' for this very reason.

During the development of *Quality in Play* (Conway and Farley 2001) (a quality assurance system for school-age play provision), when we were piloting evidence-gathering techniques and playworkers' reflective records, we found playworkers were tending to record the children's response to the specific play environment, rather than 'pure' children's play behaviours. They tended to talk more about how children used a swing or took part in a programmed activity than they did about fundamental play behaviours and the 'why' of what children were doing when they played. In a way this is very understandable because the designated play space is a given rather than a response to children's play needs, because in reality even the best playworkers aim to meet a highest common denominator of play needs, rather than responding to individual needs of children.

Clearly we can't be expected to tear down the whole caboodle and start again every time a new child turns up to play, but we do need to concentrate on continuously modifying and enriching the environment to meet the widest possible range of play needs, as opposed to expecting individual children to like it or lump it because their play needs don't fit into an average range. It is not as hard as it sounds to do this, but care needs to be taken!

The first step is to forget for a moment the given environment with its resource problems and all the other constraints on what we can actually provide, and go back to first principles. The objective is to concentrate on the modes and intrinsic purposes of children's play rather than the delivery or outcomes of playwork in particular play spaces and times, by looking at the play assumptions and values, play types, play cues and the theoretical research and thinking which underpin them. Then we need to ask ourselves what kind of provision in an ideal world could we create to meet these principles. When we've done this we can come back to what we've actually got and can provide, and start to map it against the principles and the ideal world. The objective here is to shift our thinking away from the template approach to play provision where the given environment intervenes in and directs children's play rather than the other way around.

There are a number of techniques for doing this, one of the best being the evaluation spiral developed by Bob Hughes (2001: 92–6) from an earlier idea of the Merseyside Playwork Training Project. The 'spiral' is a drawing of five concentric circles divided into any number of sectors by lines. The example shown in Figure 7.1 has eight sectors.

The inner circle scores 1 and the outer 5, and any word, concept or aspect of a play environment can be assigned to the sectors. Shading in the sectors to score from 1 to 5 produces a quick visual record of whatever you want to map or measure. For example, a spiral can be made with 15 sectors – one for each play type (NPFA 2000: 33), and used by playworkers to score how well the play environment meets the play types now, and then repeated after some time has elapsed and something has been done, to get a picture of what has changed, both in perception and in reality.

The real beauty of the spiral for playwork is that children can use it as a play activity which produces real data over which they can have control for planning or change. At its most basic it is a much more pleasurable colouring-in exercise than having to do homework-like writing or tick box exercises, but unless children understand the purpose and can trust that it will genuinely lead to improvement, they have every right and incentive to subvert the whole process. At a more sophisticated (and difficult) level for playworkers it could be used to find out what children really think about the human and physical play environment by mapping their perceptions of the playwork response.

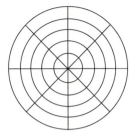

Figure 7.1 Evaluation spiral with eight sectors

In one example, a play project made simple spirals with sectors for the boys' and girls' toilets, and other areas of the building. The girls scored their toilet fairly high, and the boys' toilet very low. The boys scored the girls' toilet very high and their own toilet very low. There were animated discussions among the children about the scores when all the spirals were compared, and the outcome was that the boys realized for the first time that the poor state of their toilets was something to do with the way they treated them, rather than the result of some universal law which says that boys' toilets are by definition disgusting.

Another very useful tool for examining the play environment is Simon Nicholson's 'How not to cheat children: the theory of loose parts' (1971) which contains fundamental insights into what children really need in order to engage in play to the fullest possible extent. Nicholson was an architect who became intrigued by his observations that children played in much more creative, challenging, adaptive and combinatorial ways on the building sites during construction than on the designed and formally designated play spaces installed in the finished development. The simple reason was that the building site was in effect an unstaffed adventure playground, with a huge amount of different materials and junk (loose parts) lying around which the children could use in any way they wanted, while the finished designated play space was typically nothing like this kind of play environment. Nicholson also used the example of a seashore as a near ideal play environment because of the richness and variety of materials and transitions between natural forms and textures (continue the list for yourself from your own memories and experiences of being on a beach, while imagining me kicking myself as I remember the children's beach back at Bermondsey!).

Thinking about what we did as children with the bits and pieces lying around, and looking at what children actually do when playing in the light of play types, loose parts and the other play concepts, will help us create genuinely enriched play environments, and avoid stupid mistakes as in the next example.

Over many years I had noticed how much children loved to build camps and dens, not just on adventure playgrounds, but anywhere and everywhere. The problem with their camps, as I then saw it, was that they leaked when it rained, soaking and rotting the old cushions and fabrics used in their construction and decoration; the freestanding ones were permanently on the point of collapse and all of them contained thickets of rusting and protruding nails. My bright idea was to build an open framework in the shape of two facing streets with proper pitched roofs, close-boarded level floors and a nail-free system of wood composite panels which the children could fix to the frame by means of wooden pegs in different configurations. After the initial interest, it just didn't work for the children. The pegs were too fiddly and quickly got lost, the panels were just that bit too big, heavy and unwieldy for the children to manoeuvre, and the whole thing was on far too large a scale. The penny finally dropped when I saw four children making a perfect camp out of a table and an old sheet, and finding Eeyore-like dens (Milne 1977) made out of the haphazardly piled panels anywhere and everywhere except where they were 'supposed' to be. I realized that I had never properly observed and reflected on camp-building by children as a *process* as opposed to a *product*. My structures now have very different functions: one is used as a woodworking area and dry timber store, while the other is a covered all-weather mini-adventure playspace with fixed camp areas, platforms and scramble nets. They are used by the children, but not at all in the way originally envisaged.

By using recording techniques and tools like spirals, we can begin to think about what sort of play environment should be created and who would be involved in the design and operation of it, and try genuinely to put the principles into practice and make them a reality for children. In my view, this has to be at the heart of professional playwork practice, because as well as informing individual playworkers, it would create a written body of knowledge starting from children's needs and recording both responses which work and those which don't. This has been tried, with mixed success as the following example shows.

Some years ago Hackney Play Association set up a 'design and build' play project as an attempt to involve children in the design and construction of play environments from start to finish of the process. A school contacted us for help with remodelling the infant's playground, involving two junior classes as a curriculum-based project. The school had carried out a survey in which the children had completed questionnaires whose answers were fed into a computer database, with unexpected results. Although the children had consistently said the playground was boring, over 70 per cent of the answers indicated they didn't want any changes. It turned out that the first question had been: 'What is missing from the playground?' The children had taken the question absolutely literally, looked around at the old bike shed, the painted hopscotch lines on the tarmac and the drinking fountain, seen that everything was still there and nothing had been stolen and naturally replied 'nothing is missing'.

Our playworkers tried to use spirals with the children to explore play types, and while they liked the spirals, they had problems with the fine divisions between different types of play, perhaps because the playworkers themselves found it difficult to explain them. The children said that as far as they were concerned there were in fact just three types of play, corresponding to rough and tumble play, games with rules like football or skipping, and a third very important play type which they scientifically categorized as 'just mucking about'. After some more exploration of the play types through considerably simplifying the language, the children eventually decided on a ship structure along one wall of the playground, because it would be good for several play types such as role, fantasy, dramatic and imaginative play, while other play types such as locomotor, social and communication play were already at least partly catered for in the existing playground. The playworkers stifled a groan – this was the third project in a row where children had come up with a ship structure as their preferred design.

'Design and Build' kept a comprehensive record of photographs, children's drawings and spirals, and planning and costing schedules throughout its three-year life, but it was only towards the end of the project that we began to realize that something fundamental was missing – we had never properly evaluated the information we had collected. We commissioned Bob Hughes (1999) to carry out an independent evaluation, and he had some tough things to say about the project. The environmental and time constraints had in many cases overridden the initial aim, which was that the children should cause and drive the playwork response. To quote from the report: 'this is very typical of a good and enthusiastic playworker who wants the play space to be right for children, although sometimes apparently even in spite of the children themselves!'

The report also noted that while individual components often varied, what was called 'the silhouette' of a lot of the larger and more permanent structures was very similar, revealing that we had in fact been unconsciously designing and building to templates. The evaluation had a lot of very positive things to say as well, but if we had only done more evaluation (internally or externally) earlier on, we would probably have avoided many of the mistakes we made. Better still, if we had started off by thinking through the fundamentals of children's play needs before setting the project in the concrete of the grant application, we might well have ended up with many more truly enriched play environments.

A year or so later during the Quality in Play development programme, we also found there was a fantastic amount of monitoring of play provision through playworkers' reflective records, quarterly, monthly or even weekly returns, annual reports, business plans and general bean-counting, but virtually no evaluation of what they contained. Filing cabinets and computer systems in both play sites and local authority offices were stuffed full with information which wasn't used in any meaningful or useful way to plan the enrichment of children's play experiences. Playworkers were infuriated by the admission of some managers and monitoring officers that they didn't have time to properly analyse the collected information, but then had to admit to an equal shortage of time to evaluate their own collected information.

My suspicion is that what really lay behind the failure to evaluate was the lack of an evaluation model rather than a shortage of time. Josephine Seccombe (1999) has developed a startlingly simple evaluation framework which easily adapts to playwork. It starts from the premise that you should only collect information which is necessary and useful for evaluation, which in turn is not about looking back at successes and failures in the traditional way, but is about looking forward and focusing on the positive. The framework is based on simple questions, asking what worked and should be continued; what was missing and should be changed; and what should be discontinued, with reasons for each decision. Another question asking what would make 'it bigger' is deliberately vaguely phrased in this way to encourage a more holistic approach to thinking about improvement. The overall idea is to let go of what doesn't work as painlessly as possible; avoid our psychological tendency to blame someone else, or the overall environment for our failures; and accept that our most cherished approaches or constructs may no longer be useful. It is also designed to encourage us to celebrate and continue success, and to try innovation without fear of future failure. All best practice emerges from pathways littered with the wreckage of ideas which simply didn't work.

Here is an example of how this approach leads to a much more sophisticated analysis of the success or failure of an activity or project. A dance troupe had been commissioned to run a series of workshops on a tree theme with children in several playgrounds and school-based play centres across a local authority, culminating in a performance at a large playday event in a park when a tree would be planted. The project was deemed unsuccessful because the dance troupe didn't manage to involve enough participants, and it was decided not to attempt a similar project in future.

But when the Seccombe evaluation model was applied, a quite different picture began to emerge. When it was asked what elements should be continued and why, it became obvious that a dozen or so children had put a lot of energy and effort into creating and performing a very high quality tree-themed song and a dance routine of which they were extremely proud. A particular playworker had actually done most of the support and coordinating work with this group of children, and it was their combined enthusiasm which had made the project a success, if not on the scale originally envisaged. Informal *ad hoc* dance activities had often previously happened on the playground, because they were very much part of the pop music video culture of the children, and the playworker had always responded to this as an enjoyable part of his work on the playground. So there was no reason why dance, both totally informal and the more structured development of performances, shouldn't continue to be part of the life of the playground as long as the children wanted to do it. Perhaps the playworker and children could run the sessions at other play provision sessions and work up a performance with more participants next time. The only thing that should be discontinued was the engagement of the particular dance troupe, not the idea of dance as an activity or project.

I want to finish with an observation made by the 'design and build' project. Over three years in 68 locations involving over 3000 children the project team noticed a wide variation in what they ended up calling the 'play literacy' of the children. The variation didn't necessarily depend on the type or ethos of the play space, but on other factors. For example, on one particular adventure playground the majority of the children were noticeably confident and highly competent across a whole spectrum of skills, from using tools to initiating quite large-scale cooperative ventures, while on other apparently similar adventure playgrounds this was less in evidence. The determining factors seemed to be the overall attitude of playworkers, their response to the children's play and the availability of loose parts. While all the playgrounds were child-centred, this one spent a lot of time and effort looking at and reflecting on what children actually did when they played. It also had a strong culture of encouraging children to take part in, question and develop each and every aspect of the playground, ranging from tools and materials always being freely available and 'mess' being tolerated, to the children organizing and running the AGM as a pantomime in which the adults had to explain what they did and why they did it (much to the auditor's astonishment when he found himself having to play the scripted part of a Scrooge-like ship's purser).

In this responsive environment, the children's play was in many ways very much like the play of children everywhere, but it extended much further up the hierarchy of responsibility and spread into every nook and cranny of the life of the playground. Here is something very like Bruner's dictum in action (NPFA 2000: 6) with a playful approach to a very wide spectrum of actions being the norm, compared to a narrower play repertoire and range of competencies observed on the other playgrounds. The play literacy of the children on this playground is in my view a direct result of what I've called the symbiotic relationship between their play and the playwork culture, in which children's play shapes and drives the playwork response, and which I have now belatedly learned to see as the core of professional playwork practice.

Chapter 8

Adventure playgrounds in the twenty-first century

Tony Chilton

Why is play important?

In the UK today, the most common adult perception of the value of play includes the idea that it is an activity with educational content. Play is seen as a precursor to formal learning; an activity that occupies the child's time in a productive way or provides a diversion from other areas of life. It is often more acceptable when it is non-messy, quiet, undemanding of adults, constructive and productive – i.e. there should be tangible results. Although there is a general acceptance that it aids physical and intellectual development, and contains elements of creativity, all of these are seen to be best accommodated through an adult controlled process. It is rare for children to get the opportunity to determine their own space, or to have a say in what it should contain, how it should be shaped, and how much time they should spend there.

In reality however, play is active, noisy, messy, informal, unstructured and unadulterated (Else and Sturrock 1998). It is a medium that enables children to explore with unmitigated freedom. Sadly, modern society's apparent obsession with the social control of young people results in few places where children can be their natural selves (Chilton 1985), and adults today spend less time with children than 30 years ago. Else (2001) suggests that many parents would prefer their children to use fixed equipment playgrounds because they are 'cleaner, more convenient and they believe safer'. Changes in employment patterns, mass communications, car ownership, etc. have allowed adults greater freedom than ever before – freedom to explore different forms of entertainment, leisure, sports and social activities. Inevitably there is a tendency for those adults to think their children should be engaged in the same sort of organized and structured activity.

Hand in hand with greater social control comes greater investment in safety than ever before. Provision for children is delivered on that basis, and most parents ask the question 'Is it safe?' before considering any other criteria associated with play value. In a recent survey, a leading playground equipment manufacturer identified 'safety, safety, safety' as the prime consideration in terms of play value (Brown 2002). Of course this is an adult's view of safety, not a child's view – i.e. safety is seen as a function of the engineering characteristics of the equipment, rather than the children's usage of it and the play site as a whole.

More and more, children are being expected to fit into a world where the parameters are dictated by adults. Political and social agendas are leaning towards institutionalized provision for children at every stage of their lives. The modern built environment has been colonized by adults for their own use, with little consideration of children's need for space within which they can express their natural and innate behaviour. There is a tendency to see play as a performance-based activity as opposed to a behavioural process. As a result we are inhibiting individual growth and the development of personality. Children are being denied the opportunities for self-expression, exploration, experimentation, innovation and creativity that are so essential to their healthy development (Hughes 1996a).

All this may result in a detrimental influence on the child's ability to establish a sense of independence, particularly in decision making processes (Bruner 1972). The opportunity for perceiving, encountering and subsequently managing risk is being removed. It follows that in later life these young people will be more vulnerable to accidents and injury, and because of the lack of development of social skills may suffer social exclusion.

Early adventure playgrounds

Historically, most adventure playgrounds were established in urban areas in response to the decreasing availability of suitable space for children to play creatively. The early advocates of such provision were concerned about the detrimental impact that modern development of the physical environment could have on the child's ability to pursue a variety of play opportunities (Ward 1978). Large, densely built residential areas were springing up all over post-war Britain, with limited thought given to the play needs and play habits of children. Such harsh, sterile environments did little to stimulate the natural play instincts of children. Adventure playgrounds, originally called 'junk playgrounds' by Sorensen (1931), were seen as an opportunity to give children the chance to create their own self-centred play environments. The vision of people like Abernethy (1968) and Allen of Hurtwood (1968) was not simply a reflection of the value of such play space, but also included the strong advocacy of the employment of playworkers, perhaps the most important ingredient of the adventure playground (Chilton 1985). Essentially, playworkers were seen to be people with skills and qualities geared to developing personal relationships with children, while at the same time not only protecting children's access to play, but enhancing it through the provision of resources and, most importantly, allowing children the time to play at a pace they dictated.

In the early days, adventure playgrounds were established on sites that were unusable, unwanted eyesores, which were not considered economically viable (Benjamin 1974). Many local authorities, having given little thought to the purpose of adventure playgrounds, were willing to hand over such areas. The management of these projects was usually left to local communities, with minimum support from local authorities other than support for funding applications to external sources. Very few of the sites contained indoor accommodation, and they normally had little revenue funding. The acquisition of resources, in terms of materials and equipment, was left entirely in the hands of the playworkers and the local community, who worked together to identify sources of support. Children and young people were very much a part of the process. The playground structures were built by a combination of children, playworkers and members of the local and wider community. The early sites had no manufactured equipment and most of the material being used was recycled.

Children's freedom to come and go as they please was seen as important, and Sorensen warned against too much supervision, saying 'children ought to be free and by themselves to the greatest possible extent . . . one ought to be exceedingly careful when interfering in the lives and activities of children' (Allen of Hurtwood 1968: 55). Therefore, it was regarded as a fundamental tenet of adventure play that children dictated the pace at which things were done. Guidance from the playworkers was mainly focused on the safety of large timber structures. Children were free to explore their capacity for doing things themselves (e.g. building dens, water and mud play areas, large towers, swings and climbing apparatus). However, it would be wrong to give the impression that these facilities were called adventure playgrounds because of the adventurous structures that characterized their skyline. In fact the 'adventure' was what went on in the child's mind (Abernethy 1968). Life on an adventure playground was also about making fires, dressing up, role play, rudimentary cooking (mainly soup and baked potatoes), and organizing impromptu social events, such as parades and carnivals. Large scale flour and water fights and bonfires were a regular feature in the summer holidays. A number of sites kept animals, which children adopted, using rota systems.

The essential feature was that children were allowed the time, and given the encouragement, to do things for themselves. Help and guidance was only given when asked for (explicitly or implicitly). Playworkers were expected to use intuitive skills and knowledge, rather than those acquired through formal training. Such 'progress' came much later. Playworkers were more concerned with the practical and philosophical application of playwork, rather than didactic theoretical approaches. Great reliance was placed on knowledge of individual children, their family circumstances and the local community. Children had opportunities to confront and deal with conflict without the intervention of adults, unless the scenario was life-threatening. *All* children, whatever their circumstances, were welcome.

Although the majority were in London, adventure playgrounds spread throughout the UK, and were generally located in urban areas. A few were part of new town developments, such as Peterborough, Stevenage and Telford. Money came from the new town corporations, but in most other situations there remained a heavy reliance on temporary funding schemes from central government, in particular the Urban Aid Programme (Heseltine 1978–84). Few adventure playgrounds were placed in rural areas because of the planners' perception that children in those areas had free and easy access to play opportunities – a fallacy that persists today. Even the experts made this mistake. Sorensen thought the aim of adventure playgrounds was 'to give the children of the city a substitute for the rich possibilities for play which children in the country possess' (Allen of Hurtwood 1968: 55).

The early adventure playgrounds opened at times when children needed them most – after school until late in the evening, at weekends and during school holidays. When staffing allowed they were open seven days a week, showing clearly that the prime concern was the needs of the children, rather than the organization providing the facility, or the playworkers themselves. Playworkers did not take time off during school holidays. Adventure playgrounds were an essential and lively component of the communities in which they were based. Playworkers often lived in close proximity to the site, and were available when the children needed them. However, this sort of *total commitment* approach to the working environment carried with it overwhelming responsibilities and attendant stress factors. There was no obvious career structure, the pay was poor and there was often a high turnover of staff. As a consequence of all this, the quality and calibre of playworkers diminished. When this was coupled with a lack of substantial funding for projects, and a dramatically changing political climate, it is not surprising that the number of adventure playgrounds reduced considerably during the 1980s. Save for a few local authorities, there was little support for adventure playgrounds. Ironically, many of the things that made them attractive to children were now viewed in a negative light by adults. They were seen as noisy, dirty, untidy eyesores, which were intimidating and attracted large numbers of young teenagers.

The biggest negative impact on the initially child-centred approach to adventure play came from the perceived implications of the Health & Safety at Work Act (1974), which embraced such provision as adventure playgrounds. The freedom to build structures, dens and fires, and the use of tools, all carried a risk element. This was considered by many local authorities to be unacceptable, and a potential source of litigation. As a consequence, many local authorities closed their adventure playgrounds, and those that remain are less likely to be the genuine creation of the children.

Reflections

The following recollections are intended to give a flavour of what life used to be like on an adventure playground. Although the nature of the work has changed substantially over the last 30 years, there is no reason to think that children's basic needs have changed greatly. Some of the lessons from these stories remain just as powerful today. Hence my reason for including them.

Recollection 1: Anthony

Anthony was a regular attendee of the adventure playground, a 10-year-old who had been excluded from every school he attended (even a special school), largely because of his bloodthirsty and pathological urge to bite people. Anthony never bit any of the staff at the adventure playground. He did however bite a number of the older children who were foolish enough to provoke him. And could he bite! No half measures with Anthony. He gave lessons in biting to Staffordshire Bull Terriers. Once he had hold of you, he locked on and would not be shaken off! As a playworker employed by the Education Department I often used to confront issues concerning children and young people who lived on the estate where the adventure playground was located. I was thus invited to Anthony's case conference, where it became apparent that the Department were at a complete loss to find the best way of accommodating his educational needs. Home tutoring seemed the best option, but Anthony's home circumstances were not conducive to such an approach. After lengthy discussions, it was agreed that the wooden hut on the adventure playground which I used as an office, first-aid centre, tool store, emergency escape hole and refuge should be used on four mornings a week for 'home' tutoring. Anthony, his personal tutor and I spent four months in these cramped conditions, but eventually it paid off. The biting stopped, and he was gradually reintegrated back into school. Following further sessions with educational psychologists, we finally found a Rudolph Steiner School able to accommodate his needs. Anthony still lives in the town where the adventure playground is located, and remembers with considerable warmth the time he spent at there.

Recollection 2: Darren

Darren was a regular user of the playground – a 15-year-old, 15-stone bully, excluded from school – and yet he responded magnificently to the programme of integration we introduced at the playground. At last he seemed able to play gently and calmly with the disabled children who were being gradually acclimatized to the structure and different activity areas of the site. When our regular users were discussing with me the best way for children with disabilities to use the facilities, it was finally agreed that they should be treated no differently, simply given more time to get around the site, and that no activity should be denied them. There were times when Darren took this too literally. On one occasion he was pushing one of our wheelchair users (a boy called Michael) across the rickety bridge over the sandpit. 'I want to play in the sand,' said Michael. Darren upended the wheelchair and tipped him off the bridge into the sandpit. When the playworkers protested they were met with the confident response of someone who knows they're in the right: 'That's the rule! We agreed – they just get treated like everyone else.' Michael's laughter silenced any further debate.

Recollection 3: the twins

Some of the older users of the playground constructed a tree house that spanned two huge trees in the middle of the site. It was only accessible to those able to negotiate the carefully located rungs on the base of the tree. The first was over a metre from the ground so that smaller children could not get to it. Among the regular 'disabled' children to use the site were two extremely lively and demanding 9-year-old twins. They were profoundly deaf, and had no verbal communication. Although neither staff nor other children could use sign language, a very effective communication system was developed, mainly through the use of eye and physical contact. One afternoon I received a phone call in 'Tony's Hole', the name the kids had painted on my wooden hut, from the twin's mother asking me to send them home. I was exploring the site in search of them, when I felt what I thought was rain – strange because it was a sunny afternoon. I looked up to discover the twins running around the platform that surrounded the tree house, in hysterics. I still don't know what that warm liquid was, but the tree house became known as the highest toilet in the town! Anyway, I was so shocked and frightened at seeing the twins up at such a height, I didn't think too much about being soaking wet. But things got worse. Every time I tried to make eye contact to insist they come down, they would suddenly move their heads either to one side or upwards. Eventually I climbed up to the tree house to encourage them to descend. On my way up, I passed them coming down. They reached the bottom before I did and proceeded to lose themselves elsewhere on site. Needless to say their mother didn't appreciate my wonderful playwork skills!

Recollection 4: the untouchables

Michelle, Lisa, Barbara and Becky were all around the ages of 12 and 13. During a long period of fine weather the four 'untouchables', as they liked to be known, requested tools, materials and a piece of land where they could 'build a swimming pool'. I duly obliged and they began with enthusiasm. The girls resisted all offers of help from the boys, and for two days work continued at a frenzied pace. On the third day reality set in, and they changed their original plans, seeking advice about how to build a paddling pool. With the introduction of the new plan, enthusiasm was renewed and work entered into with increased energy and commitment. Throughout the whole exercise Joey, one of the disabled children, watched with increasing interest. Occasionally one of the girls would push his wheelchair closer to the action, from where he could offer his architectural observations. Construction work complete, there was the problem of identifying a source of water. The playground building was about 35 yards away and we only had one bucket, and anyway the water supply was not yet connected! The ensuing discussions resulted in all the blame for the lack of water being attributed to the 'stupid playworker' who 'should have told us about this'. Eventually we arrived at a solution – an extended hose-pipe leading from my house across the road! During the trial run to discover whether the system would work, the inner lining, a very large and heavy haulage tarpaulin, had not been fixed into the paddling pool. Consequently the area rapidly became a mud bath which the girls and others found to be tremendous fun. But at last the playground had its paddling pool.

Recollection 5: Joey

It had taken considerable persuasion before Joey's parents would let him come to the adventure playground. One of their conditions was that I would take personal responsibility for 'supervising' him. Another was that he should not participate in 'rough' games and other physically demanding activities. I agreed to everything with the secret thought that eventually Joey would determine his own level of participation given sufficient time. Unfortunately I felt that time had come too early, for on the day of the mud bath Joey became fully involved! While the water and mud play was in full swing I had become distracted for slightly too long. On emerging from the building I took a casual look around the site and was stunned to see Joey out of his wheelchair covered from head to foot in black mud. He was hysterical with joy, but that poignant moment was short lived for me, because his parents were due to collect him very soon. Having no water supply made the task of cleaning Joey almost impossible. I was trying desperately to transform him back to something like his normal self when the door opened and in came his parents. I began spluttering out my excuses to no avail. Joey's father, all 6'7" and 17 stone of him, had tears in his eyes which I thought were tears of rage. He roared at me to get out of the way, and pushed me to one side. Joey's mother, meanwhile, was transfixed. Joey was beaming, the wide grin shining through the black mud. His dad lifted him up in his enormous hands, but quickly freed one to grasp one of mine. 'Tony, thank you so much,' he said. 'His mother has had a flannel to his face for fifteen years. This is the first time I've ever seen him with mud on him, he's just like every other child!'

Issues facing adventure playgrounds today

There are still some adventure playgrounds in existence, the majority being in London. Many contain manufactured equipment. A number are still trying to relate to the original concept, but they are governed by adverse funding criteria and political agendas. In the UK today, adventure playgrounds tend to be contained and controllable by adults, at the very time when the original philosophy is most needed. If the original philosophy and operational practices were allowed, then we would not be subjecting children and young people to the vagaries of adulterated play environments. Adventure playgrounds are perhaps the only opportunity to provide comprehensive choice in relation to the changing play needs and behaviour of today's children. Without this, there is a real risk that society will lose out. It is not just a question of restricting children's physical activity, it is also about enabling them to cope with problems (Sylva *et al.* 1976). Children need a thoroughly rounded socialization that includes social challenges, risks and conflicts, and the development of social identity. With a reduced capacity for children to understand differences in other human beings, and a reduction in the opportunities to understand group pressures and social challenges, plus concepts such as cooperation and mutual respect, children will miss the opportunity to develop to their full potential. If society continues to impress upon children the importance of successful performance in everything they do, they will have difficulty in coming to terms with their limitations. If society focuses entirely on institutionalized provision, we will be guilty of restricting the emergence of personality and individuality. We will be creating a society that is more and more reliant on systems, institutionalized structures and state control, rather than one that is organically motivated and driven by human development. Six main issues arise, and these are discussed in the following sections.

Issue 1: the child care lobby

Because of the increasing demand by adults for safe out-of-school care, it is now possible for children to be in the same setting (i.e. the school) from 8.30 a.m. until 6.30 p.m. for most of their childhood. They may be attending breakfast club, school, and then an after-school club at the same venue. This is not a process weighted in favour of a child's healthy and rounded development, mainly because they will have little contact with their immediate physical and social environment, and thus little opportunity to experience freedom, choice and personal time. They will also miss out on the informal play opportunities that occur on the way to and from school, which often divert children into unexpected yet stimulating activity. They will have little knowledge of what exists in their local community in terms of its geographical and physical layout. Nor will they understand the characteristics of the community, or the characters who matter. All this has consequences for later life. They may be missing opportunities to meet new people and make new friends. Their social identity will be limited, because the local community will not know them. This might mean that the community will neither trust them nor protect them. On another level, they may miss a range of large-scale physical activities, team games and interaction with children from different cultures. There may also be strong elements of social exclusion and stigmatization, especially in diverse communities.

Good quality child care is important and there is clearly a strong need for it. However, it should not be the only type of provision. It needs to be part of an integrated strategy for out-of-school provision. Increasingly, it is seen by many people as the only type of provision they are comfortable with. In general, it caters for a limited age range, and while play is included in the programme of activities, the prime concern is *care*, and the primary features are safety and protection. The problem is one of agendas. Child care follows an adult and political agenda. Playwork, on the other hand, takes the child's agenda as its starting point. Things are done for and on behalf of the children, rather than with them. Perhaps it is time for providers of out-of-school care to review who it is they are catering for. If all they are doing is responding to adult agendas, then they must have enough courage to support the need for choice. If they were to make a dispassionate appraisal of what they do, they would surely see the almost desperate need for other types of provision. As things stand, they risk compromising children in terms of their ability to exercise control over their environment. There are no opportunities for deconstruction and reconstruction, and little room for spontaneous activity, or the sort of 'fun, freedom and flexibility' recommended by Brown (2000a).

But all is not doom and gloom. Recently, a number of schemes have been emerging that give more weight to developmental play, freedom of choice and spontaneity. Their common feature is that they are based in adventure playgrounds. For example, after studying the successful integration of an after-school club at Highfields adventure playground in Sheffield, Warwick adventure playground in Knottingley piloted a separate out-of-school club in their facility. Chris Morton, senior playworker at the adventure playground, and Maggie Harris, a play development worker, say that because both groups of staff understand and respect each other's ethos and embrace the common ground, the experience has benefited all. The adventure playground gains from the extra funding out-of-school groups can attract, bringing additional facilities and staff, and the out-of-school group enjoys the flexible play environment at the adventure playground, the extra activities and staff. Both groups of children have benefited from the larger, broader social group and the additional play opportunities it brings. The adventure playworkers have also gained an opportunity to extend their support, resources and philosophy of play to more children in the community. The out-of-school group has attracted children who would not otherwise have accessed the benefits of the adventure playground, because of parental needs for child care or fears for their safety. With many of those children subsequently visiting during school holidays on an open access basis, the importance and value of the play process and adventure play provision appears to be understood and valued more widely by parents and carers.

Issue 2: safety and security

The concern for physical playground safety has had a detrimental effect on adventure playgrounds. Because of media attention, there is an increasing perception among the general public that play areas are potentially dangerous places. In recent years there has been a strong clamour for safer surfacing on children's playgrounds. Thus, when people look at adventure playgrounds and see no impact-absorbing surfaces and a wide variety of structures, they assume they are unsafe places. People would prefer to keep their children at home or send them to places where it is thought they will be safe – and yet the Royal Society for the Prevention of Accidents confirms that the accident record of adventure playgrounds is far better than that of other forms of provision (Heseltine 1998).

Socially, children are more secure on adventure playgrounds. They are better equipped to deal with threatening behaviour and situations, because they have the opportunity to develop better social skills. There is a greater sense of togetherness and solidarity among the core group of children, and although the playworkers are able to confront other adults who come onto the site, the children themselves will not be afraid to challenge strangers. Their relationship with the playworkers means they are able to discuss any issues and concerns that they may have. A strong adventure playground will provide the children with good information about the mechanisms they can employ to address their problems. For example, playworkers are likely to have regular contact with social services and other support services. Furthermore, the adventure playground philosophy encourages effective family networking systems and structures.

Issue 3: the primacy of academic achievement in the education system

In playwork circles there is growing concern at the current political consensus that it is a good thing to introduce children to the formal education system at an earlier age (Else 2001). This happens at the expense of time that should be spent playing. Play, which is the most fundamental learning process available to humans, is increasingly being undervalued. There seems to be little recognition that play, as a learning phenomenon, served the human species well for thousands of years prior to the introduction of formal education in this country. Children are now being subjected to a mass of pressures as a result of the practice of academic testing every year of their lives. Playworkers support the need for good educational standards, but the balance is increasingly wrong. Children enjoy learning through play both consciously and subconsciously, and playworkers believe the process should be enhanced not diminished. Adventure playgrounds offer a wide diversity of activities, and great flexibility in the creative process because of the ready availability of 'loose parts' in the environment (Nicholson 1971). The fact that children are able 'to build and shape their own environment' instils in them a 'sense of competence and responsibility' (FPFC 2001: 18). Children in adventure playgrounds learn about their world (e.g. how to work out space, distances, height, etc.) (Hughes 1996). They learn about territory and how to manage their own bodies. They test themselves in a variety of ways in relation to the environmental and physical features of the adventure playground and the characteristics of other children. They learn about confronting problems, both physical and social (Sylva *et al.* 1976) and they develop life skills (Hughes 1996a).

As a consequence of developing competence to do things, children's confidence increases (Brown 2000a). According to Bruner (1972), play offers children the freedom to fail. Rather than being subjected to external pressures to achieve, they develop their own faculties in their own time and at their own pace. Self-discipline is far longer lasting than externally applied discipline – i.e. what we learn for ourselves stays with us longer than something an adult makes us learn against our will. Adventure playgrounds offer opportunities for creative development and intellectual stimulation (Brown 2000a). This sort of play stimulates the brain and makes children more proactive than reactive. Furthermore, adventure playgrounds offer opportunities for group games that encourage social interaction (e.g. dens are usually the result of a cooperative effort) (Parten 1933). The essence of adventure play is that the child is in control of their play environment. There is no predetermined programme or curriculum to adhere to, but help, guidance and support are there when required.

Issue 4: social inclusion

Playworkers on adventure playgrounds expect to deal with *all* children, whatever their personal, physical, emotional or social circumstances. They adopt a 'holistic view of the child . . . the hate and aggression as well as the love and the joy' (Taylor 1997). Therefore, addressing the issue of social exclusion is part of their everyday work. By virtue of their siting, adventure playgrounds are usually quite vulnerable facilities. As King (2001) says, 'to survive and thrive they need to come to terms with the most challenging kids – otherwise they'll wreck the place'. Thus, almost by definition they are generally well placed to respond to the most difficult children, and well suited to the task of addressing social exclusion for a number of reasons. They offer a long-term commitment to the children, and a focus for community development. They are usually located in areas of social deprivation, which makes early intervention possible. They offer children the chance to create their own private space, while at the same time being flexible enough to provide specialist activities aimed at alleviating the negative effects of stimulus bias in the wider environment (Hughes 1996a).

Children at risk are faced with a confusing array of professionals – each bringing their own agenda to their relationship with the child. King (2001) suggests that adventure playgrounds are ideally placed 'to hold things together in the face of professional intervention'. For disturbed and troubled children, playwork offers several effective avenues of support and developmental guidance. Because of its inherently flexible approach, adventure play helps to promote self-confidence, self-acceptance and an ability to cope with day-to-day problems (Brown 2000a). Furthermore, it provides an essentially therapeutic environment suitable for children who have been damaged by life's events (Else and Sturrock 1998). This is the focus of the approach offered by The Venture, an adventure playground in Wrexham which has recently been awarded funds from the central government initiative, the Children's Fund (King 2001).

Issue 5: finance and the quality of staffing

Modern funding systems favour less socially and politically challenging forms of provision. The problem is our fear of allowing children the freedom to choose what, where, when, how and with whom they play. There is a perception on the part of many decision making bodies that adventure playgrounds are almost anarchistic breeding grounds for rebellious spirits. There is a fear that adventure playground children will be more challenging and less malleable. Because these children do not fit the image of middle-class provision, and because those involved are often seen as anti-establishment figures, adventure playgrounds do not receive the same levels of funding as more formal types of provision. The funding criteria are often geared towards finished products, in terms of performance based outcomes, measurable returns and economic sustainability. Those are things that do not sit comfortably with the free, flexible philosophy of adventure play (Brown 2000a), where process is regarded as more important than product.

The lack of funding and the absence of a meaningful career structure inevitably has an impact on staffing levels and the length of employment that playworkers are prepared to give. Rates of pay are poor, when set alongside related fields of work with comparative levels of responsibility (e.g. teachers, social workers, youth workers). Playworkers also suffer problems regarding status and recognition. All too often the importance of their role is misunderstood, and yet they are in one of the most demanding occupations. Where children attend a facility entirely by their own choice, they come on their own terms. As a consequence, discipline structures are less clear, and the playworker's authority derives almost entirely from the strength of their personality and their ability to form relationships. Else (2001) suggests that the skilled playworker will 'have a repertoire of responses to the child that will include the ability to be controlling without being aggressive, and encourage free play without being weak or passive'. The final section of this chapter contains a summary of the characteristics that might be considered relevant when appointing staff to an adventure playground (see p. 127).

Issue 6: national organizations – a source of optimism

The National Playing Fields Association (NPFA) was the major organization promoting adventure playgrounds in the late 1950s and throughout the 1960s. The director of their Children and Youth Department, Drummond Abernethy, took the message about child development extremely seriously. Abernethy, who was almost evangelical in his approach to the work, was an educationalist who had been involved in drafting the 1944 Education Act. He regarded playwork as being concerned with the correction of 'developmental imbalance' (Abernethy 1968: 20), and suggested that play consisted of a compound of fantasy, imitation, adventure, physical development and coordination. Thus, 'play in all its aspects is as essential to a child as food' (Abernethy 1973: 6).

The NPFA continued their work, and it gathered momentum with the creation of the regional officer structure in the 1970s. Most regional officers had experience of adventure playground work prior to their appointment. The NPFA supported the development of a number of bodies that were representative of the field of playwork (e.g. the Adventure Playworkers Association and the Joint National Committee for Training in Playwork). It supported regional play councils, and the regional officers were actively involved in establishing a number of adventure playgrounds. Concurrent to this was the emergence of the London Adventure Playground Association (now PLAYLINK), the Handicapped Adventure Playground Association (now Kidsactive), and a number of play associations in cities across the country (e.g. Bristol, Liverpool, Manchester, etc.).

The NPFA withdrew from the work in 1984, with the expectation that the work of their regional officers would be continued by Playboard, but that organization attempted to address a much wider constituency, and eventually went into liquidation. Subsequently there has never been a national movement to promote adventure playgrounds. Even today the Children's Play Council does not specifically lobby on behalf of adventure playgrounds. The only national organization to do so is Play Wales, which has recently persuaded the Welsh Assembly of the need for greater recognition of the value of open access play provision. As a result, the Assembly has set aside £1m per year for five years. They have also successfully lobbied the New Opportunities Fund so that section 43 C(1) of the National Lotteries Act now states 'the Fund may also fund projects that support staffed play provision' (Play Wales 2001a). As a consequence of the absence of any national organization, and the strength of the movement in the principality, Play Wales has been given a mandate to set up a UK organization (Play Wales 2001b).

What makes an effective playworker?

The following thoughts derive from an unpublished paper produced for training purposes in 1989.

Skills

- *Organizational*: activity centred and based on identified and defined needs of the children and young people, many of them diverse – to do this effectively there is a strong need for understanding, sensibility, empathy, objectivity and a deep knowledge of children's behaviour patterns, including those which take place away from the playground.
- *Management and administration*: of the physical site, personnel, finances, communication systems, committees, materials and equipment.
- *Promotional*: to attract support and involvement in the work of the playground, and to promote the interests of the children in the immediate and wider community.
- *Motivational*: to motivate and provide stimulating opportunities for the children to learn from the experiences available to them.
- *Group work*: in order to work effectively with the children, management, community and all other relevant groups in the area.
- *Communication*: to make all the above fully effective, sound communication skills are essential.

Knowledge

Effective playworkers require knowledge of the following:

- *Children's overall developmental needs*: educationally, recreationally, emotionally and socially.
- *Children's patterns and types of behaviour.*
- *Political policies*: coupled with the ability to understand how these affect the lives of children.
- *Physical provision*: building techniques, site activities, site development and maintenance, health and safety matters.
- *The local community*: its characteristics and personalities.
- *Child protection procedures.*
- *The caring agencies*: i.e. social services, health, education and other provision for children.
- *Legal matters and how these affect children's lives.*
- *Funding sources and systems, and how these work.*

Personal attributes

- Warmth, tolerance, maturity, objectivity, a sense of direction, empathy, courage, self-awareness, flexibility, moral responsibility, patience, sensibility, motivation, realism, intelligence, commitment to hard work, understanding, reliability, responsiveness, a sense of justice, anti-racist and anti-sexist attitudes, vision.

Chapter 9

Establishing play in a local authority

Stuart Douglas

Local government has been the most significant provider and supporter of playwork provision in the last 30 years. This chapter attempts to identify its current role. It is very much a snapshot of the current position, as the prevailing theme throughout is one of change. It also attempts to identify what the future holds for playwork practitioners and policymakers who are affected by local government.

The context of local government

Over the years local authorities have been responsible for many developments in play provision, and are major funders of this area of social public policy. In order to analyse how this provision has developed, and will possibly develop in the future, it is important to understand how local authorities interact with central government policy and indeed how they themselves function.

The aim of local government is to ensure that there is appropriate provision of services to meet public needs. The level and type of provision is a reflection of local aspirations, mainly driven by local party political manifestos, and national desires of central government. The democratic principle, which makes local government so distinct from other public agencies, should mean that services are geared towards what local individuals and communities need. However, it also means that decision making is slow and the need to be accountable to the voters leads to a build-up of systems that make rapid change difficult.

For most authorities the majority of their funding comes from central government, which has generally operated a degree of wealth redistribution, no matter what its political orientation. The locally set council tax is usually a minority of a council's total income – the majority of the funding comes from resources provided by central government for a wide variety of 'statutory' services. Statutory provision is the terminology used for those services local authorities are required to provide by law, such as education, social services, etc. In addition to statutory provision local authorities have the power to provide 'discretionary' services, for which they raise the funds themselves. This is normally achieved through the council tax, but councils have had to become successful at tapping into other sources of funding. Examples of this include funding from the European Community (EC), National Lottery funding and a variety of special government initiatives. This fiscal power allows central government to determine the agenda for local authorities. In Scotland, devolution has meant it is now Holyrood, not Westminster that distributes resources to local areas, and it seems likely that a form of devolved power will be introduced throughout the UK in years to come.

In addition to this relationship, central government is also able to drive forward its manifesto through quasi-autonomous non-government organizations (Quangos) who can encourage local agencies either financially or with the provision of advice. Agencies such as the Arts and Sports Councils are obvious examples of this, although the National Lottery Distribution Agencies (sports, arts, heritage, charities, millennium, and new opportunities) have been recent additions to the long arm of central government as it seeks to achieve its political ideals.

The size of authorities and their range of services varies dramatically throughout the UK. Those serving the major conurbations such as Birmingham or Glasgow have different needs and strategies compared to those serving rural areas such as Cumbria or the Western Isles. This variation reflects the conflict in trying to seek the optimum way of delivering a local service cost effectively. The population and geographical size of an authority's domain need to be significantly large enough to ensure that a council has enough fiscal power to meet its objectives. At the same time it has to be small enough to ensure that people who receive the services perceive themselves as having some form of ownership over the processes. The development of two tiers of local authority was an attempt to resolve this anomaly. County or regional councils were established to deliver the large service areas of education, social services and transport, while the very local issues of housing, leisure, cleansing and planning were delivered at a more local level by district or town councils. This system has now been disbanded in favour of a unitary system in many parts of the country as the largest authorities were seen by some as unrepresentative. In the 1980s the regional councils began to be seen as a threat to central government when several large Labour controlled authorities used whatever power they could to exert influence over a Conservative controlled Westminster parliament. The reintroduction of unitary authorities in the mid-1990s was just part of the continual process of change that local government encounters. This unification is not universal, and there are many areas that still have two levels of administration.

The need for authorities to ensure a level of provision of public services that met the demands of their voters led to the inevitable consequence that playwork provision would be funded and overseen, in one form or another, by local authorities. This does not ignore the significant work carried out by agencies such as Barnardo's, and other voluntary organizations that operate independently of local authorities. It merely states the reality that the majority of funding for playwork comes from local government. These financial resources may be used to enable other agencies, mainly local voluntarily managed projects, to deliver a play service, or an authority may run services directly. Indeed, some authorities are involved in both approaches.

Thus, we have a situation where national political party manifestos point the direction for local authorities, and although they retain a degree of autonomy to reflect local needs and aspirations, this is only made possible by the significant degree of funding received from Westminster. Playwork is a 'discretionary' provision and is therefore particularly vulnerable to cuts and budget pressures. It is also the case that play has never been high enough on the political agenda for central government to make a contribution that is significant enough to allow the development of national guidelines and substantive research. Since the demise of the ill-fated Playboard in the 1980s, a wide range of agencies have been charged with the task, but as yet none have managed to deliver much of substance. This has left local government operating in something of a void in terms of guidance and national standards.

Play in a local government context

In these circumstances it is not surprising that playwork provision takes many shapes and forms: adventure playgrounds, play centres, play buses, peripatetic playwork and play in parks, to name but a few. This range of provision is well described by other authors. In addition to fully child-centred playwork, other strands of local government provision for young people offer opportunities for a child to play (albeit as a by-product). Indeed, there are still some authorities who see sports coaching, art workshops and other 'skill development' activities as being playwork. However, as these activities do not have at their core the objective of encouraging and enabling children to play, their role will not be considered in this chapter.

Despite their reputation of being slow, bureaucratic and cumbersome (which they are), local authorities have gone through a period of dramatic change, particularly in the last decade. This change has been the result of one government initiative after another. These initiatives have had a significant role in the rise and fall of play services. Some history may be useful to explain this. The 1960s and 1970s saw the creation of a number of new play centres and adventure playgrounds. The major conurbations were able to attract funding through the Urban Aid Programme (in its many guises), and via the Manpower

Services Commission. This was a central government plan to provide a short-term 'quick fix', aimed at both reducing unemployment and trying to build a social fabric in the decaying cities. In the 1980s and early 1990s there was a drive, at first initiated by Playboard, towards establishing 'play policies', which were seen as documents that would commit a local authority to ensuring that children's play needs were met within their areas of jurisdiction. The thinking underpinning these policies was in a similar vein to that at the root of many equal opportunities polices. Authorities, particularly Labour controlled ones, realized they were not fully addressing the interests of everyone within their community. A plethora of guides were produced on the subject, and readers should consult these for a more detailed analysis (e.g. Playboard 1985). However, most of the guidance may be summarized under a number of common points:

- planning processes should consider children's play needs;
- play areas should conform to British Standards;
- lead departments should be identified to be responsible for play provision;
- the role of the voluntary sector should be confirmed.

It is interesting to note that the children's involvement was not seen as important then, and it is only since the UK's ratification in 1991 of the United Nations (UN) Convention on the Rights of a Child that it has become common to see statements about children being consulted and involved. While many authorities adopted policies (some more thorough than others), few gave serious thought to strategic or measurable objectives. One positive outcome was in encouraging a situation where the benefits of play were discussed and debated at council level by elected members and senior managers within the organization. This allowed some provision to flourish, with the result that the power of play and the way it could cut across council services began to be recognized. However, many policies contained fine words, but failed to commit resources, and imposed no performance measures. The latter part of the twentieth century saw an ever-increasing demand on the financial resources of local authorities. As a result of all this, the period saw a decrease in open access playwork provision. The economic imperative to have as many people in the workforce as possible has led to a significant growth in out-of-school child care provision, often to the detriment of open access provision. This is another example of how central government policy is carried through at a local level.

Many play policies reflected the growth of research showing how complex the play process is, and as a consequence emphasized the impact of all public services on children's right to play. Public social policy is such that there are insufficient resources to meet all the demands placed on it, not just by play campaigners but also by educationalists, environmentalists and other lobby groups. Play provision is, generally speaking, starting from a low base and improvements can only be made in a coordinated and measured way. Local authorities are generally resistant to radical change. A vast and sudden increase in spending on a new area of provision could only happen if another area of provision were to suffer. It must be understood that any existing areas of provision equate to a degree of financial and human resources managed by, and seen as important by, an individual or group of individuals. In other words, by their very nature, all existing areas of provision will have supporters with the power to influence decisions. Those with such power do not relinquish it lightly. This is one of the reasons that authorities have been reluctant to change.

Development plans

The way out of this impasse was a 'strategy' or 'development' plan, which could be used to demonstrate the benefits of a particular service at the same time as showing how broad council objectives could be met in an unthreatening and resourceful way. The steps are straightforward:

- identify where you are with an audit of policy and provision;
- identify where you want to be and in what amount of time;
- break the process down into manageable sized pieces;
- set measures that are realizable and time limited;
- work out how much the process is going to cost;
- now that you realize you cannot afford it, go back to Stage 2 and repeat!

The benefits of a play development plan include:

- It focuses financial and human energies on the key issues to be addressed. This is a particularly important consideration for play provision because, by its very nature, it can be so divergent. Very often play providers try to impact on all areas of a child's play space and experience. With the current resource limitations this is simply impossible and the result can be a patchwork of under-resourced projects. Each authority is likely to have its own key objectives, and a distinct style of delivery. For a strategy to be successful it should identify what parts of play provision will be achievable, within the context of objectives and style, and focus on these. Another crucial part of this blend is to remember that politicians like to see their resources making a positive impact so it is important to ensure that the plan builds on previous successes.
- A strategy can be used as a tool for advocating the power of play. Outlining how important play is in terms of child and community growth is critical for the development of a service, but these issues must be translated into how they meet key council objectives.
- It should identify what strengths can be built on and what weaknesses can be eradicated or minimized.
- It should identify who does what, eradicating duplication and the waste of resources.
- It should identify who the key partners are or could be.
- A well constructed plan can have the potential to attract new partners and new funding.

- It should develop an agreed set of measurement techniques, and can therefore be a very useful management tool.

However, not everyone agreed with the introduction of strategies and some found them too constrictive, with an inability to be flexible and responsive. Others found them not challenging enough: 'The word "strategy" is now being employed in areas of public Social policy as a management ruse, not for delivering co-ordinated, relevant and improved public services to our communities, but as a disguise or a delaying tactic for not delivering services' (Chandler 2000: 16–17).

Best Value

With the election of New Labour in 1997 came a series of new measures for local government, one of which was the Local Government Bill of 1998, which placed on all councils the duty to secure continuous improvement in the economy, efficiency and effectiveness with which they exercised their functions. All authorities had to undertake a 'Best Value Review' (BVR) (DETR 2001) of all their services within a five-year cycle. This would be the principle means by which authorities would consider new approaches to service delivery and set performance targets. The principles of BVR were known as the 'four Cs': challenge, compare, compete and consult:

- The service has to *challenge* its thinking and practices. This means that fundamental questions such as 'Is the service necessary' need to be asked. While it is always easy to answer 'Yes' the outcomes of the provision need to be aligned with the council's key objectives. Research findings have to be used to show that play provision marries well to these key objectives. The many positive benefits of play make this an achievable task. The next question to be asked is: 'Is the service needed in its present form and to its present extent?' This is not so easy to answer, but there are different forms of delivery models available that can be adapted to suit local purposes. In addition it allows the service to analyse the users and locations of the service to see if they are the desired recipients. If nothing else this process provides an opportunity to make sure the service is focused on what it is trying to achieve.
- Services should *compare* themselves to other local authorities. This is less than straightforward as no two authorities are exactly the same. Is it appropriate to compare the services of a rural authority that has a small, sometimes affluent population, with a city that has a large, concentrated and often socially excluded population? Even comparing close parallels can be difficult. However, the end results can be used to point out that a particular authority is investing less than other providers in play, or conversely to argue that there is significant investment that politicians should be proud of and continue to support. Services should also be compared to non-public sector providers. This is difficult in the case of open access

playwork, as there is little to compare with. Child care practitioners, however, may be able to make comparisons with private providers.

• Services should ensure that they are *competitive*, in the sense that they bear comparison with the best, and that competition has been properly employed to bring about continuous improvements in service.
• Services should *consult* with local taxpayers, service users and the wider business community in the setting of targets. It can be a time consuming and demanding task to achieve consensus on what targets are realistic and achievable. If there is a range of different providers in the area, then having discussions on each other's role in reaching the targets can be a useful strategy for developing partnerships for the future. Ensuring that different agencies are clear on the roles and responsibilities of the local authority is also a useful outcome. Consultation with the local community, in order to give them a real voice in determining the quality and type of services that they use and pay for is another prerequisite. In addition to children and adults in the communities local to play projects, a grouping of people with a common interest in play provision can also be regarded as a community.

The processes involved in a BVR are certainly not new to people involved in playwork. A reflective playworker would always be challenging the way they are working with young people. They will be learning from other providers, and they will be consulting with young people as a matter of practice. Playworkers are also acutely aware of the competition provided by alternative provision, and that a play service is more valuable. So playworkers should not be daunted by the prospect of being involved in the BVR process.

One of the key areas is the establishment of performance measures and the use of benchmarking (a benchmark being the terminology for a point of reference or standard against which things are measured). There is still much debate about whether a play service is usefully served by quantitative measures, but until the production of *Best Play* (NPFA 2000) there was little to influence the qualitative debate. In order to kick-start that debate, *Best Play* identified seven key objectives that could be measured (NPFA 2000: 18):

1 The provision extends the choice and control that children have over their play, the freedom they enjoy and the satisfaction they gain from it.
2 The provision recognizes the child's need to test boundaries and responds positively to that need.
3 The provision manages the balance between the need to offer risk and the need to keep children safe from harm.
4 The provision maximizes the range of play opportunities.
5 The provision fosters independence and self-esteem.
6 The provision fosters children's respect for others and offers opportunities for social interaction.
7 The provision fosters the child's well-being, healthy growth and development, knowledge and understanding, creativity and capacity to learn.

These may appear to be useful and positive ways to identify the outcomes of any particular play experience. However, the responsibility to specify and inspect performance indicators lies with the Audit Commission (in England and Wales), and it seems unlikely they will grab these performance measures with open arms. Many of the real outcomes of good quality play experience show themselves in adulthood, which is no good in a political system that requires politicians to be judged by their results on a four- or five-year cycle! Nor does it suit a Best Value regime that requires services to review themselves every five years. Those seeking to develop qualitative data collection should refer to *Best Play* (NPFA 2000). However, there are some traditional counting methods still available:

- *Number of visits* is a simplistic account of the number of visits 'through the door'. A thousand visits could be the same child visiting a thousand times in a year, or it could be a thousand children coming to a one-day event.
- *Number of users* is the number of individual children who attend the service. A service could have a thousand users, but they may only come once a year, or it may have twenty users who come seven days a week, 52 weeks of the year.
- *Number of play hours* is the total number of hours the service is available to its users over the year.
- *Cost per play hour* is the total service cost divided by the number of play hours. A service that operates 20 hours every week of the year at a cost of £100,000 would have a cost/play hour of £96.15.
- *Cost per visit* is the total service cost divided by the number of visits. A service that costs £100,000 and had 100,000 visits in a year has a cost/visit of £1.
- *Spend on play per head of child population* is the total cost of the service divided by the child population the service is providing for.
- *Spend on play per total population* is the cost of play provision divided by the total population. This figure allows for benchmarking against other service providers and is often a useful tool in arguing for more resources, as it will nearly always be less.
- *Spend on play as a percentage of council spend* is a mechanism for comparing with other authorities. Two different authorities could both spend £1m on play but one could have a total spend of £2bn and the other £5m, so this is not a straightforward comparison.
- *Number of users impacted by social exclusion* is becoming a useful indicator. Targeting services at those who are most excluded is becoming a government mantra and a service should be able to show it is meeting this agenda.
- *Number and variety of activities* can be collected as an indication of the range of the service.

No single indicator is enough on its own, so a basket of measures needs to be developed, the scope and range of which will probably be identified within the council's own BVR guidelines. These quantitative measures must be seen in relation to the quality of the experience. However, in the real world these figures do matter, to benchmark your own service. The approach allows providers to demonstrate their effectiveness, seek continual improvement and add to the arguments for increased funding. If you can prove you are providing a good quality service, that is excellent. If in the first year you are providing a good quality service for 1000 youngsters, but in the second year the indicators show you are delivering the same good quality service but to only 100 young people for the same amount of money, that may not be so good, but it depends on what your targets are.

At the risk of having some play purists spluttering in their herbal tea it must be recognized that it is naive to say that quantitative indicators do not matter. Simply to stick our heads in the sand saying, 'It's the quality that counts' will not get the hoped-for response. Instead we must ask 'Is £X an appropriate subsidy for every child that comes to a play project?', because it is more than likely that someone else will ask that question, and we need to be ready with the answers. Of course the cost benefits can be identified in the form of reduced strain on health budgets, reduced social services costs on families under stress, reduced costs for policing and so on, but these need to be quantified. For example, if it costs in the region of £500 per day to keep a child with a disability in respite care, and your service can prove that it could do it with £300 per day, with the double benefit of a quality experience for the child, and providing respite for the parents, then the service is in a position of strength to increase its service profile. The financial factors, combined with the ability to demonstrate we can provide a good quality service, put play services in a powerful position.

Current trends

Whatever process has been undertaken, one of the common elements is the ability to speak the same language as government, both central and local. Talking about the benefits of play for a child's development to elected members and chief officers is often like speaking a foreign language. Play practitioners and policymakers need to be able to translate their own values and principles into the language of the day. At the moment that language is about social inclusion and social justice. It's about health, community safety, partnerships, joined-up working and stakeholder participation. This is not a difficult transition for play people to make. Most play projects are based in areas of social exclusion, or work with people who are socially excluded. The physical and mental health of our young people is of great concern to politicians (not particularly out of concern for young people, but because there are serious long-term implications for the future workforce and the cost to an already overstretched health service). Articulating that concern by talking about play in terms of stress reduction, cardiovascular improvement etc. is all possible.

In the past, one of the great difficulties for playwork has been that it was often seen as 'somebody else's responsibility'. The drive for the process of joined-up working, and cutting across sectors, puts playwork in a prime position as its benefits spread through many sectors. The ability to deliver playwork in a variety of environments and situations can also aid this process considerably. Like all language this will change – the political landscape that affects local authority provision is in a constant state of flux. The most recent New Labour drive is for partnership working, stakeholder involvement and authorities looking to enable provision rather than provide. The issue of providing or enabling is one of the great debates of playwork, and unfortunately a source of antagonism between the two styles (voluntary vs. local authority provision). Voluntary organizations will argue that locally managed projects are more responsive to local needs, encourage volunteering, are part of the process of community capacity building and provide added value by securing resources that councils cannot attract. The negative aspect of relying solely on this style of delivery is that the provision is often at the behest of the local adult community. If the community has suffered from unemployment for generations, has a collective low self-esteem, is too scared to go outside or is scarred by violence, then it may be difficult for individuals to be sufficiently motivated to get involved in community ownership. In these circumstances, play provision may never start, or may be difficult to sustain. It can take a very long time to resolve some of these issues, and a whole generation of children can easily miss out on the benefits of playwork provision. It has been recognized that many community work projects focus on adult needs, although this is often about reducing the conflict between adults and young people. In Children and Communities Hasler (1995: 181) makes the case that: 'There is a clear challenge to community work to look more closely for opportunities to work directly with children and young people and to listen to their "voice".'

From a pragmatic point of view it is sometimes the case that small, local, voluntarily managed projects employ managers who spend large amounts of their time seeking funding, rather than spending that time managing a child-centred, play-focused project. Proponents of local authority provision will argue that by directly managing provision they can ensure that the resources are focused on delivering a service for young people. In large authorities, where there is a range of provision, there can be an economy of scale that allows for a more cost-effective service; not only in terms of purchasing power, but by having a streamlined management structure, accessing training for staff development and ensuring that health and safety, financial and legal issues are taken care of in a way that does not divert the focus of those who deliver the service. The drawback is that local authorities, by their democratic nature, are slow to respond to initiatives, may get bogged down in procedures, and staff often feel they are not working for the people but for some large uncaring monolith.

In the past, the route chosen by individual local authorities depended on how the corporate organization saw its main strategies for dealing with its delivery. However, the current thinking is more of partnership. This correctly identifies that in many instances neither of the two methods above is perfect.

Unfortunately, there is a lot of history and in some cases antagonism between the two methodologies. For true partnerships to work these differences need to be set aside and the debates should focus on how to raise the profile, quantity and quality of playwork provision. The development of 'play trusts' is an emerging technique for pulling together some of these anomalies and contradictions. Trusts are established independently of local government as non-profit making organizations, or possibly charities. They have a board of directors made up of relevant stakeholders who will provide input into policy and development. They can then deliver services that the authority is prepared to pay for. With the cross-cutting nature of playwork it could be possible to have projects, such as training for local development agencies, funded by different departments of a local authority as well as other agencies. A play trust can also attract resources from grant-giving trusts and charities that are unable to fund local government provision. If there is a sufficient level of provision then this will allow for the economies of scale that a conglomeration of projects can bring. Rather than play-specific trusts it may well be that play provision will be part of a wider brief by a community or housing association, or a leisure trust.

In the future, then, a range of agencies will meet provision: local voluntary organizations, housing associations, community associations, play trusts, etc. The current government's desire is to modernize local government, with the role of the authority changing to one of standard setting, monitoring and evaluating. It will also have a role in the identification of gaps in provision and in seeking ways to ensure these gaps are filled, working in partnership with a variety of agencies. In order that services meet the demands of their local community, and have a significant impact on young people, these agencies will need to have appropriate policies and strategies in place that will not be dissimilar to those discussed above.

Crystal-ball gazing

A feature of this chapter has been the constant change that faces local authorities. This has had a significant impact on the personnel profiles of these organizations. Reducing and streamlining services has resulted in a rapid decline in the number of people employed by councils. Indeed, when seen collectively over the UK, the number of local government employees who have lost their jobs in the last five years would be seen as a national disaster if it happened to any industrial sector. This has to be measured against the need to develop new areas of work as government agendas change. Authorities are then in the position where they have to recruit and train new staff, which is a costly exercise. The developing solution is one of 'multi-skilling', where staff are trained to be able to carry out a range of functions in order that the peaks and troughs of a service can be managed more effectively and change taken on board more efficiently. Paradoxically, this is happening just as playwork has become much more professional in its approach. This is particularly due to the development of S/NVQs and higher and further education courses, along with agencies such as the National Training Organization for Sport and Recreation and Allied Occupations (SPRITO) who are taking the subject seriously. However, it can be argued that multi-skilling is an advantage for playworkers. There is the scope for playworkers to transfer their skills to work with younger or older children, with community work projects, with health projects, social work agencies and schools. This could have benefits for playwork, in that the profession may become much more fundamental to the range of agencies it can support, causing agencies that have traditionally been hostile to playwork to improve their understanding of the standard and values of the profession. A Third Column of playworkers infiltrating all the other public sector agencies is an interesting way of raising the play debate. The concept of multi-skilling is also a potential solution to the seasonal fluctuations that have agencies running around trying to find people to cope with huge demand during the summer season. All these aspects could result in an increase in salaries and job opportunities. On the other hand, multi-skilling could also result in the demise of playwork (again!) if there is not a consistent and credible argument put forward for the development of provision.

Devolution is starting to make an impact at a local level in Scotland. The Scottish Parliament is using its new found political strength to target areas that are of particular concern in Scotland. Social justice is a key area for the new Parliament and this means prioritizing resources in favour of those who are excluded from the mainstream of provision – and young people are high on the priority list. There is the potential for this political process to be taken forward with large English regions being created that develop policies appropriate to their needs. How such policies will impact on play provision remains to be seen. One thing is for sure: if playwork is not being measured, its results not being monitored and its benefits not being argued, then it will not grow. As central government forces authorities to look for more for less, how will this impact on play? Certainly there are many good models developed in playwork of how communities can take a leading role in developing provision, but how can a service that fundamentally needs financial support from government (local or national) deliver more for less? Creative ways of working in partnerships with training agencies, early years, youth and community organizations etc., need to be developed. There needs to be concrete evidence that an increased spend on play will make an impact on the spending of the health services, the police and social welfare institutions. Playwork must be able to show that it can meet key national and local objectives, whether they are health, lifelong learning, community safety, social regeneration or whatever. What is needed are hard measurable facts, not wishy-washy sentiment.

While much of what has been written in this chapter refers to recent change there are some trends that will affect playwork provision in the longer term that need to be given some thought. The current way the school year operates is coming under increasing attack, which is no surprise considering it was originally based on the farming calendar. The introduction of shorter, more frequent holidays would force a rethink on the part of providers who lay such heavy emphasis on school holiday provision. A report by the Children's Play Council (CPC) found that 53 per cent of respondents' programmes were offered during school holidays (CPC 2001). Unfortunately, this is due to a perceived need to meet the demand created by 'bored children with nothing to do'. Playwork practitioners argue that playwork provides life-enhancing play experiences when children are not at school, but as mentioned previously, this argument has not received the understanding or support that it might. Teachers are currently contracted to work face to face with children for 195 days of the year, and such is the power of the teaching unions it is highly unlikely that this will increase. An even spread of holidays throughout the year could unleash new opportunities for much more frequent, year-long provision for the 170 non-school days in a year. This would alleviate the six or seven week madness that occurs every year as play providers struggle to deliver a service when everyone else is sitting on a beach sipping their pina coladas. Conversely, if the 'boredom' argument wins, then summer provision may disappear altogether.

Employment patterns are changing. Gone are the days of 9 a.m. to 5 p.m. working. Service sectors need to operate 24-hour services, seven days a week. Developments in information technology (IT), the cost of office accommodation and the gridlocking of our towns and cities has resulted in a dramatic increase in home working. How will this affect play provision? Will there be a requirement for more, because parents need space and time to work at home, and having a safe, exciting play facility nearby will meet their flexible needs? Or will provision be less, as home-working parents change their working patterns to spend more time with their children and seek to access private provision?

The consequences of global warming may seem far away, but how will a play service cope with a climate that is increasingly hostile, and when pressure on land becomes greater as the sea levels rise and the population of low-lying towns and cities moves to higher ground? What will be the use of outdoor play provision if it rains more often than not, or being outdoors leads to exposure to harmful rays of the sun? These factors may result in a demand for exciting and creative use of indoor space to enable young people to play. Maybe the answer will be giant indoor play spaces where it never rains and the grass is always green! But then there is the disturbing thought of having to artificially manufacture igloo building, mud pie building and kite flying!

The need for research

This book is another example of the growth in authoritative material that has aided the playwork movement to take its arguments forward. The need for hard evidence has already been raised within the chapter. However, a lot of the current research has focused on general play needs, rather than the specific benefits of playwork delivered in a local community context. There is the correct assumption that adult intervention in the play process is wrong, but this is often misconstrued as 'adult *involvement* is wrong'. This misconception needs to be challenged for playwork to progress in acceptance, and to do this some hard evidence must be produced. The development of qualitative outcomes puts playwork practitioners in a prime position to provide the data for such evidence. If, as a result of *Best Play* (NPFA 2000) and the Best Value process (DETR 2001), play projects throughout the UK begin to measure outcomes in a standardized way, then there is the potential for a significant base of information. If this data were to be collated nationally, then there would surely be the potential to show that community-based playwork provision does make a significant difference to children, young people and the communities within which they live.

Chapter 10

It's not what you know, but who you know!

Jackie Martin

Networking: some initial thoughts

The examination of networking in the context of playwork can lead us down a labyrinth of fascinating pathways. While our starting point may be 'How can I utilize the networks to maximize the opportunities available to the children in my play project?' the process of analysing networks takes us into a complex web of both personal and professional territory. In order to comprehend fully the various aspects of networking we need to go back to basics and look at the core purpose, philosophy and underpinning value base of our play project. In parallel with this organizational analysis, we also need to examine personal issues such as who we are (our personal identity) and how we function (our strengths, weaknesses and ways of operating).

This chapter addresses the purposes of networking in playwork, the key characteristics of networks and strategies which can be adopted to enable us to network more effectively. Three case studies are examined: a local play project, a city-wide project and a national project. Drawing on soft systems methodology (Checkland and Scholes 1990), a model is explored which can be applied to any play project, regardless of whether that project is face-to-face or developmental, local or national. The model is applied to the local project in order to explore the different dimensions of the networking conundrum. The assumption underpinning the chapter is that the role of the playworker goes beyond that of a facilitator of children's play opportunities and includes a multiplicity of other associated roles which link senior playworkers in particular with a range of other agencies and people in their local community. This may be a debatable starting point, but if we take the notion of the play project as a compensatory play space, designed to ameliorate the effects of a paucity of such spaces in the community, then we must view play projects as being an integral part of that local community. This implies that playworkers need to engage with a range of people and agencies who may be active in their community. Play projects that do not have full-time senior playworkers are inevitably hampered in taking on this broader remit by the lack of human resources. For example, many out-of-school child care projects operate on a self-financing model with only part-time workers, and therefore have a limited ability to network with local agencies.

So what is a network? According to *The Concise Oxford Dictionary* (Pearsall 1999) a network is 'a group of people who exchange information, contacts and experience for professional or social purposes'. Networks can be aligned to spheres of influence. They are the people we come into regular contact with. They can include children, their parents and carers, local funding organizations, the business community, local schools, suppliers, health visitors, arts projects, trainers, local councillors, MPs or the Early Years Development and Child Care Partnership. Networks are often based on informal membership. A collection of individuals, sometimes representing organizations or local authority departments, sometimes just representing themselves and their agencies, can make up a network. Playwork networks can contain a very diverse range of people from different professional backgrounds, with different lifestyles and ways of working, but usually with an interest in children and their play needs.

Playworkers may need to network for a variety of reasons. Information exchange is often the primary purpose, but networks can also be utilized to influence, to lobby and campaign or simply to inform. Playworkers can gain knowledge, learn new skills and meet people who may challenge their ideas and beliefs. Playworkers are often extremely good at utilizing networks to seek resources. This can range from collecting 'jumble' to sourcing major grants; from obtaining signed footballs for raffle prizes to finding junk materials for creating carnival floats. Some volunteer parents have amazing talents when it comes to utilizing networks in this way, though they might not recognize it as a valuable skill. Networks are also often used as a form of support. In a field which is still not widely understood, comments such as 'You earn money just for playing with kids?' can be very irritating and demoralizing. Networking with other playworkers with similar frustrations can be an important source of support.

Without a formal constitution, committee structure or set of elected officers or workers with roles and positions, one might assume that network members operate on an equal basis. However, the power dynamics within networks can be quite complex. A number of factors can influence how much power each member has. Position and role will inevitably have an influence. Directors of national play organizations carry a certain status by virtue of their position, and therefore inevitably have a degree of power and influence. This is enhanced even further if they also control resources such as grant aid. Knowledge and information also enhances personal power and status. If the knowledge is legitimated through training or qualifications, it can add more weight, and consequently carry more power. Personal charisma can also be a powerful dynamic, even if people do not have a formal role. Assessing your own power base and analysing the power base of others can be a useful exercise if your aim is to maximize the networking potential of different situations (Williams 1988).

Through networking it is often possible to find out what individual positions are on a particular issue. If individuals are not at a formal meeting they don't have to espouse the party line, follow formal protocol, or be accountable through a set of minutes for what they say. If they are in a position to exert influence, you can use the opportunity to validate personal views; inform them about projects, policies or initiatives; act as a sounding board to help articulate a particular perspective; or contribute to the gathering of evidence to strengthen a particular view. In this way you can be quite influential by 'changing hearts and minds'.

If your starting point is a shared value base, the process is often easier. People with similar beliefs tend to network more comfortably. Shared language, ideas and priorities form a common bond. Playworkers meeting together often have a starting point which does not need explaining. If you don't have to go back to basics to explain why you receive a salary to play with children, the potential for moving a discussion forward to a mutually beneficial exchange is much stronger. Networking with people from different professional backgrounds can be problematic if there is a conflicting value base. The youth work value base of informal education linked to curriculum objectives can be at odds with a child-centred approach which values freely chosen, personally directed behaviour. Similarly the teaching value base underpinned by the formal curriculum and expectations regarding behaviour can result in conflict and misunderstanding.

Analysing networks

When we analyse our networks, the key question to be addressed is, 'Why do we want to expend energy networking?' Following on from this, we can analyse whether the networks we expend most energy on maintaining are worth the effort. People in networks may wish to pursue their own personal goals, linked to their own training and development, or their personal experiences and preferences. Alternatively they may pursue organizational objectives, finding out about issues, projects, useful people and ways of working. Individuals within an organization may have different views about the most useful or productive networks. Clearly, whatever the objective of networking activities, communication is a key process. Some playworkers have excellent skills, and are able to communicate with a wide range of people from children to trustees of charitable trusts. Others may lack confidence and be reluctant to network actively with people they do not normally come into contact with. This is where agencies which actively support and facilitate networking can play an important role. Training courses are a good example of opportunities for facilitated networking.

Some play projects are good at reviewing and evaluating their practice and achievements. Some projects employ consultants and have away-days or residentials. Others employ researchers to conduct long-term studies, either providing an outside viewpoint or facilitating a more collaborative approach. Training techniques such as creating 'thought showers' and 'SWOT analysis' (strengths, weaknesses, opportunities and threats) are commonly employed. However, less widespread is the use of the 'rich pictures' technique, an approach adapted from soft systems methodology. According to Checkland and Scholes (1990: A16) the rationale for using 'rich pictures' lies in the 'complexity of multiple interacting relationships which characterise the intricacies of human affairs. Pictures are seen as a better medium for expressing relationships than linear prose for encouraging holistic rather than reductionist thinking.' Some people think in terms of pictures more easily than others. They can convert quite complex ideas and concepts into a pictorial form. Out of the pictures meanings can emerge. Key stakeholders may be identified and main issues be revealed. Each picture represents only the perspective of the artist. It is therefore possible to have very different pictures representing the same organization or situation. In both drawing and analysing the rich picture a series of questions can be posed:

- Who are the key 'moving spirits'?
- Where does the power lie?
- Who is part of the network and who might feel excluded?
- Where is the majority of the networking energy expended?
- Is engagement in networks a conscious attempt at purposeful action, in pursuit of well-defined objectives, or a more arbitrary process involving unpredictable actions and outcomes?
- To what extent are networking relationships influenced by personal interest, confidence, a preference for communicating with like-minded people or a fear of operating outside personal comfort zones?

Another of Checkland and Scholes's (1990) ideas is to explore the *'Weltanschauung'* or world view. By looking beyond the immediate networks and systems we can explore adjacent and overlapping systems which currently or potentially have an impact on the network under analysis. These could include:

- prevailing societal attitudes to children;
- political influences and considerations;
- changing legislation;
- current social policy initiatives;
- new technological advances;
- attitudes to and awareness of environmental issues.

Applying this way of thinking is not necessarily about looking at a problem in a network and trying to find a solution, but of looking at ideas around a situation which some people may view as problematic. Alongside this it may be necessary to explore the customs and history of an organization. This may throw some light on why those involved view certain relationships as particularly significant, and how actions and relationships can be noticed and judged. In the process of drawing what appears to be a very simple picture, a range of issues can be explored, although the picture may not make sense to the outside eye.

Through the use of case studies, some of the questions raised will now be explored in more detail.

Case study 1: a local play project

The first case study involves an in-depth analysis of a local play project. Interviews were held with the senior playworker who is male, white, was born locally and was heavily involved in setting up the project. The aim was to explore the networks which he views as significant in the development of the project, and to support him in constructing a rich picture which could then be used as a tool to explore the issues surrounding the networking relationships. A tidied-up and simplified version of the resulting rich picture is shown in Figure 10.1.

Waring (1989) suggested using ready-made fragments as a way of formalizing the pictures. This can act as a useful starting point. I introduced some ideas for symbols which could represent issues such as conflict, cooperation and resources, but the playworker was given freedom to come up with his own pictorial representations of his perspective. Through this process, the image of a Battenberg cake emerged as a way of looking at the various networks. This links to Battram's (1998) idea of using metaphors as tools of analysis to help throw light on some of the processes involved. The history, purpose and value base of the organization was considered when mapping and analysing the project's networking relationships. Background information was collated from both interviews and written documentation. A point in time was chosen when the project was at its most successful. Subsequently the project has undergone some major changes. When projects undergo significant changes, they can become quite embroiled in internal issues and lose contact with their wider networks.

The evaluation of the exercise was very positive. The interviewee valued the opportunity to engage in conscious reflection and found the techniques useful. One of the outcomes of the process was a reminder of the networks that would need to be rebuilt to take account of the new context and of the new opportunities which had arisen and which could be capitalized upon.

In order to set the context for the analysis, the following narrative describes the background to the project. The project is located on a deprived estate in a fairly typical inner-city local authority borough where poverty is endemic. Around 75 per cent of children on the estate are entitled to free school meals and nearly all the children are entitled to a clothing grant.

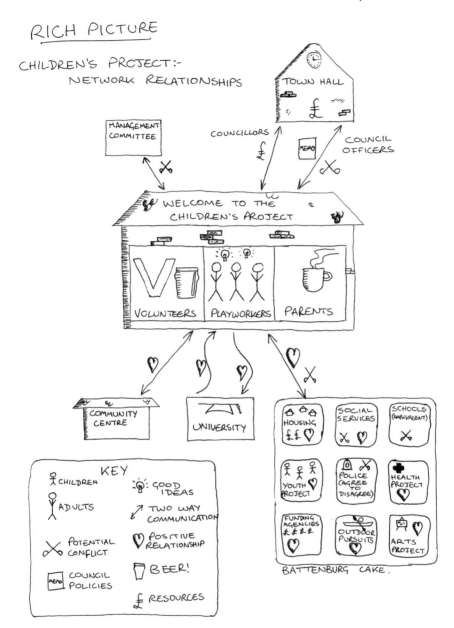

RICH PICTURE

CHILDREN'S PROJECT:-
    NETWORK RELATIONSHIPS

Figure 10.1

Long-term unemployment is the highest in the region at around 15 per cent, and in 1990 it had the highest crime rate in England. In the summer of 1991 riots broke out on the estate. In the preceding period 19 houses were set on fire in ten days, 57 arrests were made and there was ram-raiding almost every night. The estate has a strong network of local activists, mainly women involved in a range of projects from the Credit Union to the Community Rights Centre. Opposition to the poll tax was strong during the 1980s and local groups were vociferous in their demands for local services. A typical example was the campaign for a play area, which reputedly started with a mother of ten children haranguing council officials because the local kids were playing on the rubbish dump. In 1986 the campaign bore fruit and a new £140,000 playground was opened, complete with a hut and a playworker. During the following years the playworker organized local playschemes, street games sessions and arts workshops in the local Book Centre. In the lead-up to the riots, local facilities were being cut and the youth project lost most of its workers. After the riots the council suddenly became keen to invest in the community, presumably to ensure there was no repeat of the events of the summer of 1991. One of the outcomes was a new play project with a team of staff including four full-time playworkers housed in the new Community Resource Centre.

The 'children's project', as it became known, went from strength to strength, developing its own unique philosophy and practice. The foundation of the project is its 'open access' work. Children from the local community can attend the Centre for a minimal fee and stay on a voluntary basis. They can leave when they get bored, or need to go elsewhere. Staffing ratios are high enough to ensure that adequate standards of care and supervision are maintained, and a wide range of play activities are available for the children. Playschemes are well attended and provide scope for more ambitious play activities. Building on the foundation of solid relationships between the playworkers and the children, a number of additional projects have been developed. A camping group was established to take small groups of children away to experience different environments, try out more adventurous activities and take responsibility for planning their own food and programme. This more intense work has had a significant impact on the children's development. They have noticeably grown in confidence and self-esteem and have improved their social skills, levels of cooperation and communication skills. Parallel to this, a children's participation group was established for children who wanted to have a greater say in the running of the project. Group meetings and activities give children the opportunity to make their own decisions, influence other decisions, explore issues concerning children's rights and generally 'have their say'. A third parallel project to the open access work has been the 'one-to-one work' with children who have been excluded from school. Staffing levels of the project enabled very effective work to be carried out with some extremely challenging children. In overseeing all this work, the senior playworkers are involved in liaison with a range of agencies at different levels.

The children's project works closely with the housing department, which usually provides financial assistance because they see a direct correlation between the effectiveness of the summer playschemes and the levels of vandalism and car crime on the estate. While a justification of playwork based on crime reduction may present some ethical dilemmas, many projects find the offer of extra resources worth the compromise. However, it could be argued that this encourages the continued misunderstanding of the true value of playwork.

The social services department is seen as a key agency to network with. Under the Children Act (1989) the social services department has a responsibility to meet the needs of those children defined as 'in need'. Resources like the children's project can provide important respite for families under pressure. The project can also provide a positive outlet for children with emotional problems, and assist in the healing process for children who have been abused or neglected. The 'one-to-one' work is viewed as particularly beneficial by the playworkers. However, the playwork ethos is not always fully understood by social workers and can be viewed with suspicion. Playwork does not have the same well-established theoretical base, widely accepted practice models or qualification structure as social work. Issues such as expectations regarding children's behaviour, curriculum objectives, approaches to discipline or safety can all be causes of conflict.

The local health project plays an important part in the local community and has linked with the children's project by providing health and hygiene related activities. Following the publication of *Our Healthier Nation* (Department of Health 1998), recent government initiatives have broadened the role of the health visitor to include work with children over 5 years of age, and an expansion in health promotion work. This is an interesting example of the social policy agenda impacting on play networks.

The local school is an obvious point of contact, given the large amount of time children spend in schools. Schools exert a considerable influence on children's behaviour, expectations and interests, and on their self-esteem, identity and confidence. Teachers can be important sources of information about children, any problems they are experiencing, and achievements worthy of celebration. However, issues such as confidentiality and the difference in professional status between teachers and playworkers can act as major barriers to the establishment of effective networks and communication. Some play projects have been successful in developing collaborative work with schools concerning areas such as bullying, tackling antisocial behaviour, environmental projects and homework clubs. More often, contact with the local school is limited to publicizing the playschemes.

In contrast, a very harmonious relationship exists between the children's project and a nearby community centre. This is attributed by the interviewee to the existence of a shared value base. Both projects attempt to be non-judgemental in their approach to working with the local community, and both aim to target those most in need. Their approach is one of empowering, and seeking direction from 'the client'. The minimal interventionist approach advocated by Hughes (1996a) is paralleled by the community worker's approach of 'loitering with intent'. This phrase was coined by the interviewee when explaining the relationship with the community centre and can be applied to playwork: loitering with intent to pick up and respond appropriately to play cues (Else and Sturrock 1998). Connotations linked to sinister or criminal activities are not implied by this phrase.

The project also works alongside the police, but this can involve a deliberately distant relationship. This was exemplified by agreements with the police, just before the riots, not to go into the building where play activities take place. This policy was stretched to the limit when children were discovered bringing large amounts of stolen goods into the project, and boundaries needed to be renegotiated. Networking with police officers tends to be more distant and formal, on a 'need to know basis'.

Alongside work on the estate, the children's project recognizes the importance of introducing children to the wider world and to environments beyond their normal experience. By using personal networks, they have gradually built up a year-round programme of camping trips and adventure activities, supported by a local outdoor pursuits agency. These activities are heavily influenced by the interviewee's personal interest in outdoor pursuits. This highlights an example of how personal interests and motivations can have a strong influence on the direction a project takes. Identifying an organization with a similar value base was seen as crucial. Some outdoor pursuits agencies are very 'macho', with an emphasis on the development of hard skills and a competitive ethos. The children's project works closely with an agency which has a philosophy based on experiential learning.

Inevitably, resources are tight, and fund-raising is a significant feature of the senior playworkers role. Networking with local charitable trusts is another dimension of the project's activities. Fund-raising can be an arduous and time-consuming business. Written communication skills are needed, alongside the ability to present a concise case backed up by evidence. Funding agencies want to fund people who will turn ideas into reality. The children's project has been very successful in raising funds from a wide variety of sources. Following the initial written communication, networking skills have been employed, initially through telephone contact, but where face-to-face communication can be orchestrated this has been found to be more effective. Projects that can articulate clearly their mission, aims, objectives, targets and evaluation framework are more likely to be successful in the competition for funding. These relationships are represented by the squares in the Battenberg cake (see Figure 10.1).

In a slightly different category, a significant agency with which the project networks is the local university, which hosts one of the National Centres for Playwork Education, and runs a degree in playwork. Having piloted and rejected the NVQ approach to qualifications, the children's project identified the benefits of a more academic route. Over several years, they have built up a solid two-way relationship with playwork staff at the university. The children's project hosts students on placement, viewing such opportunities as an ideal way of providing an injection of ideas and enthusiasm, modelling reflective practice and reviewing professional standards. Overseas students are particularly valued as they can introduce different cultures, customs and role models. Staff in the project have taken advantage of education and training opportunities through short courses, conferences and modules offered by the university. The interviewee has also contributed to lectures about both practice issues and the work of the children's project. The experience of reflecting on and presenting the ethos of the project has provided an opportunity to sharpen thinking and apply new concepts and ideas to the way the project works. An example of what could be termed a 'windfall outcome' of networking resulted from a university conference where the children's project playworkers attended a workshop run by children from a children's rights organization. This led to a consultation exercise which resulted in the establishment of a local children's participation group. Subsequently, children from that project ran a workshop on participation at a local conference. This is a good example of how unpredictable the effects of networking can be. The workers attending the original conference did not go with the aim of learning how to set up a participation project, but were sufficiently inspired to set up an initiative which was later to have a major impact on the running of the children's project. This has led to a fundamental questioning by the playworkers of the outcomes of playwork, the value of large-scale open access work and the benefits of small-scale, highly interventionist group work (a debate which is outside the remit of this chapter). The relationships with the university and the benefits arising from those relationships are less straightforward than links with other projects because they involve ideas, thoughts and issues relating to status and professionalization. The link is therefore represented in the rich picture (Figure 10.1) by a wavy line.

Central to the rich picture are the links with parents and other adults involved in the project. A significant aid to networking has been the availability of tea and coffee. The project has developed a reputation of being a friendly place for parents and carers to have a 'cuppa and a chat'. The current community centre has a community café which assists with networking enormously, but even in the days when there was no café, parents could always find a quiet spot to sit and have a coffee. They might then be coaxed into a greater involvement in the children's project by becoming volunteers. Relationships are consolidated through social events outside the work arena, often involving 'having a pint' after work. These relationships are represented on the rich picture by the symbol of a cup of tea and a pint of beer, and raise a whole range of issues related to work boundaries. Involving parents leads to interesting debates around potentially problematic role models, parents smoking and swearing and issues of being overprotective. Some playworkers argue the play project is a place to escape from the parent's watchful eye, others argue it is part of the local community and should involve all its members, young and old. Interesting challenges face playworkers wanting to develop intergenerational work, building networks through grandparents, enabling the exploration of local history, traditional games, community identity, etc.

The senior workers in the children's project are managed by the local authority's Community Services Department, and work on a secondment basis. The project itself is run by the management committee of the community centre. A constant threat hanging over the project was the termination of the secondment arrangement and the removal of the two senior playworkers. This has now happened, and the project has been left with a smaller staffing base and less direct support from the local authority. The issue of seconded workers and grant funding from local authorities presents a complex set of relationships which impact on the networks. Within the rich picture the interviewee identified two networking channels: one with local authority officers, symbolized by a string of memos (representing policies, procedures and instruction), and one with elected members, symbolized by the flow of resources. While this is inevitably an oversimplistic representation of a complex web of interrelationships, issues of power and control can be identified and explored. To add to the complexities, the picture also shows the community centre management committee, which raises another set of issues and tensions in need of examination. The relationships are further complicated because some parents are also management committee members.

Case study 2: a city-wide project

The second case study examines a city-wide play association, which has as one of its primary aims the support of networking among paid and volunteer playworkers. It considers the extent to which effective networking contributed to the success of a major campaign against cuts in play services. The play association was established in 1975, and despite achieving a great deal in the way of benefits for children's play in its 15-year existence, it lost its funding in 1990 and ceased to operate. Taking the play campaign of 1989 as a critical point for the exploration of networks, a number of key relationships and stakeholders can be identified. One of the main stakeholders was the local authority which provided the organization's core grant aid. The play association had developed an extensive network of contacts with both councillors and council officers. These relationships involved both opportunities and tensions. In the period leading up to the play campaign, relationships with the local authority play section were complex. There was some duplication of roles and a general hostility to the voluntary sector. The service had just expanded the number of neighbourhood playworkers, and set up play forums in each of the political wards in the city. Playschemes were organized on a ward basis and the play forums were intended to be the springboard for the development of year-round play. To complement these developments the play association established a programme of 'big play meetings'. Three times a year play activists from all the play forums and local groups would come together to share information and developments, and to discuss issues of concern. Major debates at the time included the development of a new play strategy for the authority, and the introduction of the Children Act (1989), with its implications for registration and inspection. Each year a big play meeting was held after the summer holidays to evaluate the playschemes and make recommendations to council officers and councillors. Through its strong networks with other voluntary organizations, the play association secured a seat on the council's arts and recreation committee, and so could feed issues directly to councillors. Although the place on the committee was inevitably non-voting, it provided a useful platform for promoting playwork and challenging the dominant recreational philosophy.

In 1989, major cuts to the play service were proposed as a result of government policies connected with rate capping. The play association was able to mobilize the networks it had developed over a long period of time and launch an effective anti-cuts campaign. The association had around 300 members, including sympathetic voluntary organizations, parents' groups, playscheme committees, established year-round play projects, specialist arts projects, community centres and youth projects. Members had benefited from the play association in many ways, through its library, information and advice service, training workshops and regular newsletters. Some members played a role on the management committee and various subcommittees. The networks had resulted in friendships, close working relationships and a sense of loyalty and commitment. Members saw the play association as a way of meeting people from other areas of the city engaged in similar activities and with compatible values. Thus, when the need arose to mobilize forces and launch a campaign, the necessary relationships already existed. Members volunteered to lobby their ward councillors through the monthly surgery and to attend community forum meetings. By using the mechanism of a 'remit', recommendations could be sent to the main arts and recreation committee, emphasizing the importance of the local play projects and highlighting the contribution of play to children's development. Play association members who also belonged to the ruling Labour Party attended branch meetings and put forward 'resolutions' opposing cuts in play services, which were then forwarded to constituency meetings. With the support of one local activist, a paragraph was inserted into the constituency Labour Party manifesto. Alongside this lobbying strategy, the play association also organized direct action. A Sunday Labour group meeting, where the decision regarding budget cuts was to be finalized, was lobbied and a march through the town was organized with placards and petitions. Coachloads of parents and children arrived at the civic centre and stood outside the doors of the meeting in an attempt to get the 'no cuts' message across. The campaign was very successful and although some cuts were made, the playschemes were saved.

This case study illustrates how an established network can be utilized both to promote play and prevent cuts in play services. The example is characteristic of a network with a strong central focus, in the form of a development officer, with the ability to organize and mobilize resources. Regular written communication was an important tool in keeping everyone informed of progress and enabling the network to maintain its direction. The relationships which developed through the big play meetings, training events and informal contact not only benefited the campaign but had numerous other spin-offs, including: skill sharing, joint trips and sharing information about job opportunities. The play association was well respected by the voluntary sector, and with only one full-time development officer and a part-time administrator achieved a considerable amount. In comparison the fledgling neighbourhood play forum system with high staff turnover and vague objectives struggled to establish universal support. Some play forums were very effective and linked with the play association through training and campaigns; others struggled and met infrequently. Arguably, the play association posed a threat to the local authority by highlighting some of the problems within the authority's play strategy rather than highlighting the positives. The play association was also difficult for council officers to control, and following a diversionary strategy to force a merger between the play association and the local resource centre, a proposal to remove core funding from the play association was passed by the council. While the play association was able to mobilize its networks to campaign against the cuts in play it was unsuccessful in organizing a campaign to save its own funding.

Case study 3: a national project

The Joint National Committee on Training for Playwork (JNCTP) was established in 1975 to develop a national system of peer-endorsed playwork qualifications. As an essentially unfunded organization reliant on the goodwill of members to organize events, the JNCTP has done remarkably well to survive for so long, let alone to maintain the profile and respect it currently commands. In the early days a representative system was established, with members from regional groups and from different constituent parts of the playwork field (in effect a 'joint committee' as the name implies). The regional groups were supported by the National Playing Fields Association (NPFA) regional officers. Once the NPFA ceased to employ regional officers it became difficult to maintain the representative structure, and so the constitution was changed. The JNCTP is now made up of people with a general interest in playwork training. The executive committee consists of members with a firm commitment to its aims, who are willing to contribute to the activities of the organization.

An interview was conducted with one of the long-standing members of the executive committee to try to clarify some of the characteristics and benefits of involvement in relation to the networking role. The JNCTP represents a fairly extensive, albeit loose network of people involved in playwork. They aim to organize three conferences followed by a general meeting each year, all of which provide important forums for networking through both structured and unstructured means. The conferences are held in venues around the country, usually with a keynote speaker followed by a choice of workshops. Costs are kept deliberately low to keep them as accessible as possible. The workshops provide a structured opportunity for networking, information exchange and influencing new developments in training. Conferences can be a source of inspiration, a forum for support and an opportunity to meet people who it would be difficult to meet in any other situation. They also offer an opportunity to have a moan about the state of playwork, underfunding and various controversial initiatives taken by national organizations and awarding bodies. Freelance trainers can tout for business, organizations selling publications can market their wares and opportunities arise to talk face-to-face with key policymakers in an attempt to influence developments. Conferences can be useful for both creating new networks and maintaining old ones.

It is interesting to reflect on how effectively conference delegates utilize the JNCTP networks and take advantage of the opportunities which may arise. If you attend a conference, do you have a mental checklist of things to find out, ideas to explore, policies you want to influence or carefully formulated views you want to express? Do you summon up the courage to talk directly to the head of the new Office for Standards in Education (Ofsted) unit or the civil servant from the Department for Culture, Media and Sport? Do you look through the delegates list and seek out people from similar projects in different areas of the country, or with similar job titles in the hope of gaining new insights into ways of tackling your current responsibilities? Do you travel across the country ready to distribute leaflets, brochures and business cards from your own organization? Maybe you simply seek out the people you already know and have a general unfocused chat? On the other side of the debate it may be worth analysing how accessible the JNCTP conferences are to minority groups. Are conferences and debates accessible to black playworkers or to disabled playworkers? One very successful conference in Cardiff attracted a number of people from disability rights groups, but the next conference then focused on a different issue and the new network contacts were not maintained. An issue for organizations with limited resources is ensuring that venues are accessible and facilities such as child care, interpretation and induction loop systems are available. The JNCTP has a fairly detailed equal opportunities policy and action plan, and has a checklist system for ensuring such facilities are available if needed, but the fact that they are infrequently requested tells a story in itself. Playworkers who are just getting involved in local training issues can lack the confidence to attend national conferences. The possibility of not knowing anyone can be a daunting prospect.

Alongside conferences, being on the executive committee of the JNCTP can provide a very useful networking opportunity. Since meetings are held more frequently, relationships have the opportunity to develop and there is more time to explore issues, perspectives and approaches in more detail. The status which comes with being an executive member gives members a different and potentially more powerful or influential role when it comes to networking. Communicating a position on an issue which is supported through a membership organization clearly carries more weight than an individual point of view. A particularly useful forum has been the annual residential forward planning and review weekends. Informal times between structured sessions can be very beneficial in terms of networking. In addition, new ways of approaching old problems are explored, using different techniques. The 1999 residential weekend utilized some concepts from Battram's work on complexity theory. One of the ideas expounded by Battram is that 'Networks need hierarchies and hierarchies need networks' (1998: 40). The value of self-organization, where learning takes place without a central controller, can be characteristic of networks but too much networking can result in a scenario where 'the building burns down around us while we are in a meeting' (Battram 1998: 42). Organizations that have a cooperative style of management can often clearly see the benefits of networking and utilize them to good effect in pursuing their goals. The potential of the 'metaphor' as an analytical tool was referred to previously (Battram 1998: 75). An interesting exercise exploring the characteristics of the JNCTP involved identifying an appropriate metaphor to describe the organization. One particularly inspiring idea was the image of the JNCTP as a chihuahua, a little yappy dog snapping at the ankles of the policymakers. Metaphorical thinking can be a useful exercise to explore networks, relationships and objectives. The concept of operating within a 'constantly deforming landscape' (Battram 1998: 55) helped throw some light on the disadvantages of rigid three-year plans. Battram (1998: 59) advocates a more flexible approach to planning which enables 'possibility space' to be taken advantage of. At other forward planning meetings various management tools have been used to explore the complexities of the changing context within which debates around training and playwork need to be held. Utilizing drawings (including rich pictures), quick-lists and applying different frameworks to any analysis can all be useful tools.

Conclusion

Networking can be described as anarchic, 'on the edge of chaos' (Battram 1998: 138). In all three case studies, the context is different, but some of the themes are similar. Windfall outcomes arising from the networking process can result and are not always in direct proportion to the energy expended. The benefits can be amorphous and difficult to pin down, but networks can be a catalyst for unpredictable but useful possibilities to emerge. The value of networking in playwork should not be underestimated.

Chapter 11

Playwork in adversity: working with abandoned children in Romania

Sophie Webb and Fraser Brown

The Romanian context, post revolution

> The child in the cot opposite me is almost 12, but he looks no bigger than a 4-year-old. He is wearing odd shoes, his clothes are ripped and covered in dirt and he seems to be as undernourished emotionally as he is physically. He recently learnt how to walk, but still communicates by noises and gestures.
>
> (Reflective diary, 6 February 2000)

Like many children, Alex was abandoned at birth shortly before the overthrow of Ceauşescu in 1989. The old communist regime banned birth control and abortion as part of its strategy for expanding the workforce, and women were told it was their 'patriotic duty' to have babies (Moreton 2000). The result was children whose families could not afford to raise them. The children were abandoned by their parents, who probably assumed the state would take care of them. Within the 'caring' institutions the children were neglected, malnourished, unloved and unwanted. The plight of the abandoned children was not an accident of poverty or neglect, but an indirect result of political policy (Williamson 2000).

Even today children continue to be abandoned in Romania. There are still around 90,000 living in underfunded, state-run institutions, or on the streets – a number that has changed little since 1989 (Williamson 2000). The government's aim to give each orphan an experience of growing up in a family appears unrealistic in the short term, because of the severe lack of available finances brought about by a number of factors, including rampant inflation, excessive bureaucracy and institutionalized corruption (Moreton 2000). In the last 12 years, aid agencies and charities have adopted a range of approaches for helping the children. The majority of these have been well-meaning but ineffective. The problem is not one that can be solved in a few weeks by picking the children up and cuddling them. Most have never experienced any continual human contact, so when these groups leave the children are probably left feeling empty and confused.

The White Rose Initiative (WRI) recognized these problems and has been working since 1990 to alleviate disadvantage in Romania. They have focused much of their work on the ancient Transylvanian town of Sighisoara, where they have helped to refurbish three hospitals, an orphanage and a nursery. When Dr Cornel Puscas was appointed director of Sighisoara's five hospitals, he found a group of abandoned children living in the paediatric hospital. The children were not receiving satisfactory care, but without adequate resources he was unable to address the problem. He already knew of Harlow and Suomi's (1971) experiments with 'isolate reared' monkeys, and was struck by the similarity of conditions experienced by this group of children. In 1999 he approached the WRI to see if they could set up a playwork project in the hospital.

Most of the children had been abandoned at birth, and had spent most of their lives tied in the same cot, in the same small room. Their ages varied from 18 months to 12 years old. They rarely went outside, and at this stage they were exhibiting classic symptoms of neglect and malnutrition: stunted growth, rocking, absence of language, etc. (Smith *et al.* 1998). In terms of stimulation theory, the children had almost certainly experienced chronic play deprivation and extreme play bias, in the form of three of the four 'dangerous extremes' described by Hughes in Chapter 5 of this book. In September 1999, WRI provided the materials for a playroom, and employed a Romanian woman (Edit Bus) as a playworker to work exclusively with the children. After an intensive course of playwork training at Leeds Metropolitan University, Edit started work in October 1999. At the beginning of the Therapeutic Playwork Project Edit had 16 children in her care.

From the outset, the Therapeutic Playwork Project had two main aims. First, it was hoped that a combination of a stable, caring environment and good quality therapeutic playwork would go some way towards enabling the children to achieve their full potential. Given the deprivation experienced by the children, there was concern that the damage might already be too severe, and it might be too late to help them. However, once they were in a caring, supportive environment they began to make amazing progress. Within the space of five months the work had produced dramatic results, especially in terms of their physical development. The second aim, which was to some extent dependent on the success of the first, was to improve the chances of the children being able to live an ordinary family life outside the institutional environment. It is a measure of the success of the project that only three of the original 16 children still remained in the hospital 18 months later.

This chapter is based on a research study of the development of five of these children during the first year of the Therapeutic Playwork Project. Our definition of playwork, and its underpinning assumptions, are explored in Chapter 5. The observational data that forms the basis of this chapter began in February 2000 when one of the researchers (Sophie Webb) went to work at the hospital as part of her 'experiential learning'.[1] The intention was to work with the changes that had already been achieved, and to help with new ideas and encouragement. The children already appeared to be much happier from receiving care, stimulation and freedom from their cots, but there were serious problems to be overcome because their behaviour was still extremely complex. Sophie's work continued until April 2000, when she was joined for a short period by the second researcher (Fraser Brown), and the work was supplemented by a further visit in August 2000.[2]

In October 1999, at the start of the Therapeutic Playwork Project, the children had few social influences in their lives except for brief visits from the nurses to change their nappies, give them a few mouthfuls of food and water and then tie them up again. By February 2000, and throughout the lifetime of the research study, none of that altered. The only change in the daily experience of the children was provided by the Therapeutic Playwork Project. It might be tempting to claim that the developmental changes in the children were directly attributable to playwork, and in particular therapeutic playwork, but such a claim could only be tested through an extensive longitudinal study. It would also depend on our acceptance of a generic definition of the profession (see Chapter 5), and that is not to everyone's taste. Furthermore, this was only a small-scale study, and so it would not be logical to make grandiose claims. Instead, it is our contention that the developmental changes achieved were only made possible by the children's experience of the Therapeutic Playwork Project.

Research methodology

The aim of the research was to assess developmental change over a period of seven months from February to August 2000. The three distinct assessment points were in February, April and August. Five children from the original group were studied in depth during the period from February to April. By August only three of them remained, and so there are no findings and observations for two of the children in August. It was possible to observe the children each day, noting the details of their play behaviours and social interaction. Observations had to be unobtrusive, for two reasons:

- to avoid disrupting what the children were achieving in their play;
- to enable the recording of detailed notes at close quarters.

Participant observation

The method most suited to these requirements was *participant observation*, which Becker and Geer (1957: 28) define as an approach where 'the observer participates in the daily life of the people under study, either openly in the role of researcher or covertly in some disguised role, observing things that happen, listening to what is said, and questioning people, over some length of time'.

Steckler (1999) suggests participant observation can occur on four levels:

1 complete participant (role is concealed);
2 participant as observer (role is partially concealed);
3 observer as participant (role is known);
4 complete observer (role is concealed).

In this case, the participant's role as observer was known by WRI's employees, but not by the children or the nurses. From their point of view it would have seemed the researchers were complete participants (visiting playworkers from the UK). The ethical implications of this, especially in relation to 'informed consent' and privacy (Alderson 1995: 3–5), are less significant than might be thought. After thorough discussion of the implications, both WRI and the director of the hospital had given permission for the study to take place, and for the children's medical records to be used. Nevertheless, the names of all the children have been changed for reasons of confidentiality.

It might be argued that this approach was participant observation in its truest sense for only one of the researchers (i.e. Sophie Webb), since that is a method more normally associated with fieldworkers becoming totally immersed in the day-to-day culture of the group being studied (Lacey 1976). Clearly, when Sophie Webb undertook her experiential learning from February to April she was able to become something of an 'insider' (Denscombe 1998: 149), and so gain real insight into the culture of the setting. However, there were distinct elements of participant observation in the approach of both researchers. Both were able to 'join in the daily life of the group' (Moser and Kalton 1971: 249). Direct involvement enabled the researchers 'to hear, see and begin to experience reality' in the same way as the children and playworkers (Marshall and Rossman 1995: 79). It was also possible to 'listen to the symbolic sounds that characterise this world' (Chatzman and Strauss 1973: 6). All these things are fundamental elements of participant observation. It was difficult to establish a dialogue with the children because their vocabulary was limited. However, language is only one communication tool, and with careful observation of the children's play behaviour it was possible to gain insights into the 'nuances of meaning' (Chatzman and Strauss 1973: 6) from which they formed their view of the world.

There are pitfalls with participant observation. For example, it is possible for the researcher's own participation to influence the children's behaviour in an unusual way. However, in practice the day-to-day behaviour of the researchers was the same as any playworker in this setting. A further problem can arise where researchers misunderstand situations due to 'unfamiliarity with the culture' (Gold 1969: 36). That risk was addressed in two ways: first, one of the researchers had been working at the project full-time; second, via discussion with the Romanian playworker, Edit Bus. According to Denscombe 'the key instrument of participant observation methods is the researcher as a person' (1998: 152). However, in some situations there may be drawbacks. The experiential learning requirement was to live and work in the country, which meant strong attachments were formed. Recording the changing lives of these children proved to be a disturbing yet rewarding experience. In these circumstances it was necessary to guard against the risk of losing sight of the research focus.

The role of the playworker is particularly useful in terms of participant observation because the playworker takes it for granted that 'there is a low adult to child approach ratio' (Hughes 1996a: 51). In other words, it is fundamental to the philosophy of playwork that the child's agenda is regarded as the starting point for any adult-child interaction. This makes the role especially suited to Corsaro's 'reactive strategy' (1985: 28), which encourages researchers to avoid behaving like adults. Corsaro found that adults have a strong tendency to be proactive in children's settings, which affects the research outcomes. If researchers were to be effective in children's contexts, Corsaro suggested that they need to be responsive to the child and set aside their adult prejudices. The playworker's interpretative approach is well-suited to this, since it seeks to pick up on signals rather than instigate them. Thus, the playworker quite naturally tends to adopt an approach similar to that of the classic Tavistock Model (Greig and Taylor 1999), which encourages the researcher to interact with the subjects and record the behaviours and feelings of all the participants (including the researcher).

The final part of the research, undertaken during August 2000, was conducted using a different observational technique, due to the short-term nature of the visit. The follow-up visit was for ten days, as opposed to the two months spent on-site during the experiential learning phase. On this occasion the method of recording was a form of rotated peer observation which saw the researchers alternating tasks and roles – one hour working with the children, one hour of non-participant observation, and so on.

All this enabled the two researchers to complete independent assessments of the developmental progress of the children. Overall, the research process produced two separate sets of data that were subsequently collated into a single table (see Table 11.1, pp. 162–3). The collated data was given added validity by a small degree of triangulation contained within the method. Effective qualitative research involves gaining data 'from as many perspectives as possible' (Luria 1979: 177). There are several forms of triangulation according to Denzin (1978), including the comparison of data from different researchers and different time perspectives, and multiple methods: 'If such comparisons show that the findings hold, then one can have more confidence in their interpretation' (Breakwell *et al.* 2000: 280). On this occasion it was possible to triangulate the findings of two researchers at three distinct points in time. However, it is recognized that it is not possible to draw generalized conclusions from the findings on the basis of such a small 'non-probability sample' (Zikmund 1994: 455).

Table 11.1 Indicators of significant developmental change from February to April 2000, and from April to August 2000, highlighting in bold all changes of '1' or above

		Carol	Virgil	Elena	Olympia	Nicolae
Freedom	Feb	3.06	5	4.56	3.94	3.5
	April	4.8	6.27	5.76	4.72	4.16
	Feb–April	**1.74**	**1.27**	**1.2**		
	Aug	5.71			4.76	4.48
	April–Aug					
Flexibility	Feb	2.5	4.88	3.63	3.75	2.38
	April	4.53	6.13	4.63	4.43	3.29
	Feb–April	**2.03**	**1.25**	**1**		
	Aug	5.71			4.6	4
	April–Aug	**1.18**				
Socialization and	Feb	2.06	4.88	2.31	2.94	2.38
social interaction	April	4.36	6.01	4.04	4.78	3.5
	Feb–April	**2.3**	**1.13**	**1.73**	**1.84**	**1.12**
	Aug	4.92			5.42	4.12
	April–Aug					
Physical activity	Feb	3.27	5.09	4.33	4	2.18
	April	4.97	6.56	5.37	5.21	4.49
	Feb–April	**1.7**	**1.47**	**1.04**	**1.21**	**2.31**
	Aug	5.8			5.27	5.02
	April–Aug					
Intellectual	Feb	2.09	4.56	2.69	2.78	2.5
stimulation	April	4	5.89	2.98	3.65	2.78
	Feb–April	**1.91**	**1.33**			
	Aug	4.56			4.1	3.02
	April–Aug					
Creativity and	Feb	2.13	4.6	3.29	3.06	2.33
problem solving	April	5.02	6.46	3.5	4.09	3.25
	Feb–April	**2.89**	**1.86**		**1.03**	
	Aug	5.13			4.35	3.73
	April–Aug					
Emotional	Feb	4.06	4.59	3.82	4.12	2.71
equilibrium	April	4.1	5.82	3.91	4.22	3.2
	Feb–April		**1.23**			
	Aug	4.38			4.47	3.65
	April–Aug					
Self-discovery	Feb	2.81	4.86	3.67	3.69	2.5
	April	4.13	5.98	5.01	4.47	3.02
	Feb–April	**1.32**	**1.12**	**1.34**		
	Aug	5.19			4.9	3.44
	April–Aug	**1.06**				

Table 11.1 (*cont'd*)

		Carol	Virgil	Elena	Olympia	Nicolae
Ethical stance	Feb	1.8	5.5	3.6	4	1.6
	April	4.5	6.6	4.18	4.7	3.96
	Feb–April	**2.7**	**1.1**			**2.36**
	Aug	5.8			5.42	4.56
	April–Aug	**1.3**				
Adult-child	Feb	2	5	2.12	5.5	5
relationships	April	3.96	5.43	4.23	5.12	4.93
	Feb–April	**1.96**		**2.11**		
	Aug	5.04			4.82	5
	April–Aug	**1.08**				
General appeal:	Feb	3.43	5.66	3.29	4.25	2.88
fun and enjoyment	April	5.21	6.7	5.63	5.66	4.38
	Feb–April	**1.78**	**1.04**	**2.34**	**1.41**	**1.5**
	Aug	6.25			6	5.13
	April–Aug	**1.04**				

Basis for the assessment instrument

From the start, observations of the children's behaviour were recorded in a reflective diary. This contained general indications about:

- personal perceptions of what had happened during each day;
- what was planned for the next day, and why;
- reflections on the overall goals in relation to the changes that were occurring;
- what would be done next.

The diary was therefore both a data source and a tool that assisted reflection upon practice. Studying children in context made it possible to gain a deeper insight into their lives and development. The success of this approach provided the impetus for the research project: 'The researcher who hangs in there during the first period of seeing the obvious and carefully records what she sees eventually begins to notice other things, things that have been there all along but were not so obvious' (Graue and Walsh 1998: 94).

After collecting this raw data it became clear that it would be necessary to develop an assessment instrument that would enable the identification of developmental changes in the children, and would relate those changes to play and playwork theories. A derivation of the system developed by Brown (2002) for use on children's playgrounds was adopted. Under 11 general headings, the system groups a series of specific questions that serve to identify what happens when children play. Brown's original approach was reworked to produce an assessment sheet, containing 154 questions relating to the Sighisoara setting. For example:

- To what extent is there evidence of self-initiation of activities?
- To what extent is the child trying unusual combinations of behaviour?
- To what extent is there evidence of the child acquiring technical prowess and competence?
- To what extent are actions given different meanings during play?

All 154 assessments were recorded using a scale of 1 to 7. This approach has similarities to that used by the Office for Standards in Education (Ofsted) in connection with the inspection of schools. Different meanings were associated with the points on the scale, as follows:

1	2	3	4	5	6	7
never	very rarely	rarely	sometimes	often	very often	always

The assessment questions were grouped under the 11 categories used previously by Brown (2002). These categories cover the full range of children's play behaviours and/or characteristics of play, and largely derive from play and playwork theory. They are:

- freedom;
- flexibility;
- socialization and social interaction;
- physical activity;
- intellectual stimulation;
- creativity and problem solving;
- emotional equilibrium;
- self-discovery;
- ethical stance;
- adult-child relationships;
- general appeal: fun and enjoyment.

The children were observed in February, April and August 2000, and subsequently assessed using the questions in the assessment instrument. The assessments were then averaged out in each of the 11 categories, which gave an assessment grade for each child under each category. Three separate assessment forms were completed for each child, covering the period from February to August 2000. This enabled the assessment of change. The assessments for February were completed solely by Sophie Webb, and the two subsequent assessments were conducted independently by both Sophie Webb and Fraser Brown.

Table 11.1 presents our collation of the assessment grades for each child in each category for each month. Areas of substantial change are highlighted in bold type. There was evidence of change in all the children, which is explained in the next section. In order to identify significant change for individual children the approach of highlighting all changes of '1' or above was adopted and these instances were studied in greater detail. Evidence of change was all the more remarkable when set against the background of medical records describing the children as 'retarded'.

The results suggest two distinct areas for discussion:

- areas of significant change for individual children;
- areas of significant change for the whole group.

Summarizing individual change

Carol

Carol (aged 3) was tied to a cot in a room on his own. He had been separated because he was thought to be HIV positive. Due to the uncertainty of the tests, the nurses were afraid of the virus spreading so kept him away from the other children and he was treated as a nuisance. Food only came once or twice a day and his nappy was not changed regularly. He was receiving no stimulation or contact and so was continually bored and frustrated, which would often result in him playing with his own faeces. There were bruises on his back from violently rocking the cot against the wall, and each time he protested the door was closed, locked and he was ignored. Eventually the hospital staff gave permission to take Carol to the playroom each day. The side-effects of being shut away and constricted were obvious in his behaviour: 'Carol is angry, violent and attention seeking. He cries most of the time, especially when he has to go back in his room. Although he watches the busy activities of the group he makes no attempt to join in' (Reflective diary, 12 February 2000).

At this stage his play was essentially solitary (Parten 1933). During the early observations of Carol there were distinctive patterns to his play. For example, he would pick up a toy whatever its size and throw it away from him. He lacked concentration on any activity that required structure and released his frustration by throwing objects around the room. This created a chaotic atmosphere and meant the other children avoided him. It was important to offer Carol the chance of some cathartic release of his frustrations through play (Helanko 1956). The hospital regime was strict and there were limitations on the extent to which 'trajectory' play (Roberts 1995) would be viewed as acceptable. However, through therapeutic activities such as chasing bubbles or balloons, pouring water into buckets and throwing toys into a big box, Carol developed a way of freeing his aggression. After only four weeks in the playroom he began to show an interest in the other children and to engage in make-believe play:

> Today Carol had a 'conversation' with Virgil using a brick to represent a phone. He played in this way for a while and then ended the role play, pretending to leave him by walking away, waving. How did he know what a phone is?
>
> (Reflective diary, 29 February 2000)

Observations during the August period were not so striking, although Carol did show a consistent development in some areas. He was approaching children easily, with confidence and sensitivity, he had stopped throwing objects around and was now full of mischief and fun:

Today I was sitting on the floor tossing a ball gently into the air. Carol was watching me intently. First he came close. Then he backed away, all the time keeping eye contact. This was a clear play cue ('throw it to me'). I flicked the ball to him. The thrill of having someone respond to his play cue was immense. He became so excited he crammed the ball into his mouth, before returning it to me for another go.

(Reflective diary, 4 August 2000)

During this visit it was confirmed that Carol was HIV positive. His family continued to show no interest in him, and so at that time there was the very real prospect that he would spend most of his short life in the hospital.

Virgil

In February Virgil (aged 5) was already far more active and alert than the other children. However, during early observations he appeared to feel threatened when presented with new experiences, and would use objects as a defence against anxiety and stress. Previously he had been fed while still being tied in his cot:

He insists on standing on a chair to eat, instead of sitting at the table with the others, and will not let go of whatever object happens to be in his hand when the food arrives. Suddenly being given such freedom must be quite threatening.

(Reflective diary, 11 February 2000)

To begin with Virgil played on his own, not allowing other children to join in with his games. His play seemed very important to him and he would only stop when he needed to eat or sleep. He was always busy: carrying around toys, using blocks to build towers, putting things into boxes and emptying them, moving furniture around and collecting objects. He repeated these actions continually, never appearing to be tired.

By the third week Virgil showed signs of entering into 'simple cooperative' play (Williams 1984), where he involved other children in his 'work' and started to share tasks. His creative skills were also improving and he was making use of opportunities for imaginative play:

While Ion was sitting in a big yellow box Virgil started to play a game with him, involving an imaginary object. He pretended to receive something from Edit and then took it back to Ion in the box, who took it from him and put it in his lap. The spontaneous interaction between them both was fascinating to watch. Afterwards Virgil continued playing with the yellow plastic box, by putting it on his head and walking around the room.

(Reflective diary, 25 February 2000)

By week four, Virgil was beginning to be more relaxed and confident. He felt comfortable about sitting at the table to eat and started to release the objects he used for his security, suggesting he was building an inner confidence about himself and his surroundings, albeit slowly. Despite his continuing emotional instability Virgil gradually became an important member of the group with his good ideas and imagination.

Elena

Elena (aged 5) had been in hospital since birth. She had been deprived of the opportunity to play at a very early age, which delayed her progress and abilities. This was obvious when observing Elena in early February: she was afraid of people and lacked confidence, her legs were still stiff from rickets and she could not walk properly. She could not communicate or focus on activities, appearing to have little imagination, and she rocked continually, apparently unaware of her surroundings.

Her security had been within the four walls of the hospital for five years. Therefore a very gentle, gradual approach was employed when encouraging her to join in. The first experience of communicating with Elena was in the hospital room:

> She sat on my lap and started touching my hair and putting the back of her hand up to it. She was so gentle and aware of every sense, smelling my face and feeling my breath. It was a very moving experience.
> (Reflective diary, 5 February 2000)

Elena completely explored her playworker that day, interpreting the new experience in the only way she could, oblivious to what was going on around her. She used hand gestures to investigate, which was her way of communicating. When playing with a toy she would hold it to her mouth and move it around with her teeth. Both Freud and Erikson would consider this to be more typical of a child in the first year of life (Greig and Taylor 1999). In general, a 5-year-old's behaviour might be expected to have progressed to more advanced exploration such as object representation, make-believe play, problem solving, etc. (Schickedanz et al. 1993).

Elena was always by herself. While other children were forming friendships, she would sit in the corner, transfixed by an object she had picked up. If another child approached her she would run away or climb back into her cot: 'She is aware for a few seconds and then looks away. She also smiles a lot, but never at the other children. She seldom cries or makes any loud noises' (Reflective diary, 16 February 2000).

Elena was now in a stimulating environment and throughout the next six to seven weeks she started to show an interest in what was around her and became involved in the opportunities to play. Significant changes in her development included allowing other children into her space, her instigation to play games and the subtle play cues she offered (Else and Sturrock 1998):

> Elena is becoming closer to the other children, responding quicker and concentrating on activities. Today I called her name and she ran over

and grabbed my hand, pulling me into a space where she could play a game of run and jump.

(Reflective diary, 6 March 2000)

Elena began to remember this improvised game each time the playworker appeared. This was the first time she had made any connection with anyone or anything. Vygotsky (1978: 102) says, 'play contains all developmental tendencies in a condensed form and is itself a major source of development'. Elena became steadily more focused and by week five she offered another very subtle play cue in the form of a noise she often made:

I started to repeat this noise back to her and she responded by instigating the sequence when she saw me, exploring my face and trying to decide where the noise was coming from. By making myself the play environment Elena was comfortable to allow herself the freedom to communicate and investigate.

(Reflective diary, 8 March 2000)

Thus it was possible for the playworker to help the child explore her 'zone of proximal development' (Vygotsky 1976). Elena was clearly seeking to make contact in the only way she understood, and through steady encouragement was able to develop self-expression (Moyles 1989), awareness of others and flexibility within her play interaction (Trevarthen *et al.* 1996). By April, Elena was responding quickly to her name, concentrating on activities, and had become closer to the other children. Her social development in eight weeks was rapid and extremely distinct:

I watched Elena play with Virgil. It was absolutely beautiful – the best representation of play I have seen. All they were doing was chasing each other. It was so gentle and silent – as if they were flowing in and out of one another – just like two butterflies.

(Reflective diary, 30 March 2000)

Olympia

Olympia (aged 6) had a strong character and a bubbly personality, but nevertheless showed signs of frustration and a lack of self-esteem. She punished herself for attention and this jeopardized her ability to make friends (Moyles 1989). For example, when things did not go her way, or if a child took the toy she was playing with, she would hit herself or others, sometimes with a hard object or the bars of the cot. When this challenging behaviour occurred it was approached with distraction techniques – for example, offering her a toy or playing a game she enjoyed (Petrille and Sanger 1983). This technique worked well because it gave her the attention she wanted, but was channelling her behaviour into something more positive (West 1996). This started to increase her self-esteem and by week four Olympia was beginning to control her angry tantrums, which resulted in a generally calmer temperament.

The more interested she became in play activities the more she moved around the room, which helped to enhance her physical strength (Schickedanz *et al.* 1993). She also became able to choose her own activities and toys, and began to initiate ideas within her play, developing her imagination and creative skills (Moyles 1989):

> Olympia pretended to feed Ion with an empty cup, which was left over from dinner. They took it in turns to feed each other by lifting the cup to their mouths and saying 'multsumesc' (thank you).
>
> (Reflective diary, 3 March 2000)

Olympia changed considerably in the area of socialization and social interaction. She did this by evolving a way of coping with her frustration within her play. She began to share with other children and to show a very loving, caring and understanding side to her personality. Her status within the group became pivotal, taking on a mother-like role towards the other children. It was important to let her know when she had been sensitive to others, especially without punishing herself.

> Olympia's reaction to another child was quite startling today. I brought Gheorge in from another room. He had been crying for a while and was on his own. I sat him down on the floor with me and started to show him some toys (still crying). Olympia came straight over to him and started to stroke his head saying 'ahhh'.
>
> (Reflective diary, 22 March 2000)

Although Olympia had progressed further in the area of socialization and social interaction during observations in August, the change was not sufficient enough to record. She was continuing to play with other children, initiating games, and her temperament had remained the same.

Nicolae

Nicolae was born almost ten weeks premature, weighing around 700g. Now aged 9, his physical development was extremely delayed. His balance and confidence when trying to walk was similar to that of a 12- to 18-month-old child (Schickedanz *et al.* 1993). Consequently he sat most of the time, in solitary play (Parten 1933), fixing his concentration on small objects. He would make noises to himself, relying on body language to communicate most of the time. According to the medical records from the hospital he had a very immature digestive system for his age, probably due to only being given a liquid diet for years and not coping with solid food. His eating habits may also have reflected his emotional deprivation, constantly regurgitating his food and throwing it at people. This was a way of seeking attention and indicated his insecurity. He would often return to this behaviour at times of uncertainty, when he was annoyed, frustrated or upset.

Through therapeutic play and diversionary techniques his concentration moved from repetitive, obsessive behaviour on to more constructive activities. With gradual encouragement and individual attention, he began to show an awareness of the world around him:

> I've been spending time with Nicolae every morning, practising walking forwards by holding his hands and guiding him, like I would a baby. I've also offered him a choice of activities and started to include him in any group play. His progress is steady and he is starting to enjoy being around the other children.
>
> (Reflective diary, 21 February 2000)

Nicolae changed dramatically in the area of his physical abilities. Within five weeks he was able to play with the other children, because he was more confident on his feet. Therefore, the quality of his social interaction developed considerably. The more confident he became, the more interested he was in his food. His antisocial habits stopped and he showed a gradual sign of inner confidence which allowed his personality to shine through:

> This morning Edit brought some balloons into the playroom. Nicolae particularly enjoyed this, as he is now steadier on his feet and was able to stand and push the balloons around. He was able to concentrate on playing a game with Olympia where they were watching the balloon float down in front of them, then pushing it away. Their facial expressions as the balloons touched them were beautiful.
>
> (Reflective diary, 15 March 2000)

Although Nicolae changed considerably between February and April, there are fewer indications of change within the August findings. He was more confident on his feet but still staggering, and his interaction with the other children was more in the form of bullying, pinching and pushing: all of which were continued signs of inner conflict and anxiety. The brief conclusion to be made about the changes in Nicolae is that his progress has been slower than the other children.

Areas of significant change for the whole group

The significant group change took place in the early part of the project. There were three main areas:

- the nature of social interaction;
- the characteristics of physical activity;
- the sense of fun and enjoyment felt by the children (general appeal).

Socialization and social interaction

When observations began, all the children were playing on their own, irrespective of their age or stage of development. They rarely communicated and seemed focused on their own activities, unaware of each other. Clearly, the first step towards their individual development would be through group interaction. The children had not previously been encouraged to socialize, and were still being fed by a nurse while tied to their cots. The initial idea was to provide moments where the children might feel comfortable with one another, and this began through gradually encouraging them to sit at the table to eat their meals. This proved to be more than simply eating together. It became an important routine for them to socialize with one another, familiarizing themselves with close contact. This was a significant part of instigating their social play. They began to get used to each other from sitting at the table, whereas before they had no reason or inclination to be close to one another:

> This is a time of play as they explore the texture of the food (like messy play) plus the interaction with one another is vital for their play in other contexts. They all have different ways of eating too, which is delightful to watch; it's a really big event for them.
>
> (Reflective diary, 14 March 2000)

By week three, 'cooperative play' was occurring (Parten 1933), where particular children were learning how to share and join in. This was instigated by Olympia and Virgil, who sustained an important friendship. They were a vital example to the rest of the group because of the way they played together, involving others in their games:

> Virgil has started to play with the toy car and when Olympia sat on it today he started to push her around. They must have played like this for hours and hours, and when we left in the afternoon he was pulling others around. They were laughing together and really enjoying themselves.
>
> (Reflective diary, 29 February 2000)

By week four, most of the children were feeding themselves and there was also evidence of 'joining in play' (Williams 1984):

> Today Olympia began to feed Nicolae. She noticed he had finished eating and moved her cup of food over to him. She then very carefully put the food onto the spoon and fed him. This was clearly a significant achievement for both participants and the communication between them was the instigation for play.
>
> (Reflective diary, 28 February 2000)

Physical activity

According to the findings in Table 11.1, this is the area where the children as a group changed the most. Before October 1999 the children had been tied to their cots all day. Most had a form of rickets and were suffering from malnutrition due to not receiving nourishing food and exercise. By February they were a lot stronger and were out of their cots, although their physical abilities remained weak and awkward. These children needed as much encouragement with new opportunities as possible. They had been deprived of the everyday challenges which help develop children's personalities and it was necessary to encourage and extend their options and possibilities for play, without trying to stipulate their every move (Davy 1995).

The first attempt to encourage the children to play as a group (to encourage their physical abilities) was in early February and simply involved holding their hands and running with them. However, this did not work well because physically they were not able to cope with such movement as they were still staggering like babies. For example, Nicolae (aged 9) could not walk around the room without holding onto the sides of the cot or table, and could not push himself up from a sitting position. When a ball was thrown to Virgil (aged 5) he could not catch it, and could not coordinate his legs to kick. Olympia (aged 6) could not yet balance on one foot or stand on tiptoe. Their cephalocaudal skills (Schickedanz et al. 1993) had been delayed because there had been little stimulation within their environment. Gradually, through simple games such as running around the table, chase, etc. their physical strength improved considerably and they were walking confidently, running and exploring their surroundings. By the end of March a second attempt to encourage group play was far more successful, and the children were able to hold hands together and dance to music:

> Olympia was dancing to the music on the radio this morning with Virgil. They were holding hands and moving around the room. When I joined in, Carol came over and wanted to be involved and this progressed into running up and down the room with them still holding hands and wanting to stay linked together. This might appear to be something very normal, but considering how unsteady these children were only six weeks ago, it's a major achievement.
>
> (Reflective diary, 29 March 2000)

During week four (1 March 2000) there was an opportunity to take the children outside, where they were able to explore their surroundings even further. This was the first time they had been out since the previous summer. They seemed to find the experience very distressing and initially they simply stood in one place, reluctant to move around and not knowing what to do with all the space. They appeared frightened but were also showing signs of amazement. The introduction of familiar games they had been playing inside allowed them to feel more comfortable outside, and they began to explore in a new way, feeling the freedom to investigate.

General appeal: fun and enjoyment

As the children began to change and develop, they also achieved a level of familiarity within their play experiences. They started to enjoy and understand the benefits of play, and this was evident from the following examples.

In February Virgil was able to build bricks quite confidently. His proximodistal skills (Schickedanz et al. 1993) were considerably more developed than most of the other children, although the way he built the bricks was very regimented and systematic. He had obviously been shown how to do this but had not yet experienced the quality of enjoying this activity. Whereas by April, he was building the bricks and getting excited about it, laughing out loud and enjoying the anticipation as the tower of bricks fell down around him.

It was important to offer the children experiences that would not only help them to develop physically and socially as a group, but also to enjoy playing as a group. For example, a tube of bubbles was used to encourage group play:

They all gathered around me, reaching up to burst them or allowing them to pop on their faces or hands. The noises they made were lovely and I couldn't blow the next one fast enough.

(Reflective diary, 27 March 2000)

Towards the end of the first period there were other moments like this where they were completely relaxed together and playing just for the sake of it: lying on the floor with the soft toys in the playroom; playing games at the table before meal times; listening to stories by Edit; etc. Play was providing an escape from reality (Moyles 1989). It was clearly having a positive effect in terms of enjoyment, as well as social interaction and physical development.

However, there was one area where they hardly changed at all. Although the children were clearly enjoying themselves, their underlying emotional equilibrium was still fragile. Unusually sensitive reactions occurred frequently, and they appeared to stick together if someone was unfriendly or hostile towards them. When a person was not comfortable in their company it made them feel uneasy, and they rocked for security or became disruptive: 'As soon as the children are put back into their cots, they immediately start to shake them and rock back and forth. There are marks on the wall near every one' (Reflective diary, 18 February 2000).

Another example of this was on 1 March when the children had to be moved to another room to sleep in for a week. Most of them reacted to this by refusing to eat and not wanting to get out of the cots they had been placed in. Presumably they had regarded the previous room as their home, and this new room was frightening and unfamiliar territory.

Pringle (1980: 26) says children need 'new experiences, praise and recognition, opportunities to take reasonable responsibility and most of all love and security'. It was clear the children needed routines such as sitting at the table to eat, going to the playroom each morning and so on, to compensate for not having security in their lives. Alongside this, their play activities needed to be unstructured, allowing them to express themselves in whatever way they wanted. This was an area where a visiting playworker could not provide continual security. Throughout the period it was important not to appear too attached as the input was limited by time, but also because the children's basic needs (security and dependency) had not been met, and they were likely to be subjected to continuing erratic behaviour (West 1996).

Conclusion

Before the input of the Therapeutic Playwork Project each child was isolated, physically weak, lacking in social skills and generally unhappy. The findings detailed in Table 11.1 suggest that all the children underwent significant change in the areas of socialization and social interaction, physical activity and general enjoyment of play. It is also worth confirming that in every area, for every child, the results showed the changes were progressive, not regressive.

While the data seems to confirm the general benefits of play, it also highlights specific areas of interest. While Nicolae and Olympia showed significant development in some areas, they made only slight progress in others. Both children were born two months prematurely, both weighing less than 800g. The hospital records describe them as 'retarded' and informal observation tends towards the view that both children have what in the UK we would describe as 'profound and multiple learning difficulties' (DfE 1994). It might, therefore, be predicted that they would show development in the more physical, less cognitive areas, and in general that appeared to be the case. However, the findings also indicate a positive change in Olympia's creative problem-solving ability between February and April, and Nicolae began to absorb new information and made progress in the areas of intellectual stimulation and flexibility.

The findings show three children who changed a great deal in most areas: Elena, Virgil and Carol. At the start of the Therapeutic Playwork Project these children showed numerous symptoms of the damage resulting from many years of neglect and abuse. Their delayed development was clearly due to the extreme deprivation they had experienced. In these circumstances, it seems that the therapeutic benefits from the play input were particularly powerful, and at times the changes were unexpected. In February Elena appeared to be locked in her own world, showing autistic tendencies (Trevarthen *et al.* 1996). However, the findings show a significant leap forward in her social interaction skills during the period from February to April. Another example would be Virgil, who was the only child to change significantly in the area of emotional equilibrium. He seemed to find his security through play and began to come to terms with his feelings and conflicts (Axline 1969). Carol had experienced extreme neglect due to his HIV positive condition. Therefore, a marked progression in his ability to make use of opportunities for imaginative play (Hutt *et al.* 1989) might not be expected. However, this was the area where he changed the most.

The children developed dramatically in just seven months. Previously they had been tied to their cots, not regularly fed or changed and had little social interaction. From February to August nothing changed in their lives except the input of the Therapeutic Playwork Project. At night, when the playworkers left, they were tied up again and given no opportunities to play. The interaction they were receiving from hospital staff was not constructive or positive. There were no family, school or religious influences. In the absence of any positive external stimuli the children had an intense experience of play. The findings suggest, above all else, that the Therapeutic Playwork Project helped these children to become social beings, not isolated units. Every child began to form reciprocal relationships, which in turn led to a greater sense of self-worth.

It was important to work with these children, individually and as a group, considering their developmental needs, working in their space and responding to their 'play cues' (Else and Sturrock 1998). It was also essential to take a holistic approach, concentrating on the physical, mental and spiritual aspects of their progress as well as their feelings and thoughts:

> The greatest aspect for me was to watch the children come together. Even in eight weeks, I saw them change in so many ways; playing together, feeling comfortable with one another, touching, exploring, sharing, imagining, watching, becoming more confident and most of all laughing. I loved hearing their laughter.
>
> (Reflective diary, 1 April 2000)

Since the completion of the research study, the work of the Therapeutic Playwork Project has continued. WRI now employ five Romanian playworkers, whose wages are paid by sponsors in the UK.[3] The research findings show the success of the project in enabling the children to come closer to achieving their full developmental potential. This success is further demonstrated by the high proportion of children who have spent time with the Therapeutic Playwork Project and are now living with families outside the hospital. These include some of the children who are the subjects of this chapter. Olympia has now returned home to live with her family, and thanks to the work of the Luminita Copiilor Foundation, Elena and Virgil are living with foster families. Sadly, Nicolae has been transferred to a children's mental hospital.

As of April 2002 the nature of the project has changed considerably. With the successful fostering of the majority of the older children, the age range of the project has fallen and most of the children are under 2. Consequently, the work is now focused on prevention rather than cure. The aim is to provide the children with a relatively 'normal' play environment. Thankfully there is now less need for the sort of concentrated therapeutic recovery work which has been explored in this chapter.

Notes

1 See Chapter 12 for an explanation of the concept of experiential learning.
2 A more detailed summary of the research project is available from Leeds Metropolitan University.
3 For further details, contact White Rose Initiative, 23 Helston Road, Middleton, Leeds LS10 4PG.

Chapter 12

Playwork as reflective practice

Sue Palmer

For many playworkers, the term 'reflective practice' has provided a justification for the professional nature of their work with children. There is a tendency to assume that reflective practice describes an individual process of thinking about practice after the event or outlining what playwork entails with examples used to reinforce current theory. This chapter will challenge that view and offer a rationale for reflective practices that involve children as well as playworkers as part of a community of playwork practice. The experiences that inform this analysis are based on reflection with playworkers involved in the playwork course at Leeds Metropolitan University (LMU), both as students and as supporters of students. It also includes informal discussions held with playworkers on the general themes of 'What are we trying to do?' and 'What is good practice in playwork?'

The theoretical base for reflective practice

How professionals think and learn about their practice and action has been examined by a number of writers (Schön 1983; Gibbs 1988; Moon 1999). The debate may be traced back to the writings of Dewey in the early 1900s, who espoused the value of 'learning by doing'. His later work went further, and by placing theory within practice, suggested that the interaction between individual and environment operated as a series of interrelated cycles, which affected both individual and environment (Dewey and Bentley 1949). This 'evolutionary' approach to practice and theory reflected the growth of interest in Darwin's work at the turn of the century and has been taken up by later writers in developing a holistic approach to the understanding of human learning and cognition. Current debates in playwork reflect this notion. In particular, the suggestion that a child at play in a flexible environment not only develops as an individual but also inputs into the play environment (Hughes 1996a; Brown 2000a).

Most contemporary accounts of reflective practice begin with a description of the learning cycle described by Kolb (1984) (see Figure 12.1) In Kolb's model, the individual uses concrete, real-world experiences to engage in reflective observations which develop into abstract models or conceptualizations of the experience, which are then fed back into planning the next stage of interactions with the real world. Kolb's cycle of reflection, planning and experimentation has been successfully applied to many playwork-based projects, for example High/Scope, where it is represented in terms of the 'plan-do-review' cycle. It also forms the accepted base for a wide range of projects concerned with learning cycles and development for both children and adults.

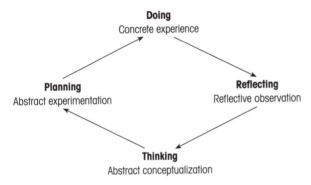

Figure 12.1 Kolb's cycle of reflection (1984)

Schön (1983) began by examining the difficulty faced by professionals in explaining their practice. He noted that, for many situations, the technical (knowing what) response identified in professional textbooks was insufficient to explain what practice required and that successful practitioners were applying a combination of practice/experience based knowledge together with reflection during and after their action (knowing how). He coined the phrase 'reflection in action' to express the process of 'thinking on your feet'. He suggested that experienced professionals do more than just carry out technical or pre-prepared actions in practice and that some process which involves thinking either consciously or unconsciously about actions takes place during action. By developing a distinction between knowing what to do and knowing how to do it, he suggested that what we know is implicit in our actions and our intuitive response to situations. He calls this 'knowing in action'. Some writers map this knowing in action cycle against Kolb's cycle of reflection (see Figure 12.2).

The two linked cycles of reflection are essential to quality practice. Reflection on action takes place after the event while reflection-in-action is the

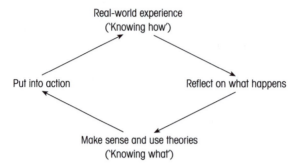

Figure 12.2 Schön's 'knowing in action' cycle (1983)

Figure 12.3 Gibbs's reflective cycle model (1988)

ongoing intuitive response and reflection that takes place during professional action. Gibbs (1988) developed a reflective cycle model (see Figure 12.3) which provides a framework for reflecting on action. This has been used in a number of professional contexts to support new practitioners in the process of recording and beginning to reflect on their experiences.

Schön (1983) indicates that reflection during action may be difficult or even impossible in some situations. For example, in a crisis situation where instinctive reaction is essential, or where reflex action is needed rather than a consideration of alternatives. He argues that this does not mean practitioners should not eventually reflect on past performance and practice. He suggests that reflecting on action at a later date has great value in developing future skills and learning from experience. Schön has been criticized for this apparent confusion of terms by using reflection on and reflection in action interchangeably (Eraut 1994). This is not surprising in that he is suggesting that both reflection on action and reflection in action are essential to advanced practice and that together they constitute a feedback loop that enables professional development.

Schön proposes a double loop learning model. It may be explained as follows. Professionals develop skills of reflecting in and on action as identified through the application of the models from Kolb and Gibbs. However, in order to engage with reflective practice, the professional must understand and re-evaluate the theoretical and intuitive bases which inform practice on a daily basis. This requires a further loop of reflection that opens up enquiry into the basis of professional practice. Schön argues that this is essential if the practitioner is to remain engaged with the client and in touch with the practice base. Otherwise reflective practice could become a self-sealing process, reinforcing established or poor quality practices. Professionals need to engage systematically with the grounding of their practices in the light of current theory and research, and in relation to their current experiences. It is also essential that such reflection takes into account the experiences of the clients with whom the professionals engage.

These suggestions for engaging in ongoing enquiry into practice have a clear relevance to playwork practice. We are concerned to engage children in a meaningful dialogue about our practices and their experience of the playwork settings. We attempt to use current understandings about the nature of play to inform our practices on a daily basis, while reflecting the value base of playwork philosophy. Bright (1996) supports this view of reflective practice and attempts to clarify the processes involved by offering an examination of reflexive practice which suggests the need to question the values and assumptions which inform practice as well as the practices themselves. He concludes that there may be a need to reflect on reflective practices in the professions to ensure that reflection is not practised superficially.

Moon (1999) uses the terms 'espoused theory' and 'theory in use' to describe the process of reflections related to action. She suggests that espoused theory is often based on previous training or education and that it remains unchanged over time regardless of counter experience or practices. The theory in use develops and elaborates over time in response to experience and pragmatic practice. The resulting theory in use applied by different individuals may therefore become a set of highly personalized approaches to practice developed from a commonly held espoused theory.

The issue that this raises for playwork practitioners is to examine the gap that may emerge between espoused theory and theory in use. For example, Hughes's (1996a: 16) assertion that 'to be playful, behaviour has to be freely chosen, personally directed and intrinsically motivated' and the definition of playwork proposed by Playboard (1984) as being 'the specific act of affecting the whole environment with the deliberate intention of improving opportunities for play' both imply a framework for playwork practice which may be difficult to attain in all settings. Observed practice on some playwork projects would indicate that the expectation of playwork practice as suggested by espoused theory does not match pragmatic practice. How many playworkers will express the need for children to have flexible environments to support their play and then practice in ways that restrict children's experience of the environment? This conflict between espoused theory and theory in use may be justified by playworkers in a number of ways, from the physical restrictions of the environment to the issue of acceptable behaviours by children in specific settings.

The mismatch between theory and practice has been investigated in a number of professional arenas. Remedies have been proposed in terms of the processes of praxis, grounded theory, the development of practical theory, discourse, mentoring and modelling of professional practice. Whichever terms are used to examine the problem, the key issue for this chapter is to find a way for playworkers to engage meaningfully with their experience of practice and to offer suggestions about how the playwork community may support the development of reflective practices.

The theories developed from Kolb's model of learning have tended to be based on a view of the mind which is sometimes described as a 'symbol processing' view. This is reflected in the work of cognitive psychologists such as Piaget who described the child as a lone scientist experimenting with the world. The mind is viewed as a 'black box' within which the individual constructs and reconstructs understandings of the world around them, using opportunities to engage with the external environment through a process of experimentation which feeds into their personal model of the world.

More recently, theorists have begun to consider a situated view of cognition that emphasizes the sociocultural processes of learning. This approach provides a rationale for the playworker in supporting children to seek further extension of their play experience. Lave and Wenger (1991) develop this idea in the arena of professional development and introduce the notion of communities of practice within which practitioners develop – first as novices who engage in legitimate peripheral practice, through to 'old timers' who provide a history and practice-based wisdom as well as the theoretical grounding for new practitioners.

This difference between the symbol processing and situated approaches to cognition may go some way to explain the difficulties which practitioners have encountered in following Schön's model of reflective practice. When he writes about reflection on action and reflection in action as being essential to expert practice he is bridging both views of the mind and may be open to criticism from either viewpoint for misunderstanding the key issues.

Schön (1983) concludes with a discussion of the role of professionals in society and, having examined the limits of reflection in action for a range of diverse professions, suggests that 'professional practitioners must discover and restructure the interpersonal theories of action which they bring to their professional lives' (p. 353). He appears to suggest that professionals need to view themselves within a context of their own professional community, which is part of wider society, rather than to conceive of themselves as individual experts concerned with their own performance regardless of the impact on others.

Reflective practice and the professions

The early 1990s saw an increase in the adoption of the concept of reflective practice in professional education and training. Much of this was a result of Schön's effort in publicizing and researching the potential for his work. For many hard-pressed professionals in education, health and social care, the notion of reflective practice appeared to provide a model for explaining the complex mix of skills and intuition applied to everyday work.

As with all models of practice, there was a tendency to reduce the complex processes described by Schön to a series of stages, which could be identified, recorded and then assessed. In the example provided by Gibbs (1988) cited earlier, professionals were eager to set out their practices in a manner which would make the complexity of the work more apparent and which could be readily understood and applied by novice practitioners.

They were also keen to find a mode of description that could be externalized and assessed. Much of the literature examining the development of reflective practice for the professions is concerned with processes that facilitate assessment of reflection on practice. This has led to a tendency to validate only those modes of reflection that can be recorded or reported to a third party (usually a tutor) by means of written communication. This is problematic for many involved in the process of recording and assessing reflective practice. Many practitioners report difficulty in written reflection, and some students who are adept at writing merely provide the tutor or assessor with the required amount of material, including reflection as required rather than as experienced. Some writers challenge the value of written material as the only means for reflecting on practice, and suggest that dialogue can be a powerful means of supporting reflection.

Good practice in fostering skills in reflective practice was reported and developed in some of the literature and included setting out the role of mentors and supervisors in supporting reflective practice. The value of reflection before action has been identified in some training situations. This would include simulations, game playing, scenario development, mental rehearsal and preparatory thinking and planning. The language used to examine reflective practice developed a distinction between reflection and reflexion, where:

- *reflection* looks at practices and experiences of action;
- *reflexion* refers to self-examination in relation to feelings and practice.

The clients, or users, of the services of professionals are also identified as relevant to examining professional practice. The description of the reflective practitioner following a learning cycle of critical reflection within the context of professional technical knowledge and action, while developing a level of professional freedom and creativity which involves and engages the client, was widely reported and promoted during the 1990s. Bines (1992), Palmer *et al.* (1994), and Yelloly and Henkel (1995) all commented on the complexity of professional practice in terms of the need to interact with clients who would bring changing dimensions to each situation.

Some writers have challenged the notion that reflective practice may be taught or assessed. They point to the apparent contradiction of setting out competence criteria for high level cognitive skills where an understanding of context and complexity are appropriate in making a judgement in relation to components such as creativity, risk taking, imagination and innovation (Dyke 1997; Ixer 1999).

In common with related professions, playwork has adopted the language and discourse of reflective practice in describing the processes of playwork. Hughes (2001) has used the term 'reflective analytic playwork' to describe an advanced form of playwork practice that relates intuitive playwork practices to current understandings of play and playwork theory. Else and Sturrock describe an approach to playwork that relies on the practitioner's ability to relate theory to practice in their involvement with the play process. They suggest that 'the playworker can be subjective about the playing child and objective about their practice' (Else and Sturrock 1998: 28).

These arguments highlight the complexity of practice and reflection in playwork and move towards accepting Schön's double loop of learning. The first loop is in reflecting on practice as it has occurred and as it is in action and the second loop examines the underpinning values and attitudes of mind and behaviour that inform practice. It is essential for playworkers to be aware of both loops in their practice so as to keep their objective review of playwork practices informed by their subjective and intuitive experience of playwork practice.

Reflective practice development at Leeds Metropolitan University

The Diploma of Higher Education in Playwork at LMU, formerly Leeds Polytechnic, enrolled a first intake of playwork students in 1989. Throughout the course development process it was recognized that the promotion of playwork practitioner skills would be essential to the success of the course. One key aspect of this highlighted by the validation panel was a concern that playwork practice did not have a sufficient profile in the course programme. The proportion of theoretical input to practice-based experience was around 9:1 in the original course document (LMU 1988).

In March 1989, an action research project funded by the National Centre for Children's Play and Recreation (NCCPR) was established to undertake practice development during the first two years of the course's operation. This project was set in the context of an agreed national programme of work for the NCCPR which included an education and training strategy to illuminate key aspects of the emerging framework for the professional development of playworkers.

The Diploma of Higher Education in Playwork at Leeds Polytechnic was the first higher education based playwork course in the country and it was felt that considerable information on the processes of teaching and learning for playworkers in higher education settings could be gained through the practice development project. The benefits of setting playwork qualifications at the same level as social work and youth & community work were also viewed as valuable to the establishment of playwork as a profession.

The primary aims of the project, as set out in the project brief, were:

- to identify and develop practice placement opportunities for students on the two-year full-time playwork diploma;
- to supervise and support practice teachers and students at these placements.

An action research methodology was applied to the project. It was judged that the two-year time-scale from the start of the project to the production of a report in August 1991 would lend itself to two full iterations of the placement process in the course. This allowed the course team to investigate approaches to supporting playwork students in their learning through practice, and preparing them for the practice experience. In addition, it allowed the course team to examine the purpose and philosophy of practice in relation to the playwork course. Recordings of stages of the project were made and learning throughout the process was compiled into a report (Palmer 1991) which contributed to the first review of the course in 1991.

The practice learning and development project set out the framework for students to undertake *experiential learning* as part of their studies on the diploma and identified learning outcomes for the process, as well as guidelines for setting up appropriate contracts with agencies offering support. Much of the material developed as part of the project is still in use on the current course and has continued to inform the course team's view of the nature of practice learning in playwork.

From the start, it was apparent that the number of agencies offering high quality playwork provision in the locality of the course (West Yorkshire) was limited. This was clearly a shortcoming in terms of the student experience as the course team's preference would be to send all students out to a perfect play setting near to the university where they would be expertly supported and supervised by skilled and experienced playworkers. There was also the further issue of differential experiences, in that some students would be placed with fine examples and others would be expected to make the most of the agency they were based at. Given the issues that this raised in terms of the quality of individual experience in the practice period, and the potential for success at different agencies, it was decided to develop an experiential learning system which did not require high quality playwork provision at the agency involved. All that was expected was 'good enough' playwork practice – defined by the course team as being an agency where playwork practice by students would be encouraged and supported.

A number of different modes for the practice learning experience were considered, and it was finally agreed that the most effective means for enabling students to benefit from experiential learning would be to offer a ten-week block in each of the first two years of the full-time course. This meant that a 'good enough' agency would still allow sufficient time for the student to engage with playwork practice and for the agency to accommodate playwork practices and philosophy.

Experiential learning now accounts for 40 per cent of the existing course in terms of block practice. In addition, students are encouraged to undertake contact work with playwork agencies on either a paid or voluntary basis as part of their studies. This provides a foundation for discourse related to current playwork practices that takes place during university-based sessions.

The decision to maximize the experience from practice in terms of the student/university experience and input, rather than the quality of the agency/supervisor input, had two key 'knock on' effects for the playwork team. First in terms of reframing the practice experience as experiential learning undertaken at a distance from the university, and second in the adoption of a reflective practitioner framework to describe the process of learning through practice.

Experiential learning not placement

The term 'experiential learning' was adopted rather than 'practice placement'. This contrasted with other professional courses at the time (e.g. youth & community work and social work). On those courses, students undertook a period of work-based learning as part of their professional development programme, carrying out projects defined by the host agency. The usual practice would include supervision by a practitioner based at the agency who would take responsibility for student learning throughout the placement. It is still common practice for social work courses to pay for the services of practice teachers and to establish partnerships for the provision of practice teaching. The professional body for social work has been key in supporting this work by providing financial support to the pay salaries of practice teachers based with voluntary sector agencies. This additional funding has resulted in an expectation that students' practice placements would be funded through the institutions involved. The playwork course was never in a position to pay for placement and so the definition of experiential learning has helped in setting out a different contract with agencies.

The shift away from the agency as the most important aspect of the process, and the focus on the university as central to the learning to be undertaken during practice redefined the nature of practice learning for the playwork course. This meant that contracts for experiential learning focused the responsibility for student learning during practice with the playwork team at LMU, rather than with the agency. The host agency was therefore released from the requirement to provide teaching during practice and was expected only to provide an environment within which a student could undertake playwork practices that could lead to the learning specified by the university. This led to an increase in the number of agencies willing to take playwork students.

The process of identifying what students would learn through experiential learning was achieved by specifying the work to be undertaken during experiential learning. A set of assignment briefs were developed which provided students with the opportunity to demonstrate outcomes from their experiential learning which were both focused in terms of specific work and flexible in allowing students to negotiate a piece of work which would record their experience as playworkers. Specifically, assessments take the form of two short pieces plus a longer (4000 word) project. In the first year, the two short pieces consist of an agency study plus a description of playwork practice with children. In the second year there is a teamwork profile of people in the agency, plus a rationale for playwork development at the agency. In each year, the project is negotiated between student, agency and university. Typically a first-year project would consist of descriptions of playwork practices at the agency set in the context of current play and playwork theory, while a second-year project would include consideration of the implications for the development of playwork practices and research.

Reflective practice and practice learning

Reflective practice was identified as an overt aim for the period of experiential learning. The playwork course team at LMU believed that it was essential that students should take responsibility for their own learning during their time away from the university. This was specifically supported by the design of the reflective diary. Throughout the period of experiential learning students are expected to maintain a reflective diary. This has to include recordings of what happened each day plus notes on how the student feels about the experience and the work of the agency. Each week a summary is made and this includes notes on issues to examine in the coming week (looking back to look forwards). At the end of the experience students are required to complete a self-assessment based on a series of headings which examine such things as teamwork, relating theory to practice, etc. Students are expected to cross-reference responses in the self-assessment to the reflective diary. The visiting tutor from the university and the supporting supervisor based at the agency use the same set of headings to provide feedback on the student's practice. The playwork team at the university pick up any serious mismatch between student/agency/university perceptions.

By identifying reflective practice as an essential characteristic of the playwork practitioner the course team moved on to define the learning outcomes related to reflective practice in the course. An introduction to the concept of reflective practice as outlined by Schön (1983) is embedded in the teaching of the course. Specific input preparing students for experiential learning and reflecting on practice makes use of reflective practice concepts. The playwork team has an awareness of the nature of reflective practices and seeks out opportunities to model reflective practice with students where possible. This may take the form of reflecting on their own experiences as playwork practitioners, or their approach to managing the course on a day-to-day basis.

From 1991 to 2001

The annual process of sending students out on experiential learning is still a key element of the playwork diploma. The system of assignments, preparation and assessment of experiential learning has not changed substantially. The annual review process and discussion with past students has highlighted five themes relevant to the development and support of reflective practice.

Recording issues
Many students initially report difficulties in keeping the reflective diary, others find the invitation to reflect on their experiences an interesting and challenging process. Difficulties often include problems in identifying events that may form the basis for learning about practice. The question of recording for recording's sake is often raised in the debate to identify what makes a good set of notes. The value of having a contemporaneous record of what happened is clear when students discuss the diary, particularly at a later date when memory can play games with time and the sequencing of events. It is clear from discussion with playworkers who have developed the skill of keeping reflective recordings that this approach to developing practice is a valued element of playwork.

Learning to reflect
The suggestion that reflection in action is not easy to report, and sometimes happens too quickly to recall, is often offered as a reason for limited reflection in the diary. Some students find it difficult to recognize reflection, particularly 'intuitive' workers who feel that some sort of balance could be upset if they think too much about what they are doing.

For some, the process of developing reflective practice can be a very disturbing experience, particularly in terms of life-changing events such as embarking on a degree and being asked to review previous attitudes and values.

Relating practice to theory
The expectation that theories should be in mind when recording the reflective diary is often raised as an unreasonable requirement. For many novice playworkers, trying to juggle theory, practice experience, self and others is a complex and difficult process. Just like learning to drive, it takes time for some parts of playwork practice and theory to become embedded. However, as already discussed, it is essential that playworkers ensure that their espoused theories and theories in use do not become disengaged. A return to theory and practice through a reflective diary is a good self-checking mechanism.

Sharing the record
The potential for shared perspectives and reflection through the use of a group diary for expressing reflective practice in a team setting is often

overlooked. My own experience of learning to reflect on practice began with a group diary held at a playwork project which was contributed to by all the workers on a daily basis.

Personal reflection
For many students, the personal nature of recordings can conflict with the process of assessment at LMU. Some people feel uncomfortable writing deeply personal reflections of their experience in practice. When working in difficult or extreme situations, playworkers can have emotional experiences to record. Ethical issues in relation to sharing such recordings should always be considered.

Developing and supporting reflective practice for playworkers

Four interlinked components can be identified in providing a supportive environment for the development of reflective practice in playwork. First there is a need to define the playwork community of practice, including children, new and experienced practitioners and others with a contribution to make. Second, this needs to be underpinned by a consideration of the nature of discourse in the playwork field – how do we talk about practice and is our talk encouraging of reflection and development in practice? Third, an examination of the skills and techniques that support reflection provides a 'tool-kit' for reflective practice. Finally we need to ensure that our reflective practices are closely linked to the values and beliefs held by playwork as a profession and that our processes of reflective practice feed into the discourse of the playwork community of practice.

How do we define the playwork community of practice?

The nature of the learning process for playworkers in the university setting can be described as a process of legitimate peripheral participation. They are learning how to behave and talk as members of the playwork community of practice. This concept of a practice community can be applied to the experience of all playworkers, whether involved in a specific playwork course or defined as playworkers by their employment or practices.

In this community of practice, novices have access to 'old-timers' as well as contemporaries providing rich grounds for the development of theory and understanding of the processes of playwork practice. Children are an essential part of the community of playwork practice. They contribute to the investigation of how best to support their play experiences. Membership of the community of practice includes academics, researchers and skilled practitioners. They all contribute to discourse on grounded theory and the identification of future research in a climate of mutual respect and support.

There is no reason why the playwork community of practice should be bounded by one physical space. The physical settings for the community include playwork agencies, training settings, people's front rooms, lecture rooms, cyberspace and e-mail. In fact, anywhere where playworkers can contact each other to engage in debate about practice. One of the early concerns of the playwork course team was the lack of contact with playworkers across the UK. This has changed in recent years with the expansion of activity on the internet and in particular with the growth in use of playwork-based discussion groups via e-mail.

Discourse in the community of practice

Everyone has some experience to offer to the discourse of the community. The value of narrative and storytelling has been highlighted through the experience of the playwork course at LMU. We have found that offering the opportunity for students to share their experiences from playwork practice and to 'tell the story' enables the group to develop a coherent view of quality practice in playwork. Stories do not need to be long to be effective, but they do allow the teller to gain insights into the experience through the process of telling the story. The process also allows others to share the experience and to engage in reflection before action and reflection on action.

The opportunity to reflect on practice and to model reflection on action with groups is also an important aspect of the teaching approach offered in the LMU course. The teaching team take the opportunity, when appropriate, to reflect on their past practice and their current practices as part of the process of discourse. It is often disturbing for students when staff appear to disagree in front of the student group, but this approach to discourse is viewed as valuable to the health of the playwork course and to the playwork team. Discourse in playwork is by its nature contentious. There are many disagreements in the playwork field about the best way to describe and justify playwork practice. The theoretical base is full of contested theories and unproven assertions. It is therefore essential that the nature of debate and discourse in playwork continues to reflect this diversity of opinion. Learning to talk as a playworker about practice involves a process of learning to deal with the uncertainties and complexities that affect practice rather than seeking out a set of 'true' statements that underpin practice.

The processes of reflecting on practice and asking questions about current research findings and assertions about playwork should become part of the playworker's everyday work. Our discourse should reflect the values of playwork and relate to the uncertainties inherent in work with children in playwork settings.

The opportunities for sharing discourse about practice are not limited to the written word applied to e-mail or papers submitted for publication. Playworkers value the opportunity to meet and share ideas about practice. We should also begin to consider the potential of different media for sharing ideas and discourse while valuing the opportunity to meet at conferences and other events to promote discussion of playwork practice and values.

One final thought on the nature of discourse into practice: critique is not always negative or destructive. There is a tendency to approach the statements of others with a critical view that may be taken as a negative. For this reason, many playworkers are reluctant to put pen to paper or to offer their thoughts, for fear of being shouted down or identified as lacking in rigour. We need to move away from this defensive approach to discourse in playwork, and to encourage as wide a range of opinions and viewpoints as possible within the discourse. It is only by responding to the critics that we will be able to develop robust arguments for playwork practice which are relevant to current practices in playwork. We do not need a set of clichés to describe our work; we need statements about playwork practice which are a true reflection of the relationship between practice and current theory.

A tool-kit for reflective practice

The key techniques and approaches for developing and supporting reflective practice and enquiry in playwork have already been examined. To summarize, the following tools are of value in developing skills as a reflective practitioner.

Diaries or logbooks
These may be individual or group-based recordings. Some practitioners prefer a structured approach to recordings and use a series of headings or even different sections in the diary. The most effective diaries offer the opportunity for the practitioner to recall events and record them at the time, then to review the experience in terms of seeking out patterns or essential characteristics. This is followed by the opportunity to reflect on what findings from the diary may mean for current and future practice.

Reflecting before action
The value of a range of activities including games, simulations and role playing in preparing playworkers for practice is recognized by many training providers. The opportunity to step into difficult situations in a simulation exercise, or to imagine the worst possible scenario, provides good grounding in preparing for practice and developing practitioners' skills for situations where the time for reflection in action may be limited.

Reflective dialogue with self
This is a little different from talking to yourself. This allows the worker to engage in an internal dialogue about experiences in practice and may be most valuable for people who are not fully comfortable with recording their experiences in writing. Alternative approaches could include the use of a Dictaphone or video diary.

Telling the story
Taking the opportunity to tell or invent stories which give insights into practice is a further valuable approach to recording and sharing reflective

practice in playwork. Playworkers need to feel comfortable learning from each other's stories and reflections as well as their own.

Linking reflective practice to values and action

To return to Schön's (1983) assertion that our beliefs are implicit in our actions, it is apparent that any process of reflective practice needs to complete the loop, making our practices reflect on, and inform, our espoused theories. For playworkers, this must mean that children become part of the feedback process for practice. Children's experience of our playwork practices and the opportunity for us to reflect on their feedback are an essential part of theorizing practice and ensuring that practices are linked to the values of playwork. Playworkers are skilled at listening to children and any development of reflective practice needs to ensure that the child's view of playwork practices is included.

Conclusion

The notion that reflective practice cannot be taught and is something that some people either have or do not have has been a recurrent theme in the experience of developing reflective practitioners. This chapter has offered a framework for considering the essential climate for the support and development of reflective practice across the whole of the playwork profession. It is not something that is the property of those who have studied at a university, or those who were born as great playworkers, or those who have worked in playwork for many years. Reflective practice belongs to the whole of the playwork community. We should all value and seek to promote reflective practices through our interactions as playworkers, by talking reflectively, applying the tools of reflective practice to our own work and sharing with others the stories which promote and develop good practice in the profession – most of all, by sharing with children our values and reflective practices to improve the play environment for everyone.

Bibliography

Abernethy, D. (1968) *Playleadership*. London: NPFA.

Abernethy, D. (1973) *Playgrounds*. London: NPFA.

Adler, G. (1989) *The Dynamics of the Self*. Boston, MA: Coventure.

Alderson, P. (1995) *Listening to Children: Children, Ethics and Social Research*. Ilford: Barnardo's.

Allen of Hurtwood, Lady (1968) *Planning for Play*. London: Thames & Hudson.

Axline, V. (1969) *Play Therapy*, revised edn. New York: Ballantine Books.

Axline, V. (1976) *Dibs: in Search of Self*. Harmondsworth: Penguin.

Bailey, V. (1978) *Leisure and Class in Victorian England*. London: Routledge.

Bailey, V. (1987) *Delinquency and Citizenship 1914–1948*. Oxford: Clarendon.

Balbernie, R. (1999) Infant mental health, *Young Minds Magazine*, 39: 17–18.

Bamberg, M. (1983) Metaphor and play interaction in young children, in F. Manning (ed.) *The World of Play*. New York: Leisure Press.

Bandura, A.L. (1962) Social learning through imitation, in M.R. Jones (ed.) *Nebraska Symposium on Motivation*. Chicago: University of Chicago Press.

Barthes, R. (1993) *Camera Lucida*. London: Vintage.

Bateson, G. (1955) A theory of play and fantasy, *Psychiatric Research Reports*, 2: 39–51.

Bateson, P.P.G. and Hinde, R.A. (1976) *Growing Points in Ethology*. Cambridge: Cambridge University Press.

Battram, A. (1998) *Navigating Complexity*. London: The Industrial Society.

BBC (1998) *Horizon: Beyond a Joke*. London: British Broadcasting Corporation.

Beacock, D.A. (1943) *The Play Way in English for Today*. London: Nelson.

Becker, H. and Geer, B. (1957) Participant observation and interviewing: a comparison, *Human Organisation*, 16(3): 28–35.

Bell, J. (1993) *Doing your Research Project*, 2nd edn. Buckingham: Open University Press.

Bengtsson, A. (1974) *The Child's Right to Play*. Sheffield: International Playground Association.

Benjamin, J. (1974) *Grounds for Play: An Extension of In Search of Adventure*. London: Square Press of the National Council for Social Service.

Bennett, E.L., Diamond, M.C., Krech, D. and Rosenzweig, M.R. (1964) Chemical and anatomical plasticity of brain, *Science*, 146.

Berlyne, D.E. (1960) *Conflict, Arousal and Curiosity*. New York: McGraw-Hill.

Bines, H. (1992) Issues in course design, in H. Bines and D. Watson (eds) *Developing Professional Education*. Buckingham: SRHE & Open University Press.

Board of Education (1912) *Report of the Departmental Committee Appointed to Inquire Into Certain Questions in Connexion with the Playgrounds of Public Elementary Schools*, Cd. 6463. London: HMSO.

Bonel, P. and Lindon, J. (1996) *Good Practice in Playwork*. Cheltenham: Stanley Thornes.

Borgia, G. and Presgraves, D. (1998) Coevolution of elaborated male display traits in the spotted bower bird: an experimental test of the threat reduction hypothesis, *Animal Behaviour*, 56: 1121–8.

Box, S. (1983) *Power, Crime and Mystification*. London: Tavistock.

Bray, R.A. (1907) *The Town Child*. London: Fisher Unwin.

Breakwell, G.M., Hammond, S. and Fife-Schaw, C. (2000) *Research Methods in Psychology*. London: Sage.

Bright, B. (1996) Reflecting on reflective practice, *Studies in the Education of Adults*, 28(2): 162–84.

Brown, F. (1989) *Working with Children: A Playwork Training Pack*. Leeds: Children First.

Brown, F. (1990) *School Playgrounds*. London: NPFA.

Brown, F. (2000a) Compound flexibility: SPICE revisited. *Proceedings of 2nd Theoretical Playwork conference, 'New Playwork, New Thinking?'*, Ely, Play Education, 21–22 March.

Brown, F. (2000b) Play value research project. *Proceedings of 2nd Theoretical Playwork Conference, 'New Playwork, New Thinking?'*, Ely, Play Education, 21–22 March.

Brown, F. (2002) An evaluation of the concept of play value and its application to children's fixed equipment playgrounds. Unpublished PhD thesis, Leeds Metropolitan University.

Brown, F. and Webb, S. (2002) Playwork: an attempt at definition, *Play Action*, Spring.

Brown, J.G. and Burger, C. (1984) Playground design and preschool children's behaviours. *Environment and Behaviour*, 16(5): 599–626.

Brown, S.L. (1998) Play as an organising principle: clinical evidence and personal observations, in M. Bekoff and J.A. Byers (eds) *Animal Play: Evolutionary, Comparative and Ethological Perspectives*. Cambridge: Cambridge University Press.

Brown, S.L. and Lomax, J. (1969) A pilot study of young murderers, *Hogg Foundation Annual Report*. Austin, TX: Hogg Foundation.

Bruce, T. (1989) *Time to Play in Early Childhood Education*. London: Hodder & Stoughton.

Bruner, J. (1972) Nature and uses of immaturity, in J.S. Bruner, A. Jolly and K. Sylva (eds) (1976) *Play: Its Role in Development and Evolution*. Harmondsworth: Penguin.

Bruner, J.S. *et al.* (1976) *Play: Its Role in Development and Evolution*. Harmondsworth: Penguin.

Bruner, J.S. (1996) *The Culture of Education*. London: Harvard University Press.

Burrell, G. and Morgan, G. (1979) *Sociological Paradigms and Organisational Analysis: Elements of the Sociology of Corporate Life*. Aldershot: Gower.

Campbell, B. (1993) *Goliath – Britain's Dangerous Places*. London: Methuen.

Campbell, J. (1991) *The Masks of God, vol. 1: Primitive Mythology*. London: Arkana.

Campbell, J.M. (1917) *The Report on the Physical Welfare of Mothers and Children in England and Wales*. Dunfermline: Carnegie Trust.

Capacchione, L. (1991) *Recovery of Your Inner Child*. New York: Simon & Schuster.

Carter, R., Martin, J., Mayblin, B. and Munday, M. (1984) *Systems Management and Change: A Graphic Guide*. London: Harper & Row.

CCRPT (Central Council of Recreative Physical Training) (1937) *Playleadership*. London: CCRPT.

Chandler, P. (2000) Playing with words, *Leisure Manager*, January: 16–17.

Charon, J. (1995) *Symbolic Interactionism: An Introduction, and Interpretation, an Integration*, 5th edn. Englewood Cliffs, NJ: Prentice Hall.

Chatzman, L. and Strauss, A.L. (1973) *Field Research*. Englewood Cliffs, NJ: Prentice Hall.

Checkland, P. and Scholes, J. (1990) *Soft Systems Methodology in Action*. Chichester: Wiley.

Chilton, T. (1985) *Children's Play in Newcastle upon Tyne*. London: NPFA.

Chugani, H.T. (1995) Infantile spasms, *Current Opinion in Neurology*, 2: 139–44.

Chugani, H.T. and Conti, J.R. (1996a) Etiologic classification of infantile spasms in 140 cases: role of positron emission tomography, *Journal of Child Neurology*, 11(1): 44–8.

Chugani, H.T. (1996b) A second chance for Christian, *The Detroit News*, 9 February.

Chugani, H.T. (1998) *BBC News*, 20 April.

Chugani, H.T., Da Silva, E. and Chugani, D.C. (1996a) Infantile spasms, III: prognostic implications of bitemporal hypometabolism on positron emission tomography, *Annals of Neurology*, 39(5): 643–9.

Chugani, H.T., Muller, R.A. and Chugani, D.C. (1996b) Functional brain reorganisation in children, *Brain Development*, 18(5): 347–56.

Clutton-Brock, T. and Harvey, P. (eds) (1978) *Readings in Sociobiology*. San Francisco: W.H. Freeman.

Cobb, E. (1993) *The Ecology of Imagination in Childhood*. Dallas, TX: Spring Publications.

Conway, M. and Farley, T. (2001) *Quality in Play – Quality Assurance for Play Providers*. London: London Play.

Cook, H.C. (1919) *The Play Way: An Essay in Educational Method*. London: William Heinemann.

Cornford, L.C. (undated) The children's hour, in R.H. Caine (ed.) *Children's Hour: An Anthology of Poems and Sketches by Leading Authors*. London: CHEA.

Corsaro, W. (1985) *Friendship and Peer Culture in the Early Years*. Norwood, NJ: Ablex.

CPC (Children's Play Council) (2001) *State of Play*. London: CPC.

Cranwell, K. (2001a) Street play and organised space for children and young people in London (1860–1920), in R. Gilchrist *et al.* (eds) *Essays in the History of Community and Youth Work in Leicester*. Leicester: Youth Work Trust.

Cranwell, K. (2001b) Church Sunday schools, treats and country holidays (1888–1912). Unpublished paper given at the *2nd History of Community and Youth Work Conference*, Durham University.

Cross, G. (1990) *A Social History of Leisure Since 1600*. Pensylvannia: Venture Press.

Crowe B. (1983) *Play is a Feeling*. New York: Allen & Unwin.

Csikszentmihalyi, M. (1975) *Beyond Boredom and Anxiety: The Experience of Play in Work and Games*. San Francisco: Jossey-Bass.

Csikszentmihalyi, M. (1979) Some paradoxes in the definition of play, in A. Cheska Taylor (ed.) *Play as Context*. New York: Leisure Press.

Csikszentmihalyi, M. (1992) *Flow, the Psychology of Happiness*. London: Rider.

cummings, e.e. (1977) maggie and milly and molly and may, in M. Harrison and C. Stuart-Clarke (eds) *The New Dragon Book of Verse*. Oxford: Oxford University Press.

Damasio, A.R. (1995) *Descartes' Error: Emotion, Reason and the Human Brain*. London: Picador.

Darley, G. (1990) *Octavia Hill*. London: Constable.

Davis, M. and Wallbridge, D. (1981) *Boundary and Space: An Introduction to the Work of D.W. Winnicott*. London: H. Karnac Books Ltd.

Davy, A. (1995) *Playwork*. Basingstoke: Macmillan.

de Bono, E. (1992) *Serious Creativity*. London: HarperCollins.

de Bono, E. (1994) *Parallel Thinking*. London: Viking.

Denscombe, M. (1998) *The Good Research Guide*. Buckingham: Open University Press.

Denzin, N.K. (1978) *The Research Act: A Theoretical Introduction to Sociological Methods*, 2nd edn. New York, McGraw-Hill.

Denzin, N.K. (1982) The paradoxes of play, in J. Loy (ed.) *The Paradoxes of Play*. New York: Leisure Press.

Department of Health (1998) *Our Healthier Nation*. London: HMSO.

DETR (Department of the Environment, Transport and the Regions) (2001) Best value site. http://www.local-regions.detr.gov.uk/bestvalue/bvindex.htm, updated 25 May 2001, accessed 26 August 2001.

Dewey, J. and Bentley, A. (1949) *Knowing and the Known*. Boston, MA: Beacon Press.

DfE (Department for Education) (1994) *The Code of Practice on the Identification and Assessment of Special Educational Needs*. London: HMSO.

DfEE (Department for Education and Employment) (1999) *Networks and Networking: A Guide for Providers of Childcare and Early Years Education: a DfEE Good Practice Guide*. London: HMSO.

Dockar-Drysdale, B. (1968) *Therapy in Child Care*. London: Longmans.

Donaldson, O.F. (1993) *Playing By Heart*. Deerfield Beach, FL: Health Communications Inc.

Dyke, M. (1997) Reflective learning as reflexive education in a risk society: empowerment and control, *International Journal of Lifelong Education*, 16(1): 2–17.

Eibl-Eiblesfeldt, I. (1967) Concepts of ethology and their significance in the study of human behaviour, in W. Stevenson and H. Rheingold (eds) *Early Behaviour: Comparative and Developmental Approaches*. New York: Wiley.

Einon, D.F., Morgan, M.J. and Kibbler, C.C. (1978) Brief period of socialisation and later behaviour in the rat, *Developmental Psychobiology*, 11(3).

Eliade, M. (1974) *The Myth of the Eternal Return: Or Cosmos and History*, trans. W.R. Trask. Princeton, NJ: Princeton University Press.

Eliade, M. (1989) *Shamanism: Archaic Techniques of Ecstasy*, trans. W.R. Trask. Arkana: Penguin Books.

Ellis, M.J. (1973) *Why People Play*. Englewood Cliffs, NJ: Prentice Hall.

Else, P. (1999) Seeing the whole picture: playwork content in the playwork curriculum, key note speech, in *JNCTP General Meeting Report*, 10 June. London: JNCTP.

Else, P. (2001) Adventure playgrounds: special places for special people. Presentation for the 'Spirit of Adventure Play' seminar, Abergele, Play Wales, 17–18 May.

Else, P. and Sturrock, G. (1998) The playground as therapeutic space: playwork as healing. *Proceedings of the IPA/USA Triennial National Conference, Play in a Changing Society: Research, Design, Application*. London: IPA.

Eraut, M. (1994) *Developing Professional Knowledge and Competence*. Lewes: Falmer Press.

Erikson, E. (1951) *Childhood and Society*. Imago: USA.

Fagen, R. (1981) *Animal Play Behaviour*. New York: Oxford University Press.

Ferchmin, A. and Eterovic, V.A. (1979) Mechanisms of brain growth by environmental stimulation, *Science*, 205(3): 522.

FPFC (Fair Play for Children) (2001) Adventure playgrounds, *Play Action, Childhood Under Threat*, Spring Issue.

Freud, S. (1990) *Studies on Hysteria*, vol. 3. London: Pelican.

Froebel, F. (1826) *The Education of Man*. New York: Appleton.

Fromm, E. (1993) *The Art of Being*. London: Constable.

Frost, J.L. and Jacobs, J. (1995) Play deprivation: a factor in juvenile violence, *Dimensions*, 3(3): 6–9.

Gardiner, D. (1937) *Play Centres*. London: Methuen.

Garvey, C. (1991) *Play*, 2nd edn. London: Fontana.

Gibbs, G. (1988) *Learning by Doing: A Guide to Teaching and Learning Methods*. London: Further Education Unit.

Gold, R. (1969) Roles in sociological field observation, in G. McCall and J. Symonds (eds) *Issues in Participant Observation: A Text and Reader*. London: Addison Wesley.

Goldberg, A. (1982) Play and ritual in Haitian voodoo shows for tourists, in J. Loy (ed.) *The Paradoxes of Play*. New York: Leisure Press.

Gould, S.J. (1996) *Full House: The Spread of Excellence from Plato to Darwin*. New York: Harmony Books.

Graue, M.E. and Walsh, J.D. (1998) *Studying Children in Context: Theories, Methods, and Ethics*. London: Sage.

Greig, A. and Taylor, J. (1999) *Doing Research with Children*. London: Sage.

Grof, S. (1975) *Realms of the Human Unconscious*. New York: Viking.

Groos, C. (1901) *The Play of Man*, trans. E.L. Baldwin. New York: D. Appleton & Co.

Guilbaud, S. (1997) A role for playwork in helping children with autism to interact with others. Unpublished undergraduate dissertation, Leeds Metropolitan University.

Gunner, M. (1998) Stress and brain development. Presentation to the Michigan Association of Infant Mental Health's 22nd Annual Conference.

Hall, G.S. (1904) *Adolescence: Its Psychology and its Relations to Physiology, Anthropology, Sociology, Sex, Crime, Religion and Education*, vol. 1. New York: Appleton.

Hammersley, M. (1992) *What's Wrong with Ethnography: Methodological Explorations*. London: Routledge.

Harlow, H.F. and Harlow, M.K. (1962) The effect of rearing conditions on behaviour, *Bulletin of the Menninger Clinic*, 26: 213–24.

Harlow, H.F. and Suomi, S.J. (1971) Social recovery by isolation-reared monkeys, *Proceedings of the National Academy of Sciences USA*, 68(7): 1534–8.

Hart, R. (1995) The right to play and children's participation, in H. Shier (ed.) *Article 31 Action Pack: Children's Rights and Children's Play*. Birmingham: Play Train.

Hasler, J. (1995) Belonging and becoming – the child growing up in community, in P. Henderson (ed.) *Children and Communities*. London: Pluto.

Heather-Bigg, A. (1890) Evenings of amusement, in W. Bousefield (ed.) *Elementary Schools: How to Increase their Utility*. London: Percival.

Helanko, R.V.M. (1956) *Theoretical Aspects of Play and Socialisation*. Turku, Finland: Turn Yliopiston Kustantama.

Heseltine, P. (ed.) (1978–84) various articles in *Play Times*. London: NPFA.

Heseltine, P. (1998) Introductory presentation by RoSPA's playground safety officer to the ILAM training seminar '*Inspecting Children's Playgrounds*', Liverpool, September.

Heseltine, P. and Holborn, J. (1987) *Playgrounds*. London: Mitchell Publishing.

Hickey, E.W. (1991) *Serial Murderers and their Victims*. Pacific Grove, CA: Brooks Publishing.

Hillman, J. (1977) *Re-visioning Psychology*. New York: Harper Perennial Library.

Hillman, J. (1992) *The Myth of Analysis: Three Essays in Archetypal Psychology*. New York: Harper Perennial Library.

Hinde, R. (1982) *Ethology: Its Nature and Relations with Other Sciences*. Glasgow: Fontana.

Hoffman, E. (1992) *Visions of Innocence: Spiritual and Inspirational Experiences of Childhood*. Boston, MA: Shambhala.

Hooff, J.A.R.A.M. van (1972) A comparative approach of phylogeny of laughter and smiling, in J.S. Bruner, A. Jolly and K. Sylva (eds) (1976) *Play: Its Role in Development and Evolution*. Harmondsworth: Penguin.

Hoyles, M. (1991) *The Story of Gardening*. London: Journeyman Press.

Hughes, B. (1975) *Notes for Adventure Playworkers*. London: Children and Youth Action Group.

Hughes, B. (1982) *Play and Playwork: A Definition by Synthesis*. Ely: PlayEducation.

Hughes, B. (1988) Play and the environment, *Leisure Manager*, 6(1): 15–23.

Hughes, B. (1990) Built environmental effects on instinctive and intuitive play outcomes – some ideas, in *Proceedings of the 11th IPA World Conference*. Tokyo: IPA.

Hughes, B. (1996a) *Play Environments: A Question of Quality*. London: PLAYLINK.

Hughes, B. (1996b) *A Playworker's Taxonomy of Play Types*. London: PLAYLINK.

Hughes, B. (1997) Towards a technology of playwork, in *Proceedings of PLAYLINK/ Portsmouth City Council Conference*. Portsmouth: PLAYLINK.

Hughes, B. (1998) Playwork in extremis – the RAP approach, in *Proceedings of Childhood and Youth Studies Conference: 'Towards an Interdisciplinary Framework'*. Cambridge: Anglia Polytechnic University & DfEE.

Hughes, B. (1999) Hackney play association design and build project – an evaluation. Unpublished report. London: Hackney Play Association.

Hughes, B. (2000) A dark and evil cul-de-sac: has children's play in urban Belfast been adulterated by the troubles? Unpublished MA dissertation, Anglia Polytechnic University.

Hughes, B. (2001) *Evolutionary Playwork and Reflective Analytic Practice*. London: Routledge.

Hughes, B. and Williams, H. (1982) Talking about play 1–5, *Play Times*, 31–5.

Huizinga, J. (1955) *Homo Ludens*. Boston, MA: The Beacon Press.

Hutt, S.J., Tyler, S., Hutt, C. and Christopherson, H. (1989) *Play Exploration and Learning: A Natural History of the Pre-school*. London: Routledge.

Huttenlocher, P.R. (1990) Morphometric study of human cerebral cortex development, *Neuropsychologia*, 28(6): 517–27.

Huttenlocher, P.R. (1992) Neural plasticity, in A.K. Asbury, G.M. McKhann and W.I. McDonald (eds) *Diseases of the Nervous System*. London: W.B. Saunders.

Huttenmoser, M. and Degan-Zimmermann, D. (1995) *Lebenstraume fur Kinder*. Zurich: Swiss Science Foundation.

Ixer, G. (1999) There's no such thing as reflection, *British Journal of Social Work*, 29(4): 513–27.

Jennings, S. (1995) Playing for real, *International Play Journal*, 3(2): 132–41.

Johnsen, E.P. and Christie, J.F. (1984) Play and social cognition, in B. Sutton-Smith and D. Kelly-Byrne (eds) *The Masks of Play*. New York: Leisure Press.

Johnson, R. (1993) Enhancing early play experiences through observational techniques, *International Play Journal*, 1(2): 132–41.

Josephs, J. (1993) *Hungerford: One Man's Massacre*. London: Smith Gryphon Publishers.

Jung, C.G. ([1967] 1983) *Memories, Dreams, Reflections*. London: Flamingo.

Kelly, D. (ed.) (1989) *Deviant Behaviour: A Text-reader in the Sociology of Deviance*, 3rd edn, New York: St Martins Press.

Kelly-Byrne, D. (1983) A narrative of play and intimacy, in F. Manning (ed.) *The World of Play*. New York: Leisure Press.

King, M. (2001) Social inclusion. Presentation for the 'Spirit of Adventure Play' seminar, Abergele, Play Wales, 17–18 May.

Klein, M. (1955) The psychoanalytical play technique, *American Journal of Orthopsychiatry*. 55.

Kolb, D. (1984) *Experiential Learning: Experience as the Source of Learning and Development*. London: Prentice Hall.

Konner, M. (1991) *Childhood: A Multicultural View*. Boston, MA: Little, Brown & Co.

Lacey, C. (1976) Problems of sociological fieldwork: a review of the methodology of 'Hightown Grammar', in M. Shipman (ed.) *The Organisation and Impact of Social Research: Six Original Case Studies in Education and Behavioural Science*. London: Routledge & Kegan Paul.

Langs, R. and Badalementi, A. (1996) *The Cosmic Circle*. New York: Alliance Publishing Inc.

Laplanche, J. and Pontalis, J.B. (1988) *The Language of Psychoanalysis*, trans. D. Nicholson-Smith. London: Karnac Books.

Laquer, T. (1976) *Religion and Respectability*. London: Yale University Press.

Lash, J. (1990) *The Seekers Handbook*. New York: Harmony Books.

Lave, J. and Wenger, E. (1991) *Situated Learning: Legitimate Peripheral Participation*. Cambridge: Cambridge University Press.

LCC (London County Council) (1911) *Annual Report*. London: LCC.

LCC (London County Council) (1930) *General Purposes Subcommittee Minutes*. London: LCC.

Lewis, J. (1991) *Women and Social Action in Victorian and Edwardian England*. Stanford, CA: Stanford University Press.

LMU (Leeds Metropolitan University) (1988) *DipHE in Playwork: Internal Course Documentation*. Leeds: LMU.

LMU (Leeds Metropolitan University) (2000) *BA (Hons) Playwork: Internal Course Documentation*. Leeds: LMU.

Loizos, C. (1967) Play behaviour in higher primates: a review, in D. Morris (ed.) *Primate Ethology*. Chicago: Aldine.

Lorenz, K. (1954) *Man Meets Dog*. London: Methuen.

Lorenz, K. (1961) *King Solomon's Ring*. London: Methuen.

Lorenz, K. (1970) *Studies in Animal and Human Behaviour*, vol. 1. London: Methuen.

Luria, A.R. (1979) *The Making of a Mind*. Cambridge MA: Harvard University Press.

Magnard, M. (1989) *Sociology in Focus*. London: Longman.

Marshall, C. and Rossman, G. (1995) *Designing Qualitative Research*, 2nd edn. London: Sage.

Mary Ward Centre (undated) Uncatalogued material relating to Passmore Edwards Settlement.

Maslow, A. (1971) *The Farther Reaches of Human Nature*. New York: Viking Press.

McEwen, B.S. (1999) Stress and hippocampal plasticity, *Annual Review of the Neurosciences*, 22: 105–22.

McIntosh, C. *et al.* (1957) *Landmarks in the History of Physical Education*. London: Routledge & Kegan Paul.

MacMahon, L. (1992) *The Handbook of Play Therapy*. London: Routledge.

Meares, R. (1993) *The Metaphor of Play: Disruption and Restoration in the Borderline Experience*. Northvale, NJ: Aronson Inc.

Melville, S. (1999) Creating spaces for adventure, *Built Environment*, 25(1): 71–4.

Miller, A. (1995) *Picture of a Childhood*. London: Virago.

Miller, S. (1973) Ends, means and gallumphing: some lit motifs of play, *American Anthropologist*, 78.

Milne, A.A. (1977) *Classic Stories from Winnie the Pooh*. London: Methuen.

Mitchell, J. (1986) *The Selected Melanie Klein*. Harmondsworth: Penguin.

Moon, J. (1999) *Reflection in Learning and Professional Development – Theory and Practice.* London: Kogan Page.

Moore, R.C. (1990) *Childhood's Domain: Play and Place in Child Development.* Berkley, CA: Mig Communications.

Moreton, C. (2000) The children who forget their names, *Independent on Sunday*, 24 December.

Moser, C.A. and Kalton, G. (1971) *Survey Methods in Social Investigation*, 2nd edn. London: Heinemann.

Moyles, J.R. (1989) *Just Playing? The Role and Status of Play in Early School Education.* Milton Keynes: Open University Press.

MPGA (Metropolitan Public Gardens Association) (1887–1900) *Annual Reports.* London: MPGA.

Nachman, S. (1979) Social play on Nissan: the magical contest, in A.T. Cheska (ed.) *Play as Context.* New York: Leisure Press.

Nicholson, S. (1971) How not to cheat children: the theory of loose parts, *Landscape Architecture Quarterly*, 62(1): 30–4.

Nicholson, S. and Schreiner, B.K. (1973) *Community Participation in Decision Making* (Social sciences: a second level course, urban development Unit 22). Milton Keynes: The Open University.

Nietzsche ([1872] 1999) *The Birth of Tragedy and Other Writings*, edited by R. Geuss and R. Speirs, trans. R. Speirs. Cambridge: Cambridge University Press.

NPFA (National Playing Fields Association) (1926) *Proceedings of the Inaugural Meeting of the National Playing Fields Association.* London: NPFA.

NPFA (National Playing Fields Association) (1928–30) *Playing Fields Journal.* London: NPFA.

NPFA (National Playing Fields Association) (1928–35) *Annual Reports.* London: NPFA.

NPFA (National Playing Fields Association) (1984) *Towards a Safer Adventure Playground*, 2nd edn. London: NPFA.

NPFA (National Playing Fields Association) (2000) *Best Play: What Play Provision Should do for Children.* London, NPFA/Children's Play Council/PLAYLINK and Department of Culture, Media and Sport.

Nunn, P. (1947) *Education: Its Data and First Principles.* London: Edward Arnold.

O'Shaughnessey, E. (1983) Words and working through, *International Journal of Psycho-Analysis*, 64: 281–90.

Ogden, C. (1930) *The ABC of Psychology*, 2nd edn. London: Kegan Paul.

Ogden, T.H. (1994) *Subjects of Analysis.* London: Karnac Books.

Onions, C.T. (1983) *The Shorter Oxford English Dictionary*, vol. 1. Oxford: Oxford University Press.

Opie, I. and Opie, P. (1959) *The Lore and Language of Schoolchildren.* Oxford: Oxford University Press.

Orr, D.W. (1993) Love it or lose it: the coming biophilia revolution, in S.R. Kellert and E.O. Wilson (eds) *The Biophilia Hypothesis.* Washington, DC: Island Press.

Owen, R. (1968) *Statutes and Constitutions (of recreational clubs).* London: NPFA.

Palmer, A., Burns, S. and Bulman, C. (eds) (1994) *Reflective Practice in Nursing: The Growth of the Professional Practitioner.* Oxford: Blackwell.

Palmer, S. (1991) *Action research project: practice learning and development.* Leeds Polytechnic internal report.

Pan, H.W. (1994) Children's play in Taiwan, in J.L. Roopnarine, J.E. Johnson and F.H. Hooper (eds) *Children's Play in Diverse Cultures.* Albany, NY: State University of New York Press.

Parten, M.B. (1932) Social participation among preschool children, *Journal of Abnormal Psychology*, 27: 234–69.

Parten M.B. (1933) Social play among preschool children, *Journal of Abnormal and Social Psychology*, 28: 136–47.

Patrick, G.T.W. (1916) *The Psychology of Relaxation*. Boston, MA: Houghton Mifflin.

Pearsall, J. (ed.) (1999) *The Concise Oxford Dictionary*, 10th edn. Oxford: Oxford University Press.

Pearson-Clarke (1984) Cinderella's children: the story of after-school play centres. Unpublished manuscript in possession of Keith Cranwell.

Pepler, D.J. (1982) Play and divergent thinking, in D.J. Pepler and K.H. Rubin (eds) *The Play of Children: Current Theory and Research*. Basel: S. Karger.

Perry, B.D. (1994) Neurobiological sequelae of childhood trauma: post traumatic stress disorders in children, in M. Murberg (ed.) *Catecholamines in Post-traumatic Stress Disorder: Emerging Concepts*. Washington, DC: American Psychiatric Association.

Perry, B.D., Pollard, R.A., Blakley, T.L., Baker, W.L. and Vigilante, D. (1995) Childhood trauma: the neurobiology of adaptation and use-dependent development of the brain; how states become traits, *Infant Mental Health Journal*, 16(4).

Petrie, P. (1994) *Play and Care Out of School*. London: HMSO.

Petrille, M. and Sanger, S. (1983) *Emotional Care of Hospitalised Children*. London: Lippincott.

Piaget, J. (1951a) Mastery play, in J.S. Bruner, A. Jolly and K. Sylva (eds) *Play: Its Role in Development and Evolution*. Harmondsworth: Penguin.

Piaget, J. (1951b) Symbolic play, in J.S. Bruner, A. Jolly and K. Sylva (eds) *Play: Its Role in Development and Evolution*. Harmondsworth: Penguin.

Piaget, J. (1962) *Play Dreams and Imitation in Childhood*. London: Routledge & Kegan Paul.

Playboard (1984) *Playwork Working Group* (internal paper). Birmingham: ACPR.

Playboard (1985) *Make Way for Children's Play: A Discussion Document on a Play Policy for the Future*. Birmingham: ACPR.

PLAYLINK (1997) *Risk and Safety in Play: The Law and Practice for Adventure Playgrounds*. London: E. & F.N. Spon.

Play Wales (2001a) New opportunities for play in Wales, *Play Wales*, 5.

Play Wales (2001b) Motion passed at the 'Spirit of Adventure Play' seminar, Abergele, Play Wales 17–18 May.

Portchmouth, J. (1969) *Creative Crafts for Today*. London: Studio Vista.

Pringle, M.K. (1980) The needs of children, in J. West, *Child Centred Play Therapy*, 2nd edn. London: Arnold.

Progress (1914) Women at the House of Commons, *Progress*, 9(1): 97.

Reaney, M.J. (1916) *The Psychology of the Organized Game*. Cambridge: Cambridge University Press.

Rennie, S. (1999) The isms of playwork, in *The Proceedings of the 1999 PlayEducation Conference*, November. Sheffield: PlayEducation.

Rilke, R.M. (1964) *Selected Poems*. Harmondsworth: Penguin.

Roberts, R. (1995) *Self-esteem and Successful Learning*. London: Hodder & Stoughton.

Roper, R.E. (ed.) (1911) *Organised Play at Home and Abroad*. London: National League for Physical Education and Improvement.

Rosenzweig, M.R. (1971) Effects of environments on development of brain and of behaviour, in E. Tobach, L.R. Aronson and E. Shaw (eds) *The Bio-psychology of Development*. New York: Academic Press.

Rosenzweig, M.R., Bennett, E.L. and Diamond, M.C. (1972) Brain changes in response to experience, *Scientific American*, February.

Rubin, K.H. (1980) Fantasy play: its role in the development of social skills and social cognition, *New Directions in Child Development*, 9: 69–84.

Schickedanz, J.A. *et al.* (1993) *Understanding Children*, 2nd edn. Mountain View, CA: Mayfield Publishing Company.

Schön, D. (1983) *The Reflective Practitioner: How Professionals Think in Action*. London: Temple Smith.

Schön, D. (1987) *Educating the Reflective Practitioner*. London: Jossey-Bass.

Schwartzman, H. (1982) Play and metaphor, in J. Loy (ed.) *The Paradoxes of Play*. New York: Leisure Press.

Seccombe, J. (1999) Frameworks for evaluation. Unpublished handout from a workshop at the November 1999 Sheffield PlayEducation Conference.

Seed, P. (1990) *Introducing Network Analysis in Social Work*. London: Jessica Kingsley.

Segal, J. and Yahraes, H. (1924) *A Child's Journey*. New York: McGraw-Hill.

Selfe, P. (1993) *Work Out Sociology*. Basingstoke: Macmillan.

Shepherd, M. (2000) *Bee Biology: An Overview of Life Cycles, Nesting Habits and Habitat*. http://www.xerces.org/poll/pollbiology.htm (accessed 7 Aug. 2001).

Shiman, L. (1973) The Band of Hope: respectable recreation for working class children, *Victorian Studies*, 17(3).

Siviy, S.M. (1998) Neurobiological substrates of play behaviour, in M. Bekoff and J.A. Byers (eds) *Animal Play: Evolutionary, Comparative and Ethological Perspectives*. Cambridge: Cambridge University Press.

Smith, F. and Barker, J. (2000) Contested spaces: children's experiences of out-of-school care in England and Wales, *Childhood: A Global Journal of Child Research*, 7(3): 513–33.

Smith, P. (ed.) (1984) *Play in Animals and Humans*. Oxford: Blackwell.

Smith, P.K., Cowie, H. and Blades, M. (1998) *Understanding Children's Development*, 3rd edn. Oxford: Blackwell.

Sontag, S. (ed.) (1993) *A Barthes Reader*. London: Vintage.

Sorensen, C.Th. (1931) Open spaces for town and country, quoted in Allen of Hurtwood, Lady (1968) *Planning for Play*. London: Thames & Hudson.

Sorensen, C.Th. (1968) Preface, in Lady Allen of Hurtwood *Planning for Play*. London: Thames & Hudson.

Spencer, H. (1873) *Principles of Psychology*. New York: Appleton.

SPRITO (1992) *National Occupational Standards in Playwork*. London: Sport & Recreation Industry Lead Body.

Squiggle Foundation (1985) *Leaflet*. London: Squiggle Foundation.

Steckler, A. (1999) http://teach.Oit.Unc.Edu/script/hbhe201001ss199/scripts/serve_home (accessed Oct. 1999).

Stewart, L. and Stewart, T. (1981) Play, games and affects: a contribution towards a comprehensive theory of play, in A.T. Cheska (ed.) *Play as Context*. New York: Leisure Press.

Sturrock, G. (1997) SPICE: a redundant metaphor: towards a more extensive definition, in *Playwork as it Happens!!! The Proceedings of the 13th Play and Human Development Meeting*. Leeds: PlayEducation.

Sugarman, S. (1987) *Piaget's Construction of the Child's Reality*. Cambridge: Cambridge University Press.

Suomi, S.J. and Harlow, H.F. (1972) Social rehabilitation of isolate-reared monkeys, *Developmental Psychology*, 6: 487–96.

Suomi, S.J. and Harlow, H.F. (1976) Monkeys without play, in J.S. Bruner, A. Jolly and K. Sylva (eds) *Play: Its Role in Development and Evolution*. New York: Basic Books.

Sutton-Smith, B. (1992) Channel 4 documentary, *Toying with the Future*. London: Channel 4 Television.

Sutton-Smith, B. (1997) *The Ambiguity of Play*. Cambridge, MA: Harvard University Press.

Sutton-Smith, B. and Kelly-Byrne, D. (1984) The idealisation of play, in P. Smith (ed.) *Play in Animals and Humans*. Oxford: Blackwell.

Suzuki, T. (1977) *Living by Zen*. London: Rider & Co.

Sylva, K. (1977) Play and learning, in B. Tizard and D. Harvey (eds) *Biology of Play*. London: Heinemann.

Sylva, K., Bruner, J.S. and Genova, P. (1976) The role of play in the problem-solving of children 3–5 years old, in J.S. Bruner, A. Jolly and K. Sylva (eds) *Play: Its Role in Development and Evolution*. New York: Basic Books.

Talbot, M. (1991) *The Holographic Universe*. London: HarperCollins.

Tawil, B. (2000) The implications of compound flexibility, as applied to playwork theory and practice. Unpublished undergraduate paper, Leeds Metropolitan University.

Taylor, C. (1997) The meaning of adventure playwork for adventure playworkers, in *Playwork As It Happens*. Ely: PlayEducation.

TES *(Times Educational Supplement)* (1917) Articles dated 2 August and 22 November ('Local administration' and 'Evening Play Centres').

The Quiver (1888) Playrooms for the poor, *The Quiver*, 1888.

The Times (1906) Letters dated 6 October, 20 October and 2 November.

Thomashow, M. (1995) *Ecological Identity*. Cambridge, MA: MIT Press.

Tinbergen, N. (1975) The importance of being playful, *Times Educational Supplement*, January.

Tobin, J. (1997) A second chance for Christian, *The Detroit News*, 9 February.

Trevarthen, C. (1996) How a young child investigates people and things: why play helps development. Keynote speech to TACTYC Conference 'A Celebration of Play', London, 8–9 November.

Trevarthen, C., Aitken, K., Papoudi, D. and Robarts, J. (1996) *Children with Autism: Diagnosis and Interventions to Meet their Needs*. London: Jessica Kingsley.

Trevelyan, J.P. (1920) *Evening Play Centres for Children: The Story of their Origin and Growth*. London: Methuen.

van den Berg, C., van Ree, J. and Spruijt, B. (2001) *Play Deprivation Decreases Adult Social Behaviour, Noldus News*, 7(1).

van Lawick-Goodall, J. (1968) The behaviour of free-living chimpanzees in the gombé stream reserve, *Animal Behaviour Monographs*, 1: 161–311.

Vygotsky, L.S. (1976) Play and its role in the mental development of the child, in J.S. Bruner, A. Jolly and K. Sylva (eds) *Play: Its Role in Development and Evolution*. New York: Basic Books (original work published 1933, *Soviet Psychology*, 5, 6–18).

Vygotsky, L.S. (1978) *Mind & Society*. Cambridge, MA: Harvard University Press.

Walsh, R. (1984) *Staying Alive*. Boulder, CO: Shambhala Publications.

Ward, C. (1978) *The Child in the City*. London: Architectural Press.

Waring, A. (1989) *Systems Methods for Managers: a Practical Guide*. Oxford: Blackwell Scientific.

Weber, M. (1964) *The Methodology of the Social Sciences*, trans. and edited by E.A. Shils and H.A. Finch. New York: Free Press of Glencoe.

West, J. (1996) *Child Centred Play Therapy*, 2nd edn. London: Arnold.

Wheway, R. and Millward, A. (1997) *Child's Play: Facilitating Play on Housing Estates*. London: Chartered Institute of Housing.

Wilber, K. (1989) *The Atman Project: A Transpersonal View of Human Development*. Wheaton, IL: Quest Books, The Theosophical Publishing House.

Wilber, K. (1996) *Up from Eden*. Wheaton, IL: Quest Books.

Williams, H. (1984) *Playwork*. Milton Keynes: The Open University.

Williams, H. (1988) *Team Building: A Resource Pack for Recreation Managers*. Leeds: Yorkshire and Humberside Recreation Management Training Project.

Williams, A.S. *et al.* (2001) *The Children of London: Attendance and Welfare at School (1870–1990)*. London: Bedford Way Press.

Williamson, N. (2000) Hope in hell, *Times Educational Supplement*, 21 January.

Winnicott, D.W. (1992) *Playing and Reality*. London: Tavistock/Routledge.

Wooldridge, A. (1994) *Measuring the Mind: Education and Psychology in England 1860–1900*. Cambridge: Cambridge University Press.

Wright, R. (1995) *The Moral Animal; Evolutionary Psychology and Everyday Life*. London: Little, Brown.

Yelloly, M. and Henkel, M. (eds) (1995) *Learning and Teaching in Social Work: Towards Reflective Practice*. London: Jessica Kingsley.

Zahn-Waxler, C., Cummings, E.M. and Iannotti, R. (1986) *Altruism and Aggression: Biological and Social Origins*. Cambridge: Cambridge University Press.

Zikmund, W.G. (1994) *Exploring Marketing Research*, 5th edn. Orlando, FL: Dryden Press.

Zuckerman, M. (1984) Sensation seeking: a comparative approach to a human trait, *The Behaviour and Brain Sciences*, 7: 413–71.

Index

Index

Index

Cambridge Texts in the History of Political Thought

Titles published in the series thus far

Aristotle *The Politics* (edited by Stephen Everson)

Arnold *Culture and Anarchy and other writings.* (edited by Stefan Collini)

Bakunin *Statism and Anarchy* (edited by Marshall Shatz)

Baxter *A Holy Commonwealth* (edited by William Lamont)

Bentham *A Fragment on Government* (introduction by Ross Harrison)

Bernstein *The Preconditions of Socialism* (edited by Henry Tudor)

Bodin *On Sovereignty* (edited by Julian H. Franklin)

Bossuet *Politics Drawn from the Very Words of Holy Scripture* (edited by Patrick Riley)

Burke *Pre-Revolutionary Writings* (edited by Ian Harris)

Cicero *On Duties* (edited by M. T. Griffin and E. M. Atkins)

Constant *Political Writings* (edited by Biancamaria Fontana)

Diderot *Political Writings* (edited by John Hope Mason and Robert Wokler)

The Dutch Revolt (edited by Martin van Gelderen)

Filmer *Patriarcha and Other Writings* (edited by Johann P. Sommerville)

Gramsci *Pre-Prison Writings* (edited by Richard Bellamy)

Guicciardini *Dialogue on the Government of Florence* (edited by Alison Brown)

Harrington *A Commonwealth of Oceana* and *A System of Politics* (edited by J. G. A. Pocock)

Hegel *Elements of the Philosophy of Right* (edited by Allen W. Wood and H. B. Nisbet)

Hobbes *Leviathan* (edited by Richard Tuck)

Hobhouse *Liberalism and Other Writings* (edited by James Meadowcroft)

Hooker *Of the Laws of Ecclesiastical Polity* (edited by A. S. McGrade)

John of Salisbury *Policraticus* (edited by Cary Nederman)

Kant *Political Writings* (edited by H. S. Reiss and H. B. Nisbet)

Knox *On Rebellion.* (edited by Roger A. Mason)

Lawson *Political sacra et civilis* (edited by Conal Condren)

Leibniz *Political Writings* (edited by Patrick Riley)

Locke *Two Treatises of Government* (edited by Peter Laslett)

Loyseau *A Treatise of Orders and Plain Dignities* (edited by Howell A. Lloyd)

Luther and Calvin on Secular Authority (edited by Harro Höpfl)

Machiavelli *The Prince* (edited by Quentin Skinner and Russell Price)

Malthus *An Essay on the Principle of Population* (edited by Donald Winch)

Marsiglio of Padua *Defensor minor* and *De translatione Imperii* (edited by Cary Nederman)

Marx *Early Political Writings* (edited by Joseph O'Malley)

James Mill *Political Writings* (edited by Terence Ball)

J. S. Mill *On Liberty*, with *The Subjection of Women* and *Chapters on Socialism* (edited by Stefan Collini)

Milton *Political Writings* (edited by Martin Dzelzainis)

Montesquieu *The Spirit of the Laws* (edited by Anne M. Cohler, Basia Carolyn Miller and Harold Samuel Stone)

More *Utopia* (edited by George M. Logan and Robert M. Adams)

Nicholas of Cusa *The Catholic Concordance* (edited by Paul E. Sigmund)

Paine *Political Writings* (edited by Bruce Kuklick)

Price *Political Writings* (edited by D. O. Thomas)

Priestley *Political Writings* (edited by Peter Miller)

Proudhon *What is Property?* (edited by Donald R. Kelley and Bonnie G. Smith)

Pufendorf *On the Duty of Man and Citizen according to Natural Law* (edited by James Tully)

The Radical Reformation (edited by Michael G. Baylor)

Herbert Spencer *The Man versus the State* and *The Proper Sphere of Government* (edited by John Offer)

Utopias of the British Enlightenment (edited by Gregory Claeys)

Vitoria *Political Writings* (edited by Anthony Pagden and Jeremy Lawrance)

Voltaire *Political Writings* (edited by David Williams)

Weber *Political Writings* (edited by Peter Lassman and Ronald Speirs)

William of Ockham *A Short Discourse on Tyrannical Government* (edited by A. S. McGrade and John Kilcullen)